THE AUSTRALIAN Women's Weekly

CHRISTMAS
The Complete Collection

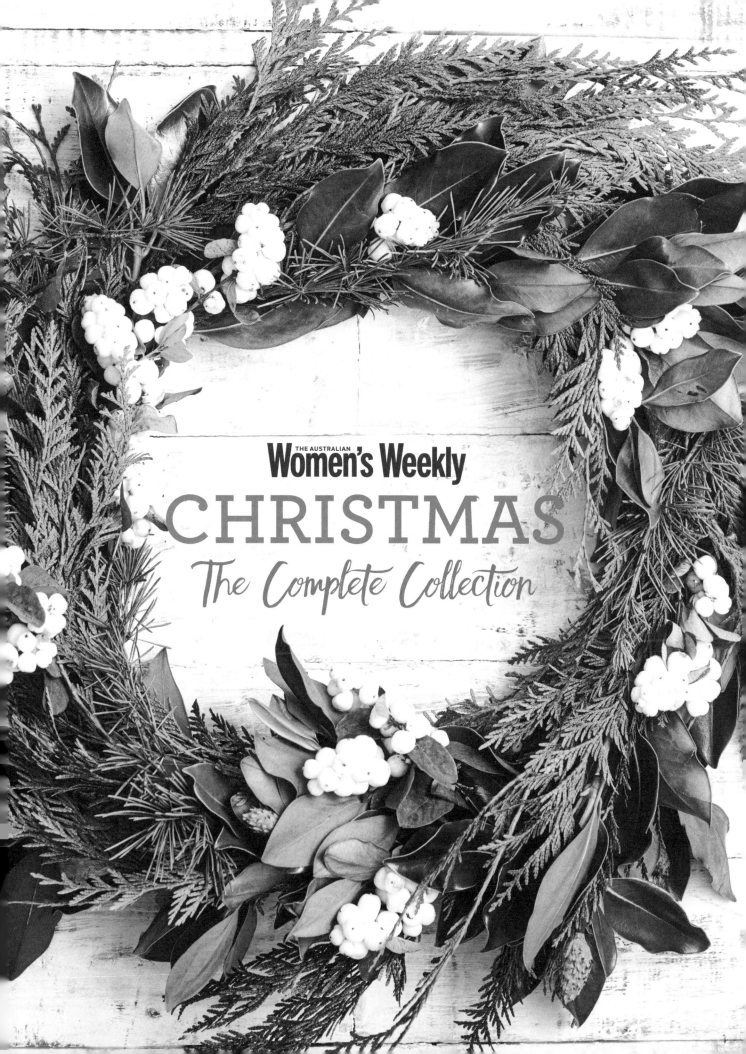

THE AUSTRALIAN **Women's Weekly**

CHRISTMAS

The Complete Collection

Contents

Christmas is Coming

It's that time of the year again. We feel it in the air, like a battalion of *glazed hams* and *fruit mince pies* marching our way. The year is coming to a close and it's gearing up for one *last big celebration* – Christmas!

For some, the word Christmas is enough to bring on an anxiety attack, while for others it's a joyous occasion they can't wait for. If you're hosting Christmas, there's a lot to consider – food, drinks, decorations, and even take-home gifts. It's a lot of planning and it's no wonder some hosts want to hide behind the Christmas tree. However, planning that perfect Christmas needn't be a complete nightmare. We at *The Weekly* can help you create the perfect menu.

GETTING ORGANISED

Before you even start thinking about food and drinks, choose what kind of Christmas you want to have. Do you want a traditional or a modern one? All your decisions regarding what you serve on the day will stem from this decision.

To make planning for the big day as stress-free as possible, we've divided this book into two sections: Traditional Christmas and Modern Christmas. Each includes lots of ideas on what to serve for nibbles and drinks, main meals, side dishes, desserts, cakes and puddings, and even edible gifts for your guests to take home. You'll have no trouble coming up with a fabulous menu that will dazzle your guests.

A TRADITIONAL CHRISTMAS

If you're planning a traditional Christmas, then the day is all about honouring the past and paying respect to Christmases gone by. Your tradition may have involved drinks on Christmas Eve; a glass of bubbles at 11am on Christmas Day; a lunch of stuffed turkey with homemade cranberry sauce and gravy followed by mum's famous trifle; and a board game in the late afternoon accompanied by some cheese and crackers and a glass of port. However, a traditional Christmas doesn't mean you have to do the same thing every year when it comes to the food. You don't have to cook the turkey the way you mother did or glaze the ham with the same marmalade. You can opt for different desserts to the steamed pudding and fruit cake that were a fixture on your table every year. This book contains many recipes with a traditional twist that will satisfy your guests. Of course, if you did want to follow your family's tradition dish for dish, then chances are you'll find those recipes among these pages too.

A MODERN CHRISTMAS

A modern Christmas is all about breaking with tradition. It's about celebrating change, embracing diversity and different cultures, as well as welcoming

new relationships. It's also about looking to the future where anything is possible. Have a buffet instead of a sit down meal; serve food and drinks on the terrace; relax in the park with a picnic, or even have a barbecue on the beach. Decorations can be lavish or homemade. Instead of buying presents for everyone do a secret santa, where each person chooses a name out of a hat and buys a gift for that person without disclosing their identity. With a modern Christmas, you can really flex your creativity with the food. You may decide to have an Asian banquet or a seafood barbecue, go cocktail and offer canapés, or serve up a roast dinner alfresco. Whichever way you decide to go, there are plenty of recipes in this book to inspire you.

A MERRY CHRISTMAS DAY

When we think of Christmas, we remember the many times we've spent with our families. We talked, we laughed, we larked about and we shared memories. We also ate – to our hearts' content. Maybe it was always Dad or Mum who cooked the Christmas lunch or dinner and perhaps now the baton has been passed to you. Or maybe it's just your turn to host Christmas this year. Whatever the case, we're delighted to be a part of your merry Christmas day!

Traditional
CHRISTMAS

Nibbles
AND
Drinks

MINI SALAMI AND
Tomato Pizzas

2 teaspoons (7g) dry yeast

1 teaspoon caster (superfine) sugar

½ teaspoon sea salt

¾ cup (180ml) warm water

2½ cups (375g) plain (all-purpose) flour

2 tablespoons olive oil

½ cup (140g) bottled tomato pasta sauce

4 medium roma (egg) tomatoes (300g),
   sliced thinly

2 cacciatore salami (135g), sliced thinly

4 bocconcini cheese (220g), sliced thinly

30g (1 ounce) baby rocket (arugula)
   leaves

¼ cup loosely packed baby basil leaves

2 teaspoons olive oil, extra

1 Combine yeast, sugar, salt and the water in a small bowl, whisk until yeast dissolves.
Cover; stand in a warm place for 20 minutes or until mixture is frothy.

2 Place flour in a large bowl, stir in oil and yeast mixture; mix to a soft dough. Knead dough
on a floured surface for 5 minutes or until dough is smooth and elastic. Place dough in a
large oiled bowl. Cover; stand in a warm place for 1 hour or until dough has doubled in size.

3 Preheat oven to 240°C/475°F. Oil two large oven trays.

4 Turn dough onto a floured surface; knead until smooth. Roll out dough until 3mm (⅛-inch)
thick. Using a 6cm (2½-inch) cutter, cut 40 rounds from dough, re-rolling scraps as required.

5 Working in batches, place 10 rounds on each tray. Spread half the sauce on pizza bases;
top with half the tomato slices, half the salami and half the bocconcini. Bake for 15 minutes
or until pizza bases are golden and crisp. Repeat with remaining rounds, sauce, tomato,
salami and bocconcini.

6 Combine rocket, basil and extra oil in a small bowl.

7 Just before serving, top pizzas with salad leaves.

VENICE DUSK

SCROPPINO WITH STRAWBERRY PUREE

LYCHEE & RASPBERRY FIZZ

BARBADOS

Christmas Eve DRINKS

VENICE DUSK

PREP TIME 15 MINUTES (+ FREEZING)

MAKES 8 CUPS

Cut rind from 1kg (2-lb) piece seedless watermelon; cut flesh into 2cm (¾-in) cubes, place in a ziptop bag. Freeze for at least 1 hour or until ready to use. Half fill a jug with ice cubes, frozen watermelon and 6 wide strips mandarin rind. Stir 1 cup (250ml) chilled vodka and ¼ cup (55g) caster (superfine) sugar in a small bowl until sugar dissolves; stir mixture into a jug with 1 cup (250ml) chilled apéritif, 3 cups (750ml) chilled soda water, 1 cup (250ml) strained mandarin juice, ⅓ cup (80ml) strained lemon juice, serve immediately.

TIP Apéritifs are made by infusing herbs and/or fruit in alcohol and water; they have a bitter taste and are characterised by their dark red colour. Use an apéritif such as Aperol or Campari.

SCROPPINO WITH STRAWBERRY PUREE

PREP TIME 15 MINUTES (+ REFRIGERATION)

MAKES 6

Place six glasses in the freezer to chill. Meanwhile, blend or process 185g (6oz) chopped strawberries and 1½ tablespoons elderflower cordial until smooth. Transfer to a jug; refrigerate until needed. To make the scroppino: place 2 tablespoons chilled vodka in a blender, slowly pour in 1½ cups (375ml) prosecco (Italian sparkling wine), then add 1.5 litres (6 cups) lemon sorbet. Blend, in bursts, until combined. Pour 1 tablespoon of the strawberry puree into the base of six chilled glasses, top with scroppino. Serve immediately.

TIPS This traditional frozen Venetian drink is made with gelato and has a texture more akin to a slushie; we've used sorbet instead. If you serve in tall glasses, serve with long spoons or straws.

LYCHEE & RASPBERRY FIZZ

PREP TIME 15 MINUTES (+ FREEZING)

MAKES 12

You need 2 x 12-hole ice-cube trays and 24 white sugar cubes. Place a sugar cube in each hole of the ice-cube trays; stain each cube with two drops of Angostura bitters. Strain 560g (1 pound) canned lychees in syrup over a bowl, reserving syrup; quarter lychees. Divide lychees and 125g (4oz) frozen raspberries into ice-cube trays. Combine reserved lychee syrup and 1 cup (250ml) chilled water; pour into trays; freeze for 4 hours. Unmould ice-cubes into a chilled bowl. To serve, place two ice-cubes into each cocktail glass, top each with 1 teaspoon brandy; pour over 2 x 750ml bottles chilled prosecco (Italian sparkling wine). Serve immediately.

BARBADOS

PREP + COOK TIME 25 MINUTES

MAKES 6 CUPS

Remove pulp from 8 passionfruit; reserve. Place 1½ cups (330g) caster (superfine) sugar in a large heavy-based frying pan over medium heat; cook, stirring, until a dark caramel colour (the sugar will start to dissolve, then form clumps; as you continue to stir it will eventually liquefy). Carefully add 1 cup (250ml) water and reserved passionfruit pulp to the sugar (the mixture will spit); when the bubbles subside, stir the mixture until smooth. Pour mixture into a large stainless steel bowl, add 1 peeled, halved and thinly sliced pineapple; turn to coat in mixture. Cut 1 orange into slices. Juice 3 oranges. Add orange juice and slices to the bowl with 1 cup (250ml) chilled dark underproof rum and 2 cups (500ml) chilled lemonade; stir to combine. One-third fill a jug with crushed ice. Add rum and fruit mixture; serve immediately.

TIP The caramel will burn if it touches your skin, so be extra careful when adding the liquid to the melted sugar. Add the liquid down the side of the pan, not over the top, keeping your arm well out of the way of boiling caramel.

Notes

Use a zesting tool to create the long thin strips of rind. If you don't have one, remove wide strips of rind with a vegetable peeler, then cut into thin strips with a sharp knife.

Chicken liver, thyme
AND BRANDY PÂTÉ

½ cup (125ml) brandy

6 sprigs fresh thyme

2 cloves garlic, bruised

600g (1¼ pounds) chicken livers

250g (8 ounces) butter

2 eggs

2 tablespoons orange rind strips
  (see notes)

REDCURRANT JELLY

300g (9½ ounces) bottled redcurrant jelly

1 tablespoon red wine vinegar

1 Preheat oven to 160°C/325°F. Oil a 1.25 litre (5-cup) ovenproof dish.

2 Place brandy, thyme and garlic in a small frying pan over high heat; bring to the boil. Boil, uncovered, for 2 minutes or until reduced by half. Remove from heat. Discard thyme and garlic; cool.

3 Meanwhile, trim sinew from livers. Heat 25g (¾ ounce) of the butter in a large frying pan over medium-high heat; cook livers, stirring, until changed in colour, but rare in the centre.

4 Process liver mixture and cooking juices with brandy, eggs and remaining chopped butter until almost smooth. Strain mixture through a fine sieve into a large jug. Spoon mixture into the dish.

5 Place the dish in a large baking dish. Pour enough boiling water into the baking dish to come halfway up the side of the ovenproof dish.

6 Bake pâté for 15 minutes or until just set in the centre. Remove dish from water bath; cool slightly. Cover; refrigerate overnight.

7 Make redcurrant jelly.

8 Pour jelly over chilled pâté; refrigerate until set. Just before serving, top pâté with rind and season with freshly ground black pepper.

REDCURRANT JELLY Melt jelly in a small saucepan over low heat until smooth; stir in vinegar until combined.

SERVING SUGGESTION Serve with fruit and nut crispbread and baby green leaves. To make your own crispbread, cut fruit and nut bread into wafer thin slices; place on a baking-paper-lined oven tray, in a single layer, in a 100°C/200°F oven until crisp.

CRAB SALAD, AVOCADO & CUCUMBER SANDWICHES

PREP TIME 30 MINUTES **MAKES** 24

4 green onions (scallions), sliced thinly

2 fresh long red chillies, seeded, chopped finely

460g (14 ounces) fresh cooked crabmeat

⅓ cup (80ml) coleslaw dressing

2 lebanese cucumbers (260g)

2 small avocados (400g), sliced thinly

16 slices white bread (720g)

1 Combine onion, chilli, crab and dressing in a small bowl. Season to taste. Using a vegetable peeler, slice cucumbers into thin ribbons.
2 Top 8 slices bread with cucumber, then avocado and crab mixture. Top with remaining 8 slices bread. Trim crusts; cut each sandwich into three fingers.

DO-AHEAD Sandwiches can be made several hours ahead; refrigerate, tightly covered. If making ahead, drizzle a little lemon juice over the avocado before using to stop it from discolouring.

PRAWN COCKTAIL WITH ZUCCHINI & MINT SALAD

PREP TIME 25 MINUTES (+ STANDING) **SERVES** 6

⅓ cup (80ml) lemon juice

1 tablespoon red wine vinegar

2 tablespoons olive oil

2 small zucchini (180g), cut into ribbons

3 radishes (110g), trimmed, sliced thinly

1 baby cos (romaine) lettuce (180g), leaves torn

½ cup loosely packed fresh mint leaves

1 large avocado (320g), cut into small wedges

18 cooked medium king prawns (shrimp) (800g), shelled, deveined

1 Combine juice, vinegar and oil in medium bowl. Add zucchini ribbons, turn to coat in dressing. Stand for 20 minutes. Add radish, lettuce and mint. Toss gently to combine; season to taste.
2 Divide zucchini salad and avocado into six serving glasses; top with prawns, drizzle with any remaining dressing.

Notes

Finger limes are an aromatic native Australian citrus available from selected greengrocers from March to June. Cut in half lengthways to scrape out the juice sacs (vesicles). Watermelon radishes are available from specialist greengrocers. If you can't find them, use the regular red variety.

SALMON *Carpaccio*

Freeze the piece of salmon for about 1 hour before cutting; this will make it easier to slice as thinly as possible. Using a long thin knife held at a 45 degree angle, cut the salmon into thin slices.

2 tablespoons lime juice

2 tablespoons extra virgin olive oil

4 finger limes, halved lengthways, seeds removed (see notes)

500g (1-pound) piece sashimi salmon, sliced thinly

1 shallot (25g), chopped finely

4 watermelon radishes (140g) (see notes), trimmed, shaved thinly

1 tablespoon fresh dill sprigs

1 cup (130g) watercress sprigs

1 Combine juice, oil and finger lime seeds in a small jug or bowl.

2 Arrange salmon slices on serving plates; top with shallot, radishes and dill. Drizzle finger lime dressing over salmon. Season.

3 Cover; refrigerate for 1 hour. Serve carpaccio with watercress.

SERVING SUGGESTION Serve with thinly sliced toasted bread.

Mustard beef
CANAPÉS

2 tablespoons wholegrain mustard

2 tablespoons horseradish cream

2 beef new york-cut steaks (440g)

2 teaspoons olive oil

¼ cup (60g) sour cream

24 baby spinach leaves

CROSTINI

1 small french bread stick (150g)

cooking-oil spray

1 Combine half the mustard and half the horseradish in a small bowl; spread over steaks. Cover; refrigerate until required.

2 Meanwhile, make crostini.

3 Heat oil in a large frying pan; cook steaks until cooked as desired. Transfer to a plate, cover; rest for 5 minutes, then slice thinly.

4 Combine remaining mustard and horseradish with sour cream in a small bowl. Place a spinach leaf on each crostini, top with steak slices and sour cream mixture.

CROSTINI Preheat oven to 160°C/325°F. Discard ends of bread; cut bread into 1cm (½-inch) slices (you need 24 slices). Place slices, in a single layer, on oven tray; spray with oil. Toast, both sides, in oven until browned lightly and crisp.

TIP New york-cut steaks are also known as sirloin or striploin, without the bone.

Notes

This loaf pan has a base measure of 9cm x 25.5cm (3½ inches x 10 inches). Some butchers sell a pork and veal mixture; if it is not available as a mixture, buy 500g (1 pound) each of pork mince and veal mince.

Chicken, pork
AND VEAL TERRINE

1 tablespoon olive oil

1 small brown onion (80g), chopped finely

2 cloves garlic, crushed

1 tablespoon finely chopped fresh thyme

1kg (2 pounds) minced (ground)
    pork and veal

¼ cup (60ml) brandy

2 tablespoons finely chopped fresh
    flat-leaf parsley

1 teaspoon ground allspice

½ teaspoon ground white pepper

⅓ cup (55g) roasted unsalted shelled
    pistachios, chopped coarsely

1 egg

1 teaspoon sea salt flakes

12 slices pancetta (180g)

4 chicken tenderloins (300g)

1 Preheat oven to 180°C/350°F. Heat oil in a small frying pan; cook onion, garlic and thyme, stirring, until onion is soft. Transfer to a large bowl; cool.

2 Add mince, brandy, parsley, allspice, pepper, nuts, egg and salt to onion mixture; mix well.

3 Grease a 1.5-litre (6-cup) loaf pan (see notes). Line the base and long sides of pan with pancetta, extending the pancetta over the sides. Press one-third of the mince mixture into pan; top with two chicken tenderloins. Repeat layers with mince mixture and chicken, ending with mince layer. Fold over pancetta to enclose. Cover terrine with baking paper then foil.

4 Place pan in a medium baking dish; pour enough boiling water into the baking dish to come halfway up the sides of the pan. Bake for 50 minutes or until a metal skewer inserted into the centre is warm to touch. Remove pan from water bath; cool for 15 minutes. Refrigerate for 3 hours or overnight.

5 Turn terrine a onto board, remove jelly and fat. Transfer terrine to a serving plate; stand for 30 minutes before slicing.

SERVING SUGGESTION Serve with marinated figs, mustard, cornichons (baby gherkins) and crusty bread.

Spruce up your gift wrapping with botanical themed paper and a sprig of festive foilage.

Wild rice and orange
STUFFED TOMATOES

You will need about 2 oranges for this recipe.

⅓ cup (65g) wild rice

1 cup (250ml) water

12 medium vine-ripened tomatoes (1.5kg)

⅓ cup (45g) slivered almonds

10g (½ ounce) butter

1 medium onion (150g), chopped finely

1 tablespoon finely grated orange rind

¼ cup (60ml) orange juice

200g (6½ ounces) persian fetta

¼ cup loosely packed fresh flat-leaf
   parsley leaves, chopped finely

⅓ cup (95g) Greek-style yoghurt

1 tablespoon finely chopped fresh mint

HERB SALAD

120g (4 ounces) baby rocket (arugula)
   leaves

¾ cup loosely packed fresh flat-leaf
   parsley leaves

¾ cup loosely packed fresh mint leaves

1 tablespoon orange juice

1 tablespoon olive oil

1 Place rice and the water in a small saucepan over medium heat; bring to the boil.
Reduce heat; simmer, covered, for 30 minutes or until tender.

2 Preheat oven to 220°C/425°F.

3 Cut 1cm (½ inch) tops from tomatoes; reserve tops. Scoop out the pulp and seeds;
reserve for another use. Place tomato shells in an oiled medium baking dish.

4 Place nuts on an oven tray; roast for 5 minutes or until browned.

5 Heat butter in a large frying pan over medium heat; cook onion and rind until soft.
Increase heat to high, add rice then juice; stir until liquid has evaporated. Remove pan
from heat; stir in fetta, parsley and nuts. Season to taste. Spoon mixture into tomato shells;
replace tops. Roast for 10 minutes or until tomatoes are tender.

6 Meanwhile, make herb salad.

7 Combine yoghurt and mint in a small bowl.

8 Serve stuffed tomatoes with herb salad and minted yoghurt.

HERB SALAD Place rocket and herbs in a medium bowl with combined juice and oil;
toss gently to combine. Season to taste.

BISTEEYA *Sticks*

¼ cup (20g) slivered almonds

1 tablespoon olive oil

500g (1 pound) chicken thigh fillets, chopped finely

1 small red onion (100g), chopped finely

1 clove garlic, chopped finely

1 long green chilli, seeded, chopped finely

pinch saffron threads

1 teaspoon ground coriander

½ teaspoon ground ginger

¼ teaspoon ground cinnamon

1 egg

¼ cup coarsely chopped fresh coriander (cilantro)

¼ cup coarsely chopped fresh flat-leaf parsley

1½ tablespoons coarsely chopped fresh mint

8 sheets fillo pastry

60g (2 ounces) butter, melted

1 teaspoon icing (confectioners') sugar

½ medium pomegranate (160g)

1 cup (280g) Greek-style yoghurt

1 Toast nuts in a large frying pan over low heat until browned lightly. Remove from pan.

2 Heat half the oil in same pan; cook chicken, stirring occasionally, for 5 minutes or until cooked through.

3 Add onion, garlic, chilli and remaining oil to pan; cook, stirring, until onion is soft. Add saffron, ground coriander, ginger and half the cinnamon; cook, stirring, until fragrant. Transfer mixture to a medium bowl; cool slightly. Stir in egg, herbs and toasted nuts; cool.

4 Preheat oven to 220°C/425°F. Oil an oven tray; line with baking paper.

5 Layer four pastry sheets, brushing each with butter. Cut layered pastry into six rectangles. Place 2 tablespoons chicken mixture along short side of each rectangle. Roll to enclose filling. Place on oven tray, brush with butter. Repeat with remaining pastry, butter and chicken mixture.

6 Bake pastries for 20 minutes or until golden. Stand on tray for 5 minutes before transferring to a serving platter. Dust with sifted icing sugar and remaining cinnamon.

7 Meanwhile, remove seeds and juice from pomegranate. Stir juice and most of the seeds through yoghurt in a small bowl; sprinkle with remaining seeds.

8 Serve pastries with yoghurt mixture.

PORK, FENNEL & FIG SAUSAGE ROLLS

PREP TIME 15 MINUTES (+ FREEZING)
MAKES 24

1 teaspoon fennel seeds

1 teaspoon ground cumin

1 tablespoon olive oil

1 small brown onion (80g), chopped finely

100g (3 ounces) sliced pancetta, chopped finely

500g (1 pound) minced (ground) pork

¾ cup (50g) stale breadcrumbs

3 dried figs, chopped finely

⅓ cup finely chopped fresh flat-leaf parsley

2 sheets ready-rolled puff pastry

1 egg, beaten lightly

1 teaspoon poppy seeds

1 teaspoon sesame seeds

1 Dry-fry fennel seeds and cumin in a small frying pan over low heat, stirring, until fragrant. Remove from pan. Crush lightly.
2 Heat oil in same small pan over medium-high heat; cook onion and pancetta, stirring, for 5 minutes or until onion is soft. Cool.
3 Using your hands, combine pork, breadcrumbs, figs, parsley, spice mixture and onion mixture in a large bowl.
4 Cut pastry sheets in half; brush pastry with a little egg. Place a quarter of the pork mixture along one long side of each pastry half; roll to enclose filling. Wrap rolls, separately, in plastic wrap; freeze for 1 hour or until slightly firm.
5 Preheat oven to 220°C/425°F. Line two oven trays with baking paper.
6 Unwrap rolls; cut each roll into six pieces. Place pieces on oven trays. Brush rolls with a little more of the egg; sprinkle with seeds.
7 Bake rolls for 25 minutes or until golden and cooked through.

SERVING SUGGESTION Serve with tomato sauce (ketchup).

CHORIZO & POTATO FRITTERS

PREP + COOK TIME 40 MINUTES
MAKES 40

2 teaspoons vegetable oil

1 cured chorizo sausage (170g),
  chopped finely

1 small brown onion (80g), chopped finely

2 fresh small red thai (serrano) chillies,
  chopped finely

2 medium zucchini (240g), grated coarsely

450g (14½ ounces) bintje potatoes,
  grated coarsely

1 small kumara (orange sweet potato)
  (250g), grated coarsely

3 eggs, beaten lightly

1 cup (150g) plain (all-purpose) flour

1 teaspoon sweet paprika

vegetable oil, extra, for deep-frying

3 teaspoons sea salt flakes

¼ teaspoon paprika

½ cup (120g) sour cream

2 tablespoons sweet chilli sauce

½ cup loosely packed fresh coriander
  (cilantro) leaves

1 Heat oil in a medium frying pan; cook
chorizo, onion and chilli, stirring, until
onion softens. Add zucchini; cook, stirring,
for 1 minute. Cool for 10 minutes.
2 Combine chorizo mixture in a large bowl
with potato, kumara, egg, flour and sweet
paprika, season.
3 Fill a wok or large saucepan one-third
full with extra oil; heat over medium heat
to 180°C/350°F (or until a cube of bread
turns golden in 10 seconds). Deep-fry level
tablespoons of mixture, in batches, until
fritters are browned lightly. Drain fritters
on paper towel.
4 Sprinkle fritters with combined salt and
paprika. Serve with sour cream, sweet chilli
sauce and coriander.

The best gift around the Christmas tree is the presence of family.

CAMPARI, ORANGE & SODA

COSMOPOLITAN COCKTAIL

BOOZY WHITE CHOCOLATE EGGNOG

PINEAPPLE PASSIONFRUIT SPRITZER

Christmas Day DRINKS

CAMPARI, ORANGE & SODA

PREP TIME 10 MINUTES **SERVES** 8

Combine 1 cup (250ml) campari, 3 cups (750ml) chilled orange or tropical juice and 2 cups (500ml) chilled soda water in a large jug. Thinly slice 1 small orange; halve slices. Divide orange slices and ½ cup fresh or frozen blueberries into 8 serving glasses. Pour over campari mixture. Serve with ice.

TIP When in season, use blood oranges.

COSMOPOLITAN COCKTAIL

PREP TIME 10 MINUTES (+ REFRIGERATION)
SERVES 8

Place 1¼ cups (310ml) vodka, ⅓ cup (80ml) orange-flavoured liqueur, ½ cup (125ml) lime juice and 2½ cups (625ml) chilled cranberry-pomegranate juice in a large jug; refrigerate for 1 hour. Just before serving, stir in 2½ cups (625ml) chilled lemonade, 1 thinly sliced lime and ½ cup loosely packed fresh mint leaves. Serve with ice.

BOOZY WHITE CHOCOLATE EGGNOG

PREP + COOK TIME 20 MINUTES **SERVES** 8

Bring 3 cups (750ml) milk to the boil in medium saucepan. Remove from heat. Meanwhile, whisk 4 egg yolks and ⅓ cup caster (superfine) sugar in medium bowl until combined. Gradually whisk in hot milk. Return eggnog mixture to pan; stir over low heat, without boiling, until mixture is thick enough to coat the back of a spoon. Remove from heat. Add 90g (3oz) finely chopped white chocolate, 2 tablespoons brandy and 2 tablespoons rum; stir until smooth. Beat ¾ cup (180ml) thickened (heavy) cream in a small bowl with an electric mixer until soft peaks form. Pour eggnog into 8 warmed heatproof ¾ cup (180ml) serving glasses; top with cream. Serve sprinkled with nutmeg.

PINEAPPLE PASSIONFRUIT SPRITZER

PREP TIME 5 MINUTES **SERVES** 8

Combine 340g (11oz) canned passionfruit pulp in syrup, 1 litre (4 cups) chilled pineapple juice, 3 cups (750ml) chilled sparkling mineral water and ½ cup coarsely chopped fresh mint in a large jug. Serve with ice.

TIP To make an alcoholic version, replace mineral water with sparkling white wine.

Rabbit and Hazelnut
TERRINE

You will need to start this recipe at least 2 days ahead.

2 rabbits (1.8kg)

400g (12½ ounces) pork sausages

1 cup (250ml) dry red wine

3 cloves garlic, crushed

1 tablespoon finely chopped fresh thyme

½ cup (70g) hazelnuts, roasted

3 teaspoons salt

1 teaspoon freshly ground black pepper

½ teaspoon freshly grated nutmeg

18 thin streaky bacon slices (540g),
  rind removed

1 Cut the boneless rabbit loin into 2cm (¾-inch) strips; reserve. Coarsely chop remaining rabbit, removing and discarding all bones. Process rabbit meat using the pulse button until coarse. Remove and discard casings from sausages.

2 Combine chopped rabbit, sausage meat, wine, garlic and thyme in a large bowl. Cover; refrigerate for 4 hours or overnight.

3 Stir nuts, salt, pepper and nutmeg into meat mixture.

4 Preheat oven to 180°C/350°F. Line base and two long sides of a 9cm x 23cm (3¾-inch x 9¼-inch) loaf pan with baking paper, extending the paper 5cm (2 inches) over edges of pan. Line pan with bacon, overlapping the slices and allowing them to overhang the sides of the pan by about 4cm (1½ inches).

5 Press half the meat mixture into pan; place rabbit loin strips on top, cover with remaining meat mixture. Fold bacon slices over to cover meat mixture. Fold baking paper over bacon; cover pan tightly with foil. Place pan in a large baking dish; pour enough boiling water into dish to come halfway up sides of the pan.

6 Bake terrine for 45 minutes; remove foil, bake for a further 45 minutes or until cooked when tested. Remove pan from water; cover terrine with baking paper. Cool at room temperature for 1 hour.

7 Place another dish or same-sized loaf pan, filled with heavy cans on terrine to weight it down; refrigerate overnight.

SERVING SUGGESTION Serve with cornichons (baby gherkins) and crusty bread.

Notes

This terrine will keep tightly wrapped in plastic wrap for up to 1 week.

Middle Eastern
SALAD CUPS

You need three 12-hole (2-tablespoon/40ml) deep flat-based patty pans for this recipe; if you only have one pan, make the cups in batches. You also need an 8cm (3¼-inch) round cutter.

1 large potato (300g), unpeeled

2 x 26cm (10½-inch) round pitta breads

¼ cup (60ml) olive oil

2 medium lebanese cucumbers (340g)

2 large tomatoes (440g), seeded, chopped finely

½ small red onion (50g), chopped finely

2 small red radishes (70g), trimmed, sliced thinly

fresh flat-leaf parsley and mint leaves, to serve (optional)

SUMAC DRESSING

1 clove garlic, crushed

1 teaspoon sumac

1 teaspoon sea salt flakes

¼ cup (60ml) lemon juice

¼ cup (60ml) olive oil

1 Preheat oven to 200°C/400°F. Oil three 12-hole (2-tablespoon/40ml) deep flat-based patty pans.

2 Boil, steam or microwave potato until just tender. When cool enough to handle, peel, chop finely; cool.

3 Meanwhile, using an 8cm (3¼-inch) round cutter, cut out seven bread rounds; separate the rounds. Repeat with remaining bread; you will have 28 bread rounds in total. Brush the inside (rough side) of each round with a little of the oil.

4 Firmly push bread rounds, oiled-side up, into pan holes. Bake for 5 minutes or until golden; cool.

5 Meanwhile, make sumac dressing.

6 Seed and finely chop one cucumber. Combine potato, chopped cucumber, tomato and onion in a medium bowl. Add dressing, stir gently to combine.

7 To serve, using a vegetable peeler, cut remaining cucumber into thin slices; place into each bread cup with a few slices of radish. Spoon 1 tablespoon salad into each bread cup; sprinkle with a little extra sumac and top with parsley and mint.

SUMAC DRESSING Place ingredients in a small screw-top jar; shake well to combine.

TIP Buy fresh, thin-style pitta bread; if the bread is too thick it may not fit into the patty pan.

DO-AHEAD Bread cups can be made a day ahead; store in an airtight container.

ROAST PUMPKIN & FETTA BRUSHCHETTA

PREP + COOK TIME 50 MINUTES
MAKES 30

1 long french bread stick (300g)

cooking-oil spray

1.5kg (3-pound) butternut pumpkin

1 teaspoon dried chilli flakes

1½ teaspoons cumin seeds

2 tablespoons extra virgin olive oil

½ cup (50g) walnuts, roasted,
    chopped coarsely

180g (5½ ounces) persian fetta, crumbled

1 tablespoon fresh thyme leaves

1 Preheat oven to 180°C/350°F. Line two oven trays with baking paper.
2 Trim rounded ends from bread. Cut bread into 30 x 1.5cm (¾-inch) thick slices; spray both sides with cooking oil. Place bread on oven trays. Bake for 8 minutes or until browned lightly. Cool on trays.
3 Meanwhile, cut pumpkin lengthways into four slices about 3cm (1¼-inch) thick. Cut each piece into 5mm (¼-inch) thick slices.
4 Place pumpkin, chilli, seeds and oil in a large bowl; toss well to combine. Arrange slices on two baking-paper-lined oven trays. Roast for 25 minutes or until just tender.
5 Top bread with 3-4 pumpkin slices; sprinkle over walnuts, fetta and thyme.

DO-AHEAD Bread can be toasted 2 hours ahead; store in an airtight container. Pumpkin can be cooked 1 hour ahead.

POLENTA CHIPS WITH PROSCIUTTO & ROAST TOMATOES

PREP + COOK TIME 45 MINUTES
(+ REFRIGERATION) **SERVES** 4

3 cups (750ml) salt-reduced chicken stock

¾ cup (125g) instant polenta (cornmeal)

1 cup (80g) finely grated parmesan

500g (1 pound) cherry truss tomatoes

2 tablespoons olive oil

4 slices prosciutto (60g)

1 sprig fresh rosemary

1 cup (180g) ligurian olives

1 Grease a deep 20cm (8-inch) square cake pan; line base and sides with baking paper.
2 Bring stock to the boil in a medium saucepan; gradually stir in polenta. Reduce heat; cook, stirring, for 10 minutes or until polenta thickens. Remove from heat; stir in half the parmesan. Season to taste. Spread polenta in pan. Refrigerate for 3 hours or overnight.
3 Preheat oven to 220°C/425°F. Line two oven trays with baking paper.
4 Remove polenta from pan; cut into 20 thick chips. Place chips on one tray; sprinkle with remaining parmesan, turn to coat. Bake for 30 minutes or until golden and crisp.
5 Meanwhile, place tomatoes on the other tray, drizzle with half the oil; season. Roast in oven for the last 7 minutes of polenta chip cooking time.
6 Heat remaining oil in a large frying pan over medium heat; cook prosciutto and rosemary, turning, until prosciutto is golden and crisp. Drain on paper towel.
7 Arrange polenta chips, prosciutto and tomatoes on a platter; top with rosemary and serve with olives.

SERVING SUGGESTION Serve with wood-fired or Italian-style bread.

Mains

DUCK WITH
Spiced Roast Peaches

6 x 200g (6½-ounce) duck breast fillets,
skin on

2 teaspoons sea salt flakes

2 medium red onions (340g)

2 star anise

4 teaspoons thinly sliced fresh ginger

2 cloves garlic, sliced finely

6 medium peaches (900g), halved,
stones removed

1 tablespoon white (granulated) sugar

⅓ cup loosely packed fresh coriander
(cilantro) sprigs

1 Preheat oven to 220°C/425°F.

2 Trim any excess fat and sinew from duck breasts; score skin in a fine criss-cross pattern. Rub salt and some freshly ground black pepper into duck breasts and into the scored skin.

3 Place duck breasts, skin-side down, in two medium cold frying pans. Place over medium-high heat; cook for 5 minutes or until skin is browned. Place duck breasts, skin-side up, in two shallow medium baking trays.

4 Peel onions, leaving root ends intact. Cut each onion into eight wedges. Place onion wedges around duck in trays; scatter with star anise, ginger and garlic. Top with peaches, cut-side up. Sprinkle peaches with sugar. Roast for 12 minutes or until peaches are caramelised.

5 If the duck skin hasn't completely crisped up in the oven, place under a hot grill (broiler) for a minute. Stand for 5 minutes. Discard star anise.

6 Serve duck with roast peaches and onion mixture. Serve topped with coriander.

Notes

You can use 1 small brown onion instead of the shallots, if you prefer. This recipe is best made close to serving. You can use scotch fillet instead of eye fillet but allow longer cooking time as the piece is thicker.

BEEF FILLET WITH
Garlic Cream Sauce

1.5kg (3 pounds) baby beetroot (beets),
   trimmed

1kg (2 pounds) baby new potatoes

8 cloves garlic, unpeeled

⅓ cup (80ml) olive oil

1.5kg (3-pound) piece centre-cut
   beef eye fillet

2 tablespoons fresh rosemary leaves

1 tablespoon fresh thyme leaves

500g (1 pound) baby spinach leaves

GARLIC CREAM SAUCE

1 tablespoon olive oil

2 shallots (50g), chopped finely

½ cup (125ml) dry white wine

1 tablespoon plain (all-purpose) flour

300ml pouring cream

2 teaspoons dijon mustard

2 tablespoons lemon juice

2 tablespoons finely chopped
   fresh flat-leaf parsley

1 Preheat oven to 200°C/400°F. Line two shallow medium baking dishes with baking paper.
2 Scrub beetroot; place in one dish. Place potatoes and garlic in second dish. Drizzle beetroot and potatoes with 1 tablespoon of oil each; toss to coat. Roast for 20 minutes.
3 Meanwhile, tie kitchen string around beef at 3cm (1¼-inch) intervals. Heat 1 tablespoon of the remaining oil in a large frying pan over high heat; cook beef, turning, until browned all over. Season; scatter with herbs.
4 Separate garlic from potatoes. Place beef on potatoes; return to oven, cook with vegetables for a further 30 minutes or until beef is done as desired. Transfer beef to a tray; cover, stand for 10 minutes. Cover vegetables to keep warm.
5 Squeeze garlic from skins; discard skins. Reserve garlic for sauce.
6 Make garlic cream sauce.
7 Heat remaining oil in a wok or large frying pan over high heat; cook spinach for 1 minute or until wilted. Season to taste.
8 Serve slices of beef with potatoes, beetroot, spinach and sauce.
GARLIC CREAM SAUCE Heat oil in a medium saucepan over medium-high heat; cook shallots, stirring, until soft. Add wine; bring to the boil. Boil, uncovered, for 3 minutes or until reduced by half. Add flour; cook, stirring, until mixture thickens and bubbles. Gradually stir in reserved roasted garlic, cream and mustard; stir until mixture boils and thickens. Stir in juice and parsley; season to taste.

ROAST CHICKEN WITH
Cranberry Seasoning

60g (2 ounces) butter

2 large brown onions (400g), chopped finely

4 rindless bacon slices (260g), chopped finely

2 cloves garlic, crushed

⅓ cup (55g) polenta (cornmeal)

2½ cups (175g) stale coarse breadcrumbs

1 egg, beaten lightly

½ cup coarsely chopped fresh flat-leaf parsley

¾ cup (100g) dried cranberries

½ cup (80g) chopped roasted almonds

2.3kg (4¾-pound) whole chicken

40g (1½ ounces) butter, softened, extra

1 medium brown onion (150g), sliced thinly, extra

3 cups (750ml) salt-reduced chicken stock,
   approximately

7 thin slices prosciutto (90g) (see notes)

1kg (2 pounds) white-fleshed sweet potato, unpeeled

¼ cup (60ml) extra virgin olive oil

¼ cup (35g) plain (all-purpose) flour

½ cup (160g) cranberry sauce

1 Heat the butter in a medium frying pan; cook onion, bacon and garlic, stirring, over medium heat, for 10 minutes or until onion is soft. Add polenta; cook, stirring, for 2 minutes. Transfer to a medium bowl; cool slightly. Add breadcrumbs, egg, parsley, cranberries and almonds; season.

2 Preheat oven to 180°C/350°F. Pat chicken dry inside and out with paper towel. Fill chicken cavities loosely with 3 cups of the seasoning. Tie legs together with kitchen string. Pull down and secure neck skin with toothpicks; tuck wings under. Place chicken on an oiled wire rack in a medium flameproof baking dish. Rub extra softened butter all over chicken; season.

3 Place extra sliced onion and 2 cups (500ml) of the stock in baking dish. Roast chicken for 2 hours or until juices run clear when a skewer is inserted into the thickest part of the thigh.

4 Meanwhile, place prosciutto slices, side by side, and slightly overlapping, on a large sheet of plastic wrap to form a 26cm x 30cm (10½-inch x 12-inch) rectangle. Place the remaining seasoning in the centre of prosciutto lengthways; press mixture together lightly into a log shape. Bring bottom edge of the long side of prosciutto over seasoning, then, using the plastic wrap as a guide, roll up firmly. Refrigerate until required.

5 Cut washed sweet potato crossways into 3cm (1¼-inch) thick slices. Place in a bowl with oil; toss to coat. Place sweet potato, in a single layer, on a large oven tray lined with baking paper; place seasoning roll at one end. Roast with chicken for 30 minutes. Turn potato, cook for a further 10 minutes. Remove seasoning roll. Cook potato for a further 20 minutes or until browned and cooked through.

6 Place chicken and seasoning roll on a plate; cover loosely with foil. Stand for 20 minutes before carving. Meanwhile, pour juices from baking dish into a jug, leaving onion in dish; stand for a few minutes or until the fat has risen to the surface. Return 2 tablespoons of the fat to dish; discard remaining fat. Top up pan juices in jug with remaining 1 cup (250ml) of stock to make 2 cups (500ml). Place baking dish over medium-high heat. Add flour; cook, stirring, until flour mixture is well browned. Gradually add stock mixture; cook, stirring, until mixture boils and thickens. Stir in 1 tablespoon of the cranberry sauce. Add a little extra stock, if needed. Season to taste.

7 Serve chicken with gravy, seasoning roll, sweet potato and remaining cranberry sauce.

Traditional MAINS

A beautifully decorated
Christmas tree brings joy to
all who gather around.

MINTED ROAST LAMB
and Vegetables

2.5kg (5-pound) easy-carve leg of lamb

2 tablespoons dijon mustard

2 cloves garlic, crushed

2 teaspoons sea salt flakes

2 cups (500ml) water

800g (1½ pounds) baby carrots, scrubbed
 (see notes)

40g (1½ ounces) butter, chopped

½ cup (180g) mint jelly

500g (1 pound) asparagus, trimmed
 (see notes)

1 tablespoon honey

1 Stand lamb at room temperature for 30 minutes. Preheat oven to 180°C/350°F.

2 Rub lamb all over with combined mustard, garlic and salt. Season with freshly ground black pepper. Place lamb on a wire rack in a medium baking dish. Add the water to dish. Roast lamb for 1½ hours.

3 Meanwhile, trim carrots, leaving tops on. Place the carrots on a large oven tray; dot with half the butter. Roast, on a separate shelf, with lamb for 30 minutes or until tender.

4 Microwave half the jelly in a small microwave-safe bowl for 20 seconds or until melted. Brush lamb with jelly. Roast lamb for a further 40 minutes for medium-rare, brushing again with jelly halfway through cooking, or until done as desired. Cover lamb loosely with foil; stand for 15 minutes.

5 Meanwhile, place asparagus on oven tray, dot with remaining butter, season; roast for 10 minutes or until just tender.

6 Drizzle carrots with honey and toss to coat. Slice lamb; serve with remaining mint jelly and vegetables.

HERBED BUTTER ROAST TURKEY WITH
Prosciutto and Pear Stuffing

5kg (10-pound) whole turkey

cooking-oil spray

¼ cup (35g) plain (all-purpose) flour

2 cups (500ml) chicken stock

PROSCIUTTO & PEAR STUFFING

60g (2 ounces) butter

1 small leek (200g), sliced thinly

2 cloves garlic, crushed

8 slices prosciutto (120g), chopped finely

2 cups (140g) stale breadcrumbs

1 small pear (180g), chopped finely

HERBED BUTTER

125g (4 ounces) butter, softened

2 cloves garlic, crushed

2 tablespoons finely chopped fresh sage

1 tablespoon finely chopped fresh thyme

1 tablespoon finely chopped fresh
rosemary

1 Make prosciutto and pear stuffing.

2 Meanwhile, make herbed butter.

3 Preheat oven to 180°C/350°F. Discard neck and giblets from turkey. Rinse turkey under cold water, pat dry inside and out with absorbent paper. Tuck wings under body. Gentle loosen skin over breast and tops of legs using fingers or the handle of a wooden spoon (do not puncture skin). Push herb butter under skin of turkey, being careful not to break skin.

4 Fill turkey cavity with stuffing. Tie legs together with kitchen string. Place a wire rack in a large baking dish. Place turkey on rack, tucking neck flap under body; spray with oil, cover with foil. Roast for 2 hours. Remove foil; roast for 40 minutes, basting occasionally with pan juices, or until juices run clear when the thickest part of the thigh is pierced with a skewer.

5 Transfer turkey to a serving platter; cover loosely with foil. Stand for 15 minutes.

6 Meanwhile, make gravy by skimming fat from pan drippings, leaving 2 tablespoons of drippings in dish. Place dish over high heat, add flour; cook, stirring, until mixture thickens and bubbles. Gradually stir in stock; stir until mixture boils and thickens. Strain into serving jug. Serve gravy with sliced turkey.

PROSCIUTTO & PEAR STUFFING Heat butter in a medium frying pan; cook leek, garlic and prosciutto, stirring, until leek is tender. Stir in breadcrumbs; cook, stirring, for 2 minutes or until toasted lightly. Remove from heat, stir in pear; season to taste, cool.

HERBED BUTTER Combine ingredients in a small bowl.

SERVING SUGGESTION Serve with char-grilled brussels sprouts, red onion and prosciutto.

Traditional MAINS

HERBED SALMON
with Fennel Remoulade

1.5kg (3-pound) piece salmon fillet, skin on

2 tablespoons olive oil

½ cup coarsely chopped fresh
   flat-leaf parsley

½ cup coarsely chopped fresh mint

1 clove garlic, crushed

2 teaspoons finely grated lemon rind

2 tablespoons coarsely chopped capers

1 fresh long red chilli, sliced thinly

FENNEL REMOULADE

1 tablespoon dijon mustard

½ cup (150g) mayonnaise

2 tablespoons lemon juice

1 tablespoon finely chopped
   fresh tarragon

2 medium fennel bulbs (600g), shaved

1 Preheat oven to 200°C/400°F.

2 Place fillet in a large baking dish lined with baking paper. Brush with half the oil; season. Bake, uncovered, for 15 minutes or until cooked as desired.

3 Meanwhile, make fennel remoulade.

4 Combine parsley, mint, garlic, rind, capers and chilli in a medium bowl.

5 Transfer salmon to a serving platter. Sprinkle with parsley mixture, drizzle with remaining oil. Serve with remoulade and lemon wedges.

FENNEL REMOULADE Combine ingredients in a medium bowl; season to taste.

Notes

Store cold leftover ham in a calico ham bag. Ham bags are available from kitchenware stores and major supermarkets. If fridge space is a problem, take the meat off the bone first. Refrigerate, covered in plastic wrap, for up to 10 days.

Ginger marmalade
GLAZED HAM

365g (12 ounces) ginger marmalade

⅓ cup grated fresh ginger

⅓ cup (80ml) maple syrup

½ cup (110g) firmly packed light
  brown sugar

1 cup (250ml) dry ginger ale

7kg (15-pound) cooked leg of ham

2 tablespoons cloves

1 Stir marmalade, ginger, syrup, sugar and ginger ale in a small saucepan; bring to the boil. Reduce heat to medium; simmer, uncovered, for 10 minutes or until reduced by half.
2 Meanwhile, place oven shelf in lowest position. Preheat oven to 180°C/350°F.
3 Using a sharp knife, cut through the ham rind about 12cm (5 inches) from the shank end of leg. Remove rind from ham by sliding your hand between the rind and the fat layer. Discard rind. Score fat in lines at 2cm (¾-inch) intervals.
4 Place ham on a wire rack placed in a large baking dish. Wrap shank in foil. Brush ham with half the marmalade mixture. Roast ham, basting with remaining marmalade mixture, for 1¼ hours or until glaze is browned lightly. Serve ham warm or cold.

TIPS If the ham doesn't fit into your oven, or if your oven is full, bake the ham in a covered barbecue, using indirect heat, and following the manufacturer's instructions.
SERVING SUGGESTIONS Serve with cornichons (baby gherkins), mustard, caperberries, a green salad and grilled bread.

FREEFORM VEGETABLE LASAGNE
with Salsa Verde

4 medium zucchini (480g)

10 medium yellow patty-pan squash (300g)

375g (12 ounces) fresh lasagne sheets

200g (6½ ounces) buffalo mozzarella, torn

400g (12½ ounces) tomato medley, halved

SALSA VERDE

⅔ cup (160ml) olive oil

2 tablespoons red wine vinegar

1 teaspoon sea salt flakes

½ teaspoon caster (superfine) sugar

1 clove garlic, chopped

2 teaspoons drained baby capers

⅔ cup loosely packed fresh coriander (cilantro) leaves

⅓ cup loosely packed fresh flat-leaf parsley leaves

1 Trim zucchini and squash; slice thinly using a mandoline or V-slicer. Heat a large oiled grill plate (or grill or barbecue); cook zucchini and squash, in batches, for 4 minutes each side or until browned and tender.

2 Make salsa verde.

3 Cut pasta sheets into 7cm x 10cm (2¾-inch x 4-inch) rectangles; you need 8 rectangles. Cook pasta, in batches, in a large saucepan of boiling water until pasta floats to the surface and is almost cooked through.

4 To serve, divide half the vegetables, half the tomatoes and half the mozzarella among serving plates; top each with a pasta rectangle and 2 tablespoons salsa verde. Repeat layering with remaining vegetables, tomatoes and pasta; drizzle with remaining salsa verde. Top with extra fresh flat-leaf parsley, if you like.

SALSA VERDE Process ingredients until almost smooth.

ROAST PORK
with Rosemary Gravy

2kg (4-pound) rolled pork loin

2 teaspoons sea salt flakes

¼ cup (35g) plain (all-purpose) flour

2 tablespoons finely chopped
   fresh rosemary

½ cup (125ml) dry white wine

2 cups (500ml) chicken stock

CAPSICUM & CIABATTA CRUMBS

1 tablespoon olive oil

1 medium brown onion (150g),
   chopped finely

2 cloves garlic, crushed

¼ cup (40g) pine nuts

½ cup (75g) thinly sliced, drained
   sun-dried tomatoes in oil

½ cup finely chopped drained
   char-grilled capsicum (bell pepper)

½ cup finely chopped fresh
   flat-leaf parsley

200g (6½ ounces) ciabatta bread,
   torn into small pieces

½ cup (125ml) chicken stock

1 Make capsicum and ciabatta crumbs.

2 Preheat oven to 240°C/475°F.

3 Cut string from pork; open out pork and place on a board, fat-side down. Slice through thickest part of pork horizontally, without cutting all the way through. Open out pork to form one large piece; press capsicum and ciabatta crumbs against loin along width of pork. Roll pork to enclose stuffing, securing with kitchen string at 2cm (¾-inch) intervals.

4 Place pork on a rack in a large shallow baking dish. Pour enough water into dish to cover base. Rub salt over pork rind. Roast, uncovered, for 30 minutes or until rind is blistered and browned. Reduce oven temperature to 180°C/350°F; roast pork for a further 45 minutes or until juices run clear, adding more water to dish if necessary. Remove pork from oven; stand, covered loosely with foil, for 10 minutes.

5 Meanwhile, pour juices from dish into a large jug; skim 1 tablespoon of the fat from juices, return fat to dish. Skim and discard remaining fat from juices. Add flour and rosemary to dish; cook, stirring, until mixture bubbles and is well browned. Gradually stir in wine, stock and juices; bring to the boil, stirring, until gravy boils and thickens. Strain gravy into a serving jug; serve with sliced pork.

CAPSICUM & CIABATTA CRUMBS Heat oil in a large frying pan; cook onion and garlic, stirring, until onion softens. Add nuts; cook, stirring, for 2 minutes or until browned lightly. Stir in remaining ingredients; season to taste, cool

A handmade bon bon filled with tiny treasures, is a cracker way to add cheer to your table.

Notes

To check if the turkey is cooked, insert a skewer sideways into the bone in the thickest part of the thigh. If the juices run clear, the turkey is ready.

MARMALADE-GLAZED
Traditional Roast Turkey

4kg (8-pound) turkey

20g (¾ ounce) butter, melted

⅔ cup (230g) marmalade, warmed

1.5 litres (6 cups) salt-reduced chicken
   stock, approximately

⅓ cup (50g) plain (all-purpose) flour

PISTACHIO & THYME STUFFING

100g (3 ounces) butter

2 medium onions (300g), chopped finely

3 cloves garlic, crushed

1 tablespoon lemon thyme leaves

3 cups fresh breadcrumbs

½ cup finely chopped pistachios

1 Preheat oven to 180°C/350°F. Make pistachio and thyme stuffing.

2 Discard neck from turkey. Rinse turkey under cold running water; pat dry inside and out with paper towel. Fill cavities with the stuffing. Tie legs together with kitchen string; tuck wings under turkey. Place turkey on an oiled rack in a large flameproof baking dish.

3 Combine butter and marmalade in a medium bowl. Brush half the marmalade mixture all over turkey; sprinkle with salt. Pour 2 cups (500ml) of the stock into the dish. Cover tightly with two layers of greased foil.

4 Roast turkey for 1 hour 20 minutes. Remove foil; brush turkey with remaining marmalade mixture. Roast, covered with foil, for 1 hour. Remove foil; roast, uncovered, for 20 minutes or until browned and cooked through. (Check liquid in base of dish during cooking; the pan juices need to brown but not burn – you may need to drain excess liquid if it's not colouring or add extra water or stock if drying out too much or burning.) Transfer turkey to a tray or platter, cover with foil; rest for 15 minutes before carving.

5 Meanwhile, pour pan juices from dish into a large jug; stand for a few minutes or until fat has risen to the surface. Skim off 2 tablespoons of the fat from the juices, return fat to dish. Skim and discard remaining fat from juices. Top up pan juices in jug with enough of the remaining chicken stock to make 1 litre (4 cups). Place baking dish over medium heat, add flour; cook, stirring, until mixture bubbles and is well browned. Gradually stir in pan juices; cook, stirring, until mixture boils and thickens. Season. Strain gravy into a heatproof jug.

6 Serve turkey with gravy.

PISTACHIO & THYME STUFFING Heat butter in a large frying pan over medium-low heat; cook onion, garlic and lemon thyme, stirring, for 5 minutes or until soft. Transfer mixture to a large bowl. Add breadcrumbs and pistachios. Season; mix well. (Makes 3 cups)

DO AHEAD Stuffing can be made a day ahead; keep covered in the fridge. Stuff and roast turkey close to serving.

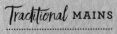

Traditional MAINS

BARBECUED *Ham*

7kg (14-pound) cooked leg of ham

2 tablespoons dijon mustard

⅔ cup (150g) firmly packed light
   brown sugar

½ cup (125ml) pineapple juice

½ cup (125ml) sweet sherry

¼ cup (55g) firmly packed light
   brown sugar, extra

2 cloves garlic, halved lengthways

¼ teaspoon ground cloves

1 medium pineapple (1.2kg), halved,
   sliced thickly

1 Cut through rind of ham 10cm (4 inches) from shank end of the leg. To remove rind, run your thumb around the edge of the rind just under the skin. Start pulling rind from widest edge of ham; continue to pull rind carefully away from the fat up to the shank end. Remove rind completely. Score across the fat at about 4cm (1½-inch) intervals, cutting lightly through the surface of the fat (not the meat) in a diamond pattern.
2 Place ham in a disposable aluminium baking dish; rub ham with combined mustard and sugar. Place on heated barbecue; cook, covered, using indirect method, following manufacturer's instructions, for 1 hour.
3 Meanwhile, stir juice, sherry, extra sugar, garlic and clove in small saucepan over heat until sugar dissolves. Simmer, uncovered, for 10 minutes or until glaze reduces by half. Brush ham with glaze; cook, covered, using indirect method for a further 45 minutes, brushing several times with glaze during cooking. Remove from barbecue, cover ham loosely with foil; stand for 15 minutes before slicing.
4 Cook pineapple on heated barbecue, brushing with remaining glaze during cooking.
5 Serve ham with pineapple.

SERVING SUGGESTION Serve with steamed asparagus and sugar snap peas.

PEPPERED BEEF FILLET
with French-style Peas

1kg (2-pound) piece beef eye fillet

2 tablespoons sea salt flakes

2 tablespoons freshly cracked
   black pepper

2 tablespoons olive oil

350g (11 ounces) shallots

100g (3-ounce) piece pancetta,
   chopped finely

2 cloves garlic, sliced thinly

3 sprigs fresh thyme

⅔ cup (160ml) red wine

½ cup (125ml) beef stock

50g (1½ ounces) butter, chopped

½ cup (60g) frozen baby peas

2 baby cos (romaine) lettuce (480g),
   trimmed, cut into wedges

1 Preheat oven to 180°C/350°F.
2 Tie beef at 2cm (¾-inch) intervals with kitchen string. Sprinkle salt and pepper on a board; roll beef firmly in seasoning. Heat half the oil in a large shallow flameproof baking dish; cook beef over high heat until browned all over. Roast, uncovered, for 20 minutes for rare or until done as desired. Remove beef from dish; cover, stand for 15 minutes.
3 Meanwhile, pour boiling water over shallots in a heatproof bowl; stand for 1 minute. Drain, peel shallots.
4 Heat remaining oil in a large heavy-based saucepan over low heat; cook shallots, covered, for 20 minutes or until tender. Add pancetta; cook, stirring, until browned. Add garlic and thyme; cook, stirring, until fragrant. Add wine; bring to the boil. Add stock; boil for 2 minutes, then simmer, covered, for 8 minutes or until liquid has reduced by about one-third. Gradually add butter to sauce, stirring, until sauce thickens. Add peas and lettuce; simmer, covered, for 2 minutes or until peas are cooked and lettuce is tender. Season to taste.
5 Cut beef into slices; serve with vegetable mixture.

SERVING SUGGESTION Serve with mashed potato.

Traditional MAINS

SPICE-CRUSTED LAMB RACKS
with Roasted Carrots

480g (15½ ounces) rainbow baby (dutch)
  carrots, peeled

¼ cup (60ml) olive oil

½ teaspoon dried chilli flakes

2 tablespoons kalonji seeds or black
  sesame seeds

2 tablespoons sesame seeds

1 clove garlic, crushed

4 x 4 french-trimmed cutlet lamb racks
  (600g)

50g (1½ ounces) red sorrel or rocket
  (arugula) leaves

½ cup loosely packed fresh flat-leaf
  parsley leaves

1 Preheat oven to 200°C/400°F.

2 Toss carrots with 2 tablespoons of the oil on an oven tray; place carrots in a single layer.
Roast for 25 minutes or until browned lightly and crisp.

3 Meanwhile, combine chilli, seeds, garlic and remaining oil in a small bowl. Place lamb on
another oven tray; rub all over with spice mixture. Roast lamb, uncovered, alongside carrots
for 20 minutes or until browned and cooked as desired.

4 Serve lamb with carrots and sorrel leaves, topped with parsley.

ROAST PORK WITH
Chestnuts and Pancetta

1.7kg (3½-pound) boneless loin of pork,
  rind on

1 tablespoon sea salt flakes

4 slices pancetta (60g), torn into pieces

4 fresh sage leaves, chopped finely

1 teaspoon fresh thyme leaves

220g (7 ounces) canned whole chestnuts,
  drained, chopped coarsely

¼ cup (35g) dried cranberries, chopped

40g (1½ ounces) butter

¾ cup (50g) stale breadcrumbs

1 teaspoon finely grated orange rind

2 tablespoons olive oil

2 medium carrots (240g), chopped

1½ cups (375ml) water

3 small beurre bosc pears (540g),
  unpeeled

1 teaspoon ground cinnamon

40g (1½ ounces) butter, extra

2 tablespoons plain (all-purpose) flour

2 cups (500ml) chicken stock,
  approximately

1 Pat pork rind dry; rub all over with salt. Cover; refrigerate overnight.

2 Preheat oven to 240°C/475°F.

3 Heat a small frying pan; cook pancetta, stirring, until crisp. Add herbs; cook until fragrant. Transfer mixture to a large bowl. Add chestnuts, cranberries, butter, breadcrumbs and rind; using your hands, mix until combined. Season to taste. Cool slightly.

4 Open out pork; season. Make a 5cm (2-inch) deep cut under the eye to make a pocket. Place stuffing across centre of the pork, pressing into the cut. Roll pork to enclose stuffing. Tie pork at 2cm (¾-inch) intervals with kitchen string. Rub rind with oil.

5 Place carrot in a flameproof baking dish; place pork on top. Pour the water into dish. Roast for 20 minutes. Reduce oven to 180°C/350°F. Discard half the oil from dish; roast for a further 15 minutes.

6 Cut pears into wedges, leaving core and stem intact. Add pears to dish; sprinkle with cinnamon. Bake for 1 hour or until pork juices run clear and pears are tender. Remove pork and pears. Stand pork for 10 minutes before slicing.

7 Drain pan juices from baking dish into a jug; place in freezer. Heat extra butter in same baking dish, add flour; cook, stirring, until browned. Skim fat from pan juices; gradually add juices to dish with half the stock, stirring, until mixture boils and thickens. Add enough of the remaining stock until mixtures reaches desired consistency. Strain into a heatproof serving jug.

8 Serve pork and pears with gravy.

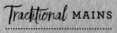

Traditional MAINS

ROAST SALMON WITH
Fennel and Apple Salad

1 cup (160g) sultanas

1½ cups (375ml) verjuice

2.5kg (5-pound) whole salmon, cleaned

1 medium brown onion (150g),
   sliced thinly

1 medium lemon (140g), sliced

4 fresh bay leaves, crushed

6 stems fresh basil

40g (1½ ounces) butter

80g (2½ ounces) fresh flat-leaf parsley,
   stems attached

1 large fennel bulb (550g)

2 small green-skinned apples (160g)

¼ cup (60ml) extra virgin olive oil

1 Combine sultanas and ½ cup of the verjuice in a small bowl. Cover; stand until required.

2 Preheat oven to 200°C/400°F.

3 Wipe salmon cavity clean; season inside and out. Fill cavity with onion, lemon, bay leaves and basil. Secure opening with skewers.

4 Line a large oven tray with foil, then baking paper; grease paper with the butter. Place salmon in the centre. Pour remaining verjuice over salmon; fold foil and paper over salmon to enclose tightly.

5 Bake salmon for 50 minutes or until cooked as desired. Stand salmon for 20 minutes.

6 Meanwhile, pick leaves from parsley, finely chop half the parsley stems. Reserve feathery fronds from fennel. Thinly slice fennel using a mandoline or V-slicer. Peel and core apples; cut into matchsticks with the mandoline or V-slicer.

7 Discard filling from salmon; peel away skin. Place salmon on a warmed large serving platter. Strain salmon cooking juices into a small saucepan; place over high heat until hot.

8 Place sultana mixture, parsley leaves, chopped stems, apple, fennel and oil in a large bowl; toss to combine. Season to taste. Sprinkle half the salad mixture over salmon.

9 Serve salmon with remaining salad and reserved fennel fronds; drizzle with warmed cooking juices.

DO-AHEAD You can prepare apple and fennel ahead of time; cover with water and a squeeze of lemon juice to prevent browning. Drain well before using.

Notes

Salmon can also be cooked
on a covered barbecue.
You can use poultry pins
to hold the stuffing instead
of skewers, if you like.

BEEF RIB ROAST
with Spiced Salt and Roasted Onions

1 tablespoon coriander seeds

1 tablespoon cumin seeds

½ cup (60g) sea salt flakes

¼ teaspoon mixed spice

1 teaspoon freshly ground pepper

3kg (6-pound) beef standing rib roast

1 tablespoon olive oil

ROASTED ONIONS

2 large brown onions (400g),
  halved crossways

4 small red onions (400g), quartered

2 bulbs garlic, halved horizontally

¼ cup (60ml) olive oil

GARLIC MAYONNAISE

1 cup (300g) whole-egg mayonnaise

1 tablespoon water

2 teaspoons lemon juice

2 cloves garlic, crushed

1 tablespoon dijon mustard

1 Preheat oven to 200°C/400°F.

2 Using a mortar and pestle, grind the seeds together until coarsely crushed. Add salt, mixed spice and pepper; mix well. Remove a third of the spiced salt mixture; reserve. Brush beef with oil, rub remaining spiced salt mixture all over beef.

3 Roast beef, uncovered, for 1½ hours for rare, or until done as desired. Cover; stand for 15 minutes before slicing.

4 Meanwhile, make roasted onions.

5 Dry-fry reserved spiced salt mixture in a small frying pan, stirring over low heat for 1 minute or until fragrant. Cool.

6 Make garlic mayonnaise.

7 Serve beef, cut into cutlets, and onions with mayonnaise and toasted spiced salt mix.

ROASTED ONIONS Place onions and garlic in a roasting pan; drizzle with oil. Season. Roast for the last 30 minutes of beef cooking time or until onions are golden and caramelised.

GARLIC MAYONNAISE Combine ingredients in a small bowl.

ROAST VEAL RACK WITH
Celeriac and Potato Gratin

2kg (4-pound) veal rack (8 cutlets)

1 cup (250ml) water

¼ cup (70g) dijon mustard

2 tablespoons horseradish cream

2 cloves garlic, crushed

1½ tablespoons plain (all-purpose) flour

2 teaspoons wholegrain mustard

2 cups (500ml) beef stock

2 tablespoons finely chopped
   fresh tarragon

1 tablespoon coarsely chopped fresh thyme

¼ cup finely chopped fresh
   flat-leaf parsley

CELERIAC & POTATO GRATIN

600ml thickened (heavy) cream

3 cloves garlic, sliced thinly

3 teaspoons coarsely chopped
   fresh thyme leaves

1 medium celeriac (celery root) (750g),
   trimmed

3 medium potatoes (600g)

50g (1½ ounces) smoked cheddar,
   grated coarsely

1 teaspoon fresh thyme, extra

1 Preheat oven to 180°C/350°F.

2 Make celeriac and potato gratin.

3 Meanwhile, place veal on a wire rack in a flameproof roasting pan; pour the water into the base of the pan. Combine dijon mustard, horseradish and garlic in a small bowl. Spread mustard mixture over veal; season. Roast veal for last 45 minutes of gratin cooking time or until done as desired. Transfer veal to a plate. Cover; rest for 10 minutes.

4 Heat roasting pan over medium-high heat, add flour; cook, whisking, until mixture is smooth and bubbly. Add wholegrain mustard and stock; stir until mixture boils and thickens. Season to taste.

5 Combine herbs; press onto veal. Cut veal into cutlets; serve with gratin and mustard sauce.

CELERIAC & POTATO GRATIN Place cream, garlic and thyme in a medium saucepan over medium heat; bring to a simmer. Remove from heat; stand for 10 minutes. Meanwhile, using a mandoline or V-slicer, thinly slice celeriac and potatoes; combine in a large bowl. Layer celeriac and potato with cream mixture and salt and pepper in a 1.5-litre (6-cup) round ovenproof dish. Sprinkle with cheese. Cover with foil; bake for 1 hour. Remove foil; bake for a further 20 minutes or until tender and golden. Top with extra thyme.

SERVING SUGGESTION Serve with roman or green beans.

PREP + COOK TIME 3 HOURS 15 MINUTES SERVES 8

ROAST LEG OF PORK
with Pears and Parsnips

2.5kg (5-pound) boneless pork leg roast,
  rind on

2 tablespoons olive oil

1 tablespoon sea salt flakes

2 small red onions (200g), quartered

2 medium parsnips (500g), quartered

4 small firm pears (720g),
  quartered, cored

8 cloves garlic, unpeeled

¼ cup (55g) firmly packed light
  brown sugar

2 tablespoons olive oil, extra

1 Preheat oven to 220°C/425°F.
2 Score pork rind with sharp knife; rub with oil then salt. Place pork in a large shallow
baking dish. Roast, uncovered, for 20 minutes.
3 Reduce oven to 180°C/350°F; roast pork, uncovered, for a further 2 hours.
4 Meanwhile, combine remaining ingredients in a large bowl. Place, in a single layer,
on an oven tray. Roast, uncovered, for last 45 minutes of pork roasting time or until tender.
Season to taste.
5 Cover pork loosely with foil; stand for 10 minutes before slicing.
6 Serve pork with pear mixture.

PREP + COOK TIME 1 HOUR 40 MINUTES (+ REFRIGERATION & STANDING)
SERVES 10

SPANISH-STYLE
Leg of Lamb

2.2kg (4½-pound) easy-carve lamb leg

1 cured chorizo sausage (170g),
   chopped coarsely

5 cloves garlic, halved

1 tablespoon sweet paprika

1 tablespoon olive oil

½ cup (125ml) dry sherry

2 teaspoons coarsely chopped fresh thyme

1 Place lamb in a large baking dish. Pierce lamb deeply all over with a sharp knife; push sausage and garlic into cuts.

2 Combine paprika, oil and sherry in a small bowl; rub mixture all over lamb. Cover; refrigerate for 3 hours or overnight, turning lamb occasionally in the marinade.

3 Preheat oven to 200°C/400°F.

4 Drain lamb; discard marinade. Place lamb in a large baking dish, sprinkle with thyme. Roast, uncovered, until done as desired (see notes). Remove lamb from oven; rest, covered loosely with foil, for 15 minutes before serving.

SERVING SUGGESTION Serve with char-grilled lemon halves and steamed snow peas.

Notes

As a general guide, roast lamb for 15 minutes per 500g (1 pound) for medium. The lamb can be cooked in a covered barbecue, using indirect heat, following manufacturer's instructions.

Notes

Use a zesting tool to create the long thin strips of rind. If you don't have one, remove wide strips of rind with a vegetable peeler, then cut into thin strips with a sharp knife.

ASPARAGUS AND
Goat's Cheese Tart

2 sheets ready-rolled puff pastry

18 thin asparagus (320g)

2 teaspoons olive oil

4 eggs

1 cup (250ml) thickened (heavy) cream

70g (2½ ounces) soft goat's cheese, crumbled

ASPARAGUS SALAD

340g (11 ounces) asparagus

⅓ cup fresh small basil leaves

2 tablespoons lemon rind strips (see notes)

2 tablespoons olive oil

1 tablespoon lemon juice

1 clove garlic, crushed

1 Preheat oven to 220°C/425°F.

2 Grease a 21cm x 30cm (8½-inch x 12-inch) loose-based fluted flan tin. Overlap pastry sheets slightly; press to join. Lift pastry into pan; press over base and sides, trim excess pastry. Prick base all over with a fork; place flan tin on an oven tray. Line pastry case with baking paper; fill with dried beans or rice. Bake for 10 minutes. Remove paper and beans; bake for a further 15 minutes or until pastry is browned and crisp.

3 Meanwhile, heat a grill plate (or grill or barbecue) to medium-high heat. Brush asparagus with oil; cook, turning, for 7 minutes or until tender.

4 Reduce oven to 200°C/400°F. Whisk eggs and cream in a large bowl; season well. Pour egg mixture into pastry case; top with asparagus and goat's cheese.

5 Bake tart for 20 minutes or until set and golden.

6 Meanwhile, make asparagus salad.

7 Just before serving, top tart with half the asparagus salad; serve with remaining salad.

ASPARAGUS SALAD Using a vegetable peeler, peel asparagus into thin ribbons. Place asparagus, basil and rind in a medium bowl. Place oil, juice and garlic in a screw-top jar; shake well. Pour dressing over salad; toss gently to combine.

Sides

ASPARAGUS, PEAS
and Zucchini with Mint

1 cup (120g) frozen baby peas

2 bunches fresh asparagus (340g),
   trimmed, halved lengthways

¼ cup (60ml) extra virgin olive oil

10 fresh mint leaves, sliced finely,
   plus extra leaves for serving

2 small zucchini (180g)

1 tablespoon lemon juice

1 Place peas in a large saucepan of boiling water; boil for 3 minutes. Add asparagus;
boil for 1 minute, drain. Rinse under cold water; drain well.

2 Place peas and asparagus in a large bowl with oil and mint; season, toss to combine.

3 Cut zucchini in half lengthways; slice thinly on the diagonal. Add to bowl; toss to combine.

4 Just before serving, drizzle with lemon juice and sprinkle with extra mint leaves.

CRISP LETTUCE WEDGES
with Creamy Lemon Dressing

300g (9½ ounces) sour cream

1 cup (300g) whole-egg mayonnaise

1 teaspoon finely grated lemon rind

1½ tablespoons lemon juice

½ medium brown onion (80g)

4 baby cos (romaine) lettuce (720g)

¼ cup (20g) fried asian shallots

¼ cup loosely packed fresh flat-leaf
   parsley leaves

1 Place sour cream, mayonnaise, rind and juice in a medium bowl. Coarsely grate onion into a small bowl. Press down on onion to extract as much juice as possible; discard onion, reserve onion juice. Add onion juice to sour cream mixture, stir to combine; season.
2 Remove outer leaves from lettuce; discard root end. Cut each lettuce lengthways into quarters (if necessary, push a 20cm (8-inch) bamboo skewer through the leaves to hold them together).
3 Arrange lettuce wedges on a large platter. Drizzle with lemon dressing; top with shallots and parsley.

SMOKED TROUT SALAD
with Salsa Verde Dressing

500g (1 pound) kipfler (fingerling)
   potatoes
125g (4 ounces) green beans
3 cups (350g) firmly packed trimmed
   watercress
1 green oakleaf lettuce, leaves separated
300g (9½ ounces) hot smoked trout,
   skinned, flaked

SALSA VERDE DRESSING

1 slice white bread (50g), torn coarsely
1½ tablespoons red wine vinegar
¼ cup loosely packed fresh flat-leaf
   parsley leaves
¼ cup loosely packed fresh basil leaves
¼ cup loosely packed fresh mint leaves
2 drained anchovy fillets, chopped
1 clove garlic, chopped coarsely
2 teaspoons drained capers
2 tablespoons olive oil

1 Boil, steam or microwave potatoes and beans, separately, until tender; drain.
Rinse under cold water; drain. Halve potatoes lengthways.
2 Make salsa verde dressing.
3 Place potatoes and beans in a large bowl with two-thirds of the salsa verde; toss gently
to combine. Place watercress and lettuce on a serving platter.; top with potato mixture
and trout pieces. Drizzle with remaining dressing.
SALSA VERDE DRESSING Combine bread and vinegar in small bowl; stand for
5 minutes or until vinegar is almost absorbed. Blend or process herbs, anchovy,
garlic, capers and bread mixture to a coarse paste. Stir in oil. Season to taste.

PUMPKIN WITH PINE NUTS
and Balsamic Dressing

2kg (4 pounds) jap pumpkin, unpeeled

1 tablespoon extra virgin olive oil

1 tablespoon pine nuts, toasted

2 teaspoons fresh thyme leaves

¼ cup loosely packed fresh flat-leaf
   parsley leaves

BALSAMIC DRESSING

2 tablespoons extra virgin olive oil

1 tablespoon balsamic vinegar

1 clove garlic, crushed

1 Preheat oven to 200°C/400°F. Line two large oven trays with baking paper.
2 Make balsamic dressing.
3 Cut unpeeled pumpkin into 2cm (¾-inch) wedges; brush both sides with oil, then season.
Place pumpkin, in a single layer, on trays. Roast, uncovered, for 40 minutes or until
pumpkin is tender.
4 Transfer pumpkin to a platter; drizzle with dressing and scatter with pine nuts and herbs.
Serve warm or at room temperature.
BALSAMIC DRESSING Combine ingredients in a small bowl.

BRUSSELS SPROUTS WITH PANCETTA

PREP + COOK TIME 25 MINUTES
SERVES 8

750g (1½ pounds) brussels sprouts, halved

30g (1 ounce) butter

1 tablespoon olive oil

1 large brown onion (200g), sliced thinly

6 slices pancetta (90g), sliced thinly

2 cloves garlic, sliced thinly

¼ cup finely chopped fresh flat-leaf parsley

1 Boil, steam or microwave sprouts until barely tender; drain.
2 Meanwhile, heat butter and oil in large frying pan. Add onion, pancetta and garlic; cook, stirring, for 10 minutes or until onion starts to caramelise and pancetta is crisp. Add sprouts; cook, stirring, until heated through. Season to taste.
3 Serve sprout mixture topped with parsley.

HEIRLOOM TOMATO SALAD

PREP TIME 10 MINUTES
SERVES 8

2 tablespoons red wine vinegar

¼ teaspoon caster (superfine) sugar

1 teaspoon sea salt flakes

¼ cup (60ml) extra virgin olive oil

1.5kg (3 pounds) mixed heirloom tomatoes

¼ cup loosely packed fresh basil leaves

1 Place vinegar, sugar, salt and oil in a screw-top jar; shake well.

2 Cut tomatoes into a mix of slices and wedges. Arrange on a platter; drizzle with dressing. Season with freshly ground black pepper and top with basil leaves.

CHERRY, WALNUT
and Fetta Salad

125g (4 ounces) mesclun

¼ cup coarsely chopped fresh chives

1 cup (125g) pitted fresh cherries, halved

½ cup (50g) walnuts, roasted

100g (3 ounces) fetta, crumbled

LEMON DRESSING

2 teaspoons finely grated lemon rind

2 tablespoons tarragon vinegar

1 tablespoon lemon juice

1 teaspoon dijon mustard

¼ cup (60ml) olive oil

1 Make lemon dressing.
2 Combine mesclun, chives, cherries, half the nuts and half the fetta in a large bowl.
Add dressing; toss gently to combine.
3 Serve salad topped with remaining nuts and fetta.
LEMON DRESSING Whisk ingredients in a small bowl until combined; season to taste.

TIP When cherries are not in season, use quartered canned baby beetroot (beets) instead.

LEMON-ROASTED POTATOES

PREP + COOK TIME 50 MINUTES
SERVES 8

1.8kg (3½ pounds) potatoes, quartered
½ cup (125ml) olive oil
1 medium lemon (140g), cut into wedges

1 Preheat oven to 180°C/350°F.
2 Place potatoes in a saucepan of cold water; bring to the boil. Boil for 5 minutes, then drain. Stand for a few minutes or until potatoes are dry.
3 Meanwhile, pour oil into a shallow roasting pan; place in the oven for 2 minutes or until oil is hot. Add potatoes and lemon to hot oil; shake until well coated, season with salt.
4 Bake for 40 minutes or until potatoes are golden and tender.

TIP For perfect roast potatoes (crispy on the outside and fluffy on the inside), use a floury potato, such as coliban or king edward; all-rounder varieties, such as sebago and royal blue, would also be suitable.
SERVING SUGGESTION Serve topped with fresh flat-leaf parsley or rosemary leaves, green olives or halved cherry tomatoes for extra flavour.

JERK-SPICED ROASTED KUMARA

PREP + COOK TIME 40 MINUTES
SERVES 8

1.5kg (3 pounds) kumara (orange sweet
  potato)
2 cloves garlic, crushed
1 teaspoon chilli flakes
1 teaspoon dried thyme leaves
½ teaspoon allspice
½ teaspoon ground cinnamon
½ teaspoon ground nutmeg
2 teaspoons sea salt flakes
2 tablespoons olive oil
1 tablespoon olive oil, extra
2 teaspoons coarsely chopped fresh chives
Greek-style yoghurt, to serve (optional)

1 Preheat oven to 220°C/425°F. Line two
large oven trays with baking paper.
2 Cut unpeeled kumara lengthways into
thin wedges; combine with garlic, chilli,
thyme, spices, salt and oil in a large bowl.
Place kumara, in a single layer, on trays.
3 Roast kumara about 30 minutes or until
browned and cooked through.
4 Place kumara on a serving platter;
drizzle with extra oil, sprinkle with chives.
Serve kumara with yoghurt.

BEETROOT, HAZELNUT
and Spinach Salad

175g (5½ ounces) baby green beans

220g (7 ounces) buffalo mozzarella
cheese, drained

120g (4 ounces) baby spinach leaves

440g (14 ounce) canned baby beetroot
(beets), drained, halved

½ cup (70g) hazelnuts, roasted,
chopped coarsely

HONEY MUSTARD DRESSING

1 tablespoon honey

2 teaspoons wholegrain mustard

2 tablespoons sherry vinegar

2 tablespoons olive oil

1 Boil, steam or microwave beans until tender; drain. Rinse under cold water; drain, halve lengthways.

2 Meanwhile, make honey mustard dressing.

3 Tear each mozzarella into quarters; place in a large bowl with beans, spinach, beetroot and nuts. Toss gently to combine. Serve salad drizzled with dressing.

HONEY MUSTARD DRESSING Whisk ingredients in a small bowl until combined; season.

ROASTED BEETROOT AND BLUE CHEESE SALAD
with Honey Pecans

12 baby red beetroot (beets) (300g), trimmed

6 baby yellow beetroot (beets) (150g), trimmed

1 tablespoon olive oil

⅓ cup (80ml) water

⅔ cup (80g) pecans

2 tablespoons honey

100g (3 ounces) frisee, trimmed

150g (4½ ounces) blue cheese, crumbled

⅓ cup firmly packed fresh chervil leaves

HONEY MUSTARD DRESSING

¼ cup (60ml) olive oil

4 cloves garlic, sliced

2 tablespoons red wine vinegar

2 teaspoons dijon mustard

2 tablespoons honey

1 Preheat oven to 180°C/350°F.

2 Toss unpeeled beetroot, oil and the water in a small ovenproof dish; season. Cover dish with foil; bake for 20 minutes or until yellow beetroot are tender. Transfer yellow beetroot to a plate; cover to keep warm. Bake red beetroot for a further 15 minutes or until tender; drain. Transfer to same plate; cover to keep warm.

3 Meanwhile, line an oven tray with baking paper. Toast nuts in a medium frying pan for 5 minutes or until golden and fragrant. Add honey; cook, stirring, for 2 minutes or until nuts caramelise. Spread nuts on oven tray; cool.

4 Make honey mustard dressing.

5 Cut beetroot in half. Place frisee, beetroot and cheese on serving platter. Sprinkle with nuts, garlic and chervil; drizzle with dressing.

HONEY MUSTARD DRESSING Heat oil and garlic in a small saucepan over low heat; simmer garlic for 5 minutes or until light golden. Cool slightly. Whisk vinegar, mustard and honey in a small bowl. Remove garlic from oil with a slotted spoon; drain on paper towel. Reserve garlic for salad. Pour warm oil into vinegar mixture in a slow, steady stream, whisking constantly until mixture thickens slightly. Season to taste.

PUMPKIN, ROSEMARY
and Thyme Gratin

1.5kg (3 pounds) butternut pumpkin,
   cut into slices

2 tablespoons olive oil

1 medium onion (150g), sliced thinly

2 cloves garlic, sliced thinly

1 tablespoon finely chopped fresh
   rosemary leaves

1 tablespoon finely chopped fresh
   thyme leaves

125g (4 ounces) swiss cheese, sliced

½ cup (125ml) thickened (heavy) cream

pinch ground nutmeg

½ cup (35g) coarsely chopped
   stale breadcrumbs

1 Preheat oven to 220°C/425°F. Line an oven tray with baking paper.
2 Place pumpkin on a tray, drizzle with oil; season. Toss well to coat. Bake for 20 minutes.
Add onion, garlic and herbs; toss to combine. Bake for a further 25 minutes or until
pumpkin is just tender.
3 Layer pumpkin and cheese in a 1.5-litre (6-cup) ovenproof dish. Combine cream and
nutmeg; pour over pumpkin, then sprinkle with breadcrumbs.
4 Bake gratin for 30 minutes or until golden and heated through.

DO AHEAD Recipe can be completed to the end of step 2, up to 2 days ahead. Store in an
airtight container in the fridge.

Vegetable FAVOURITES

PARIS MASH

PREP + COOK TIME 30 MINUTES

SERVES 4

Place 1kg (2lbs) coarsely chopped peeled potatoes in a medium saucepan with enough cold water to barely cover the potato. Boil, uncovered, over medium heat, 15 minutes or until potato is tender; drain. Using the back of a wooden spoon, push potato through a fine sieve into a large bowl. Stir 90g (3oz) butter and ¾ cup hot milk into potato, folding gently until mash is smooth.

TIP We used lasoda potatoes, but you can use any all purpose or mashing variety – desiree, sebago, coliban and king edward are all fine to use.

ORANGE & MAPLE-GLAZED BABY CARROTS

PREP + COOK TIME 25 MINUTES

SERVES 4

Melt 30g (1oz) butter in a large frying pan over medium heat; cook 750g (1½lbs) trimmed baby (dutch) carrots, turning occasionally, for 8 minutes or until almost tender. Add 2 teaspoons finely grated orange rind, ¼ cup orange juice, 2 tablespoons dry white wine and 2 tablespoons maple syrup to pan; bring to the boil. Reduce heat; simmer, uncovered, until liquid has almost evaporated and carrots are tender and caramelised. Serve sprinkled with ½ cup coarsely chopped roasted hazelnuts and micro herbs.

BRUSSELS SPROUTS WITH CREAM & ALMONDS

PREP + COOK TIME 10 MINUTES

SERVES 4

Boil, steam or microwave 1kg (2lbs) halved brussels sprouts until tender; drain. Meanwhile, place 300ml pouring cream and 2 crushed cloves garlic in a small saucepan; simmer over medium heat until reduced by half. Season. Serve brussels sprouts drizzled with cream mixture and sprinkled with ⅓ cup roasted flaked almonds.

ROASTED PARSNIPS WITH SAGE & NUTMEG

PREP + COOK TIME 50 MINUTES

SERVES 4

Preheat oven to 200°C/400°F. Cut 1kg (2lbs) parsnips in half lengthways. Combine parsnips with 2 tablespoons olive oil, ¼ cup firmly packed light brown sugar and 1 teaspoon ground nutmeg in a large roasting pan, season; roast for 30 minutes. Add ¼ cup fresh sage leaves; roast for a further 10 minutes or until parsnips are browned and tender and sage is crisp.

Traditional SIDES

CARAMELISED
Root Vegetables

1 medium celeriac (celery root) (550g),
   peeled, chopped

400g (12½ ounces) baby carrots

3 small parsnips (360g), halved
   lengthways

50g (1½ ounces) butter

1 tablespoon light brown sugar

4 green onions (scallions), sliced thinly
   on the diagonal

¼ cup (60ml) extra virgin olive oil

¼ cup firmly packed curly parsley leaves,
   chopped coarsely

½ teaspoon finely grated lemon rind

1½ tablespoons lemon juice

1 Cook celeriac and carrots in a large saucepan of boiling salted water for 5 minutes.
Add parsnips; boil for a further 3 minutes or until vegetables are just tender. Drain.
Drop vegetables in a large bowl of iced water; drain well.

2 Melt half the butter in a large frying pan; cook vegetables, in batches, for 5 minutes or
until golden. Add remaining butter as needed between batches.

3 Return all vegetables to pan; cook, covered, for 5 minutes or until tender. Add sugar;
toss vegetables until well coated and caramelised.

4 Combine onions, oil, parsley, rind and juice in a small bowl; season to taste.

5 Add half the dressing to vegetables; toss gently to coat in dressing and pan juices.
Spoon vegetables onto a serving platter; top with remaining dressing.

Notes

We used sicilian olives for their crisp, crunchy texture and refreshingly piquant, buttery flavour. You can use regular green olives instead.

Char-grilled
ZUCCHINI SALAD

8 small zucchini (750g)

2 tablespoons extra virgin olive oil

GREEN OLIVE DRESSING

2 tablespoons finely chopped pitted
   sicilian olives (see notes)

2 drained anchovy fillets, chopped finely

2 teaspoons finely grated lemon rind

2 teaspoons finely grated orange rind

1 tablespoon drained baby capers

2 shallots (50g), chopped finely

¼ cup (60ml) red wine vinegar

½ cup (125ml) extra virgin olive oil

1 Make green olive dressing.
2 Using a mandoline, V-slicer or sharp knife, thinly slice zucchini lengthways; toss gently with oil to coat. Season.
3 Cook zucchini on a heated barbecue (or grill pan) for 1 minute each side or until lightly charred and just tender. Place zucchini on a platter.
4 Just before serving, drizzle zucchini with dressing.
GREEN OLIVE DRESSING   Combine ingredients in a small bowl. Season to taste.

Desserts

CHERRY BERRY
Chocolate Pavlova

100g (3 ounces) dark chocolate (70% cocoa),
  chopped coarsely

4 egg whites

1 cup (220g) caster (superfine) sugar

1 tablespoon cornflour (cornstarch)

1 teaspoon white vinegar

250g (8 ounces) cream cheese, softened

2 teaspoons vanilla extract

¼ cup (40g) icing (confectioners') sugar

300ml thickened (heavy) cream

fresh cherries with stems attached,
  to decorate

CHERRY BLUEBERRY COMPOTE

2 cups (300g) cherries, halved, pitted

1 cup (150g) blueberries

⅓ cup (75g) caster (superfine) sugar

¼ cup (60ml) water

¼ cup (80g) cherry jam

1 Preheat oven to 120°C/250°F. Line an oven tray with baking paper. Mark an 18cm (7¼-inch) circle on paper; turn paper, marked-side down, on tray.

2 Place chocolate in a small heatproof bowl over a small saucepan of simmering water (don't let water touch the base of the bowl); stir until just melted. Cool slightly.

3 Beat egg whites in a small bowl with an electric mixer until soft peaks form; gradually add caster sugar, beating until dissolved after each addition, and mixture is thick and glossy.

4 Fold cornflour and vinegar into meringue mixture; swirl in chocolate. Dollop meringue inside marked circle on tray.

5 Bake meringue for 1¼ hours or until dry to the touch. Turn oven off, leave meringue to cool in oven with door ajar.

6 Meanwhile, make cherry blueberry compote.

7 Beat cream cheese, extract and icing sugar in a small bowl with an electric mixer until smooth; gradually beat in cream until smooth and combined.

8 Just before serving, spoon cream cheese mixture on pavlova; top with berry compote. Decorate with fresh cherries.

CHERRY BLUEBERRY COMPOTE Place cherries, blueberries, sugar and the water in a medium saucepan over medium heat; bring to a simmer. Simmer for 5 minutes or until cherries and blueberries have released juices. Using a slotted spoon, transfer cherries and blueberries to a small bowl. Stir jam into juices in pan; bring to the boil. Boil for 5 minutes or until mixture thickens. Pour syrup over berry mixture. Cool completely.

DO-AHEAD The pavlova can be made a day ahead; store in an airtight container at room temperature. Compote and cream cheese mixture are best made close to serving.

Notes

To check that you have beaten the meringue sufficiently, rub a little of the mixture between your fingers – it should feel silky smooth, without any grainy sugar crystals.

CHOCOLATE TART
with Walnut Praline

1⅓ cups (200g) plain (all-purpose) flour

1 tablespoon caster (superfine) sugar

150g (4½ ounces) unsalted butter, chopped

1 egg yolk

1 tablespoon chilled water, approximately

CHOCOLATE FILLING

150g (4½ ounces) dark chocolate
   (70% cocoa), chopped

60g (2 ounces) unsalted butter, chopped

¼ cup (60ml) pouring cream

2 eggs

1 egg yolk

⅓ cup (75g) caster (superfine) sugar

WALNUT PRALINE

1 cup (100g) walnuts

1 cup (220g) caster (superfine) sugar

1 Sift flour and sugar into a large bowl; rub in butter until crumbly. Add egg yolk and enough of the water to make ingredients come together. (Or, process flour, sugar and butter until crumbly. Add egg yolk and the water; process until ingredients come together.) Knead dough on a floured surface until smooth. Flatten slightly into a disc; wrap in plastic wrap. Refrigerate for 30 minutes.

2 Grease a 22cm (9-inch) round loose-based fluted flan tin. Roll pastry between sheets of baking paper until large enough to line tin. Lift pastry into tin; press into base and side, trim edge. Refrigerate for 30 minutes.

3 Preheat oven to 180°C/350°F.

4 Place flan tin on an oven tray; line pastry with baking paper, fill with dried beans or rice. Bake for 15 minutes. Remove paper and beans; bake for a further 10 minutes or until golden.

5 Meanwhile, make chocolate filling.

6 Pour chocolate filling into pastry case. Bake for 15 minutes or until just set. Cool.

7 Meanwhile, make walnut praline. Sprinkle praline over tart just before serving.

CHOCOLATE FILLING Place chocolate, butter and cream in a small heavy-based saucepan; stir over low heat until melted and smooth. Whisk eggs, egg yolk and sugar in a medium bowl until light and fluffy; fold in chocolate mixture.

WALNUT PRALINE Line an oven tray with baking paper; sprinkle walnuts over tray. Place sugar in a small saucepan; cook over low heat until sugar melts and starts to turn a toffee colour. Quickly remove from heat and pour over nuts (you may need to move the paper a little to ensure that all the nuts are covered in the toffee). Cool. Crack praline with the point of a knife.

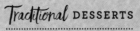

CLASSIC *Trifle*

2 x 85g (3-ounce) packets raspberry
  jelly crystals

500g (1 pound) small strawberries

250g (8 ounces) raspberries

200g (7½-ounce) sponge cake, cut into
  3cm (1¼-inch) cubes

⅓ cup (80ml) sweet sherry

500g (1 pound) mascarpone cheese

2 x 500g (1-pound) cartons vanilla bean
  custard (see tips)

600ml thickened (heavy) cream

2 tablespoons icing (confectioners') sugar

2 tablespoons flaked natural almonds,
  roasted

1 Make jelly according to directions on packet; pour into a 3 litre (12-cup) glass serving bowl. Cut 250g (8 ounces) of the strawberries in half; add to the jelly with half the raspberries. Refrigerate for 1 hour or until jelly is almost set.

2 Place cake in a medium bowl, sprinkle with sherry; toss to coat.

3 Beat mascarpone and custard in a large bowl with an electric mixer until soft peaks form. Spoon custard mixture over jelly, then top custard with sherry-soaked cake.

4 Beat cream and half the sifted icing sugar in a large bowl with electric mixer until soft peaks form. Spoon cream over cake layer.

5 Serve trifle topped with remaining raspberries and strawberries, then flaked almonds. Dust with remaining icing sugar.

DO-AHEAD This trifle can be made a day ahead up to the end of step 3; store, covered, in the fridge.

Notes

Use any good-quality thick dairy custard. You can use orange-flavoured liqueur instead of the sherry, if you prefer.

SOFT MERINGUE WITH
Pineapple and Kaffir Lime Syrup

7 egg whites

1¾ cups (375g) caster (superfine) sugar

2 teaspoons cornflour (cornstarch)

2 teaspoons white vinegar

1 small ripe trimmed pineapple (800g),
  peeled, chopped

2 limes (230g), segmented

2 tablespoons small fresh mint leaves

FILLING

250g (8 ounces) mascarpone cheese

½ cup (125ml) thickened (heavy) cream

1 teaspoons finely grated lime rind

2 teaspoons lime juice

1 tablespoon icing (confectioners') sugar

1 tablespoon finely chopped fresh mint

KAFFIR LIME SYRUP

½ cup (110g) caster (superfine) sugar

½ cup (125ml) water

1 fresh stalk lemon grass, trimmed, bruised

6 small kaffir lime leaves

1 Make filling.

2 Make kaffir lime syrup.

3 Preheat oven to 160°C/325°F. Grease a 24cm x 30cm x 3cm (9½-inch x 12-inch x 1¼-inch) pan; line base and sides with baking paper, extending paper 2cm (¾ inch) over the sides.

4 Beat egg whites in a large bowl with electric mixer until soft peaks form. Gradually add sugar, 1 tablespoon at a time, beating until thick and glossy and sugar has dissolved (about 8 minutes). Fold in cornflour and vinegar. Spoon meringue into pan; smooth the surface, then make furrows lengthways over half the meringue.

5 Bake meringue for 20 minutes, rotating the pan halfway through cooking time, or until meringue is firm to the touch. Stand meringue in pan for 2 minutes before turning out onto a large baking-paper-lined tray dusted with a little icing sugar. Carefully peel away lining paper. Line a second large tray with baking paper, dust with a little more icing sugar. Immediately invert meringue onto second lined tray. Cool.

6 Cut meringue in half lengthways. Carefully (soft meringue is fragile) place the smooth half on a platter. Spread filling over meringue, top with half of the pineapple and drizzle with a little syrup. Using a wide egg slice or long tart tin base, carefully place remaining meringue on top.

7 Place remaining pineapple in a small bowl with lime segments, mint and a little more syrup; toss to combine. Spoon pineapple mixture on meringue cake; serve drizzled with remaining syrup.

FILLING Beat mascarpone, cream, rind, juice and icing sugar in a small bowl with an electric mixer until soft peaks form; fold in mint. Cover; refrigerate until needed.

KAFFIR LIME SYRUP Place sugar, the water, lemon grass and lime leaves in a small saucepan. Bring to the boil, over medium heat, stirring until sugar dissolves. Simmer for 1 minute.

DO-AHEAD The meringue is best made on day of serving. Assemble close to serving.

Traditional DESSERTS

MOCHA, ALMOND AND
Chocolate Ice-cream

8 eggs, separated

2 cups (320g) icing (confectioners') sugar

600ml thickened (heavy) cream

1 tablespoon instant coffee granules

1 tablespoon coffee-flavoured liqueur

1 tablespoon almond-flavoured liqueur

¼ cup (20g) flaked almonds, toasted, plus extra to serve

125g (4 ounces) dark (semi-sweet) chocolate

250g (8 ounces) dark (semi-sweet) chocolate, extra

1 Beat egg whites in a large bowl with an electric mixer until soft peaks form. Gradually add sifted icing sugar; beat until sugar is dissolved.

2 Beat cream in a large bowl with electric mixer until firm. Fold cream gently through egg white mixture; divide mixture evenly into three bowls.

3 Beat egg yolks lightly with a fork; divide egg yolks evenly into three cups. Add combined coffee granules and coffee liqueur to one cup of egg yolk, then fold evenly through one bowl of egg white mixture. Pour mixture into a 23cm x 10.5cm (9-inch x 4-inch) loaf pan; level the surface. Cover with foil; freeze for 30 minutes or until ice-cream feels firm. Place remaining bowls of egg white mixture and egg yolks, covered, in the fridge until required.

4 Stir almond liqueur into another cup of egg yolks; fold into another bowl of egg white mixture along with the toasted almonds. Spread mixture evenly over coffee ice-cream layer; level the surface. Cover; freeze for 30 minutes or until firm.

5 Place chocolate in a small heatproof bowl over a small saucepan of simmering water (don't let water touch the base of the bowl); stir until smooth. Cool. Stir melted chocolate into remaining egg yolks; fold into remaining egg white mixture. Spread chocolate layer evenly over almond ice-cream layer; smooth the surface. Cover; freeze overnight.

6 Invert ice-cream onto serving plate, return to the freezer.

7 Place extra chocolate in a medium heatproof bowl over a medium saucepan of simmering water (don't let water touch the base of the bowl); stir until smooth. Cool slightly; pour as evenly as possible over ice-cream, return to freezer until chocolate is set. Serve cut into slices, topped with extra toasted flaked almonds.

DO-AHEAD The ice-cream can be made up to a week ahead; cover with foil to freeze.

Notes

To remove the seeds from the pomegranate, cut the whole pomegranate in half crossways; hold it, cut-side down, in the palm of your hand over a bowl, then hit the outside firmly with a wooden spoon. The seeds should fall out easily; discard any white pith that falls out with them.

FIG AND EGGNOG
Cheesecake

350g (11 ounces) fruit cake, cut into
   1cm (¾-inch) slices

750g (1½ pounds) packaged cream
   cheese, softened

300g (9½ ounces) sour cream

1 teaspoon vanilla extract

¼ cup (60ml) brandy

½ teaspoon ground nutmeg

1 cup (220g) caster (superfine) sugar

3 eggs

½ cup (175g) honey

¼ cup (60ml) water

1 cinnamon stick

5 fresh figs (300g), halved

100g (3 ounces) red seedless grapes

1 medium pomegranate (320g), seeds
   removed (see notes)

1 Preheat oven to 180°C/350°F. Line base of a 22cm (9-inch) springform tin with baking paper.

2 Cover base of tin with cake slices. Bake for 10 minutes or until browned lightly. Reduce oven to 150°C/300°F.

3 Meanwhile, beat cream cheese, sour cream, extract, brandy, nutmeg and sugar in a medium bowl with an electric mixer until smooth. Beat in eggs, one at a time, until just combined. Pour mixture into tin.

4 Bake cheesecake for 45 minutes or until just set. Cool cheesecake in oven with door ajar. Cover; refrigerate overnight.

5 Stir honey, the water and cinnamon stick in a medium heavy-based frying pan over high heat; bring to the boil. Reduce heat; simmer until sticky. Remove cinnamon stick.

6 Remove cheesecake from tin, place on a serving plate; top with figs, grapes and pomegranate seeds. Serve drizzled with syrup.

LIME SORBET SLICE
with Mojito Fruit Salad

1½ cups (330g) caster (superfine) sugar

2½ cups (625ml) water

¾ cup (180ml) strained lime juice

2 teaspoons egg white

LIME ICE-CREAM

2 teaspoons finely grated lime rind

¼ cup (60ml) lime juice

300ml thickened (heavy) cream

1 cup (160g) icing (confectioners') sugar

125g (4 ounces) mascarpone cheese

125g (4 ounces) Greek-style yoghurt

MOJITO FRUIT SALAD

1 medium pineapple (1.4kg), peeled, quartered,
    cored, sliced thinly

⅓ cup (80ml) passionfruit pulp

½ cup (125ml) white rum

1 medium lime (90g), cut into eight wedges

2 teaspoons white (granulated) sugar

1 tablespoon finely chopped fresh mint

1 Place sugar and the water in a medium saucepan; stir over medium heat, without boiling, until sugar dissolves. Bring to the boil; boil, without stirring, for 1 minute. Remove from heat, cool to room temperature. Combine syrup with the juice in a jug. Refrigerate for 2 hours or until cold. Reserve 1 cup of the lime syrup for the mojito fruit salad.

2 To make the lime sorbet, churn the remaining cold lime syrup in an ice-cream machine, following the manufacturer's instructions until firm, adding the egg white once the mixture starts to form ice crystals. (Or, pour mixture into a shallow, freezer-proof container; freeze until just set. Chop mixture, process until coarsely chopped; add egg white and process until combined. Freeze mixture until partially frozen.)

3 Meanwhile, line base and two long sides of a 10cm x 25cm (4-inch x 10-inch) loaf pan with baking paper, extending the paper 5cm (2 inches) above sides of pan. Spread sorbet over base of pan; smooth the surface. Cover; freeze for 1 hour or until firm.

4 Make lime ice-cream. Spread ice-cream over sorbet; smooth the surface. Cover, freeze for 6 hours or overnight until firm.

5 Make mojito fruit salad.

6 Rub the outside of the loaf pan with a warm, damp cloth. Invert pan, discard lining paper. Cut sorbet slice into thick slices; serve with mojito fruit salad.

LIME ICE-CREAM Beat rind, juice, cream and sifted icing sugar in a small bowl with an electric mixer until soft peaks form. Beat in mascarpone and yoghurt until just combined.

MOJITO FRUIT SALAD Place pineapple and passionfruit in a large heatproof bowl. Combine reserved lime syrup and the rum in a small saucepan; bring just to the boil. Pour over fruit; cool. Mash lime wedges and sugar in a medium bowl or jug to extract juice. Add lime wedge mixture (including wedges) and mint to pineapple mixture; toss gently.

Notes

You need about 9 limes and 4 passionfruit for this recipe. The slice can be made a week ahead; freeze until required. Syrup can be made a week ahead; store, covered, in the fridge.

YULE *Log*

See page 140 for step-by-step images and information on how to prepare and cook this yule log.

3 eggs

⅔ cup (150g) caster (superfine) sugar

½ cup (75g) plain (all-purpose) flour

¼ cup (60ml) irish cream liqueur

2 teaspoons dutch cocoa powder

fresh cherries with stems attached,
    to decorate

DARK CHOCOLATE GANACHE

½ cup (125ml) pouring cream

200g (6½ ounces) dark (semi-sweet)
    chocolate, chopped coarsely

HAZELNUT FILLING

125g (4 ounces) mascarpone cheese

125g (4 ounces) cream cheese, softened

1½ tablespoons dutch cocoa powder

¼ cup (85g) chocolate-hazelnut spread

1½ tablespoons irish cream liqueur

1 Make dark chocolate ganache.

2 Preheat oven to 180°C/350°F. Grease a 25cm x 30cm (10-inch x 12-inch) swiss roll pan; line base with baking paper, extending the paper 5cm (2 inches) above long sides of pan. Grease baking paper.

3 Beat eggs and ½ cup of the sugar in a small bowl with an electric mixer for 5 minutes or until mixture is thick and creamy; transfer to a large bowl. Fold triple sifted flour into the egg mixture. Spread mixture into pan; level surface. Bake for 15 minutes.

4 Place a large sheet of baking paper on a wire rack; sprinkle paper with remaining sugar. Turn cake onto baking paper; remove lining paper, immediately roll up cake from the short side. Leave to cool.

5 Meanwhile, make hazelnut filling.

6 Unroll cake, brush with liqueur; spread with filling, leaving a 3cm (1¼-inch) border on one short side. Roll up from opposite short side, using paper as a guide. Transfer to a serving platter. Roughly spread ganache over cake; dust with sifted cocoa powder. Refrigerate for 1 hour before cutting. Serve topped with fresh cherries.

DARK CHOCOLATE GANACHE Bring cream to the boil in a small saucepan; remove from heat. Add chocolate to hot cream; stir gently until smooth. Cool mixture to room temperature until ganache is spreadable.

HAZELNUT FILLING Beat ingredients in a small bowl with electric mixer until mixture is thick and creamy.

DO-AHEAD The ganache can be made 2 days ahead; store in the fridge. When ready to use, beat with an electric mixer until it is of a spreadable consistency.

Traditional DESSERTS

Yule Log

SPREADING MIXTURE INTO THE PAN

Spread the mixture to the edge of the pan, spreading evenly and gently so as not to lose any air in the mixture. Bake for 15 minutes or until sponge is golden.

PREPARING TO TURN THE SPONGE OUT

Place a piece of baking paper, cut larger than the pan, on a wire rack; sprinkle paper evenly with sugar. This paper will also act as a guide when rolling the sponge.

SPREADING FILLING ON THE SPONGE

Unroll the cold sponge; brush with liqueur. Spread with the filling, leaving a 3cm (1¼-inch) border at the end of the short side farthest away from you.

ROLLING THE SPONGE

Using the paper as a guide, roll the sponge up from the short side nearest to you. Spread and cover the roll with the ganache; refrigerate for 1 hour.

Traditional DESSERTS

CHOCOLATE AND CHESTNUT
Self-saucing Pudding

60g (2 ounces) butter, chopped

½ cup (125ml) milk

1 teaspoon vanilla bean paste

½ cup (110g) caster (superfine) sugar

1⅓ cups (200g) self-raising flour

1 tablespoon dutch cocoa powder

½ cup (100g) sweet chestnut puree

½ cup (110g) firmly packed light
  brown sugar

2 tablespoons dutch cocoa powder, extra

1 cup (250ml) boiling water

1 Preheat oven to 180°C/350°F. Grease a 1.5-litre (6-cup) ovenproof dish.

2 Heat butter and milk in a medium saucepan over low heat until butter melts; remove pan from heat. Stir in vanilla paste and caster sugar, then sifted flour and cocoa. Fold in chestnut puree. Spread mixture into dish.

3 Sift brown sugar and extra cocoa over pudding mixture. Gently pour the boiling water over pudding mixture.

4 Bake pudding for 40 minutes or until centre is firm. Stand for 5 minutes before serving.

TIP This recipe is not suitable to freeze or microwave.

SERVING SUGGESTION Serve with ice-cream or thick (double) cream.

WHITE CHOCOLATE CHEESECAKES
with Frosted Cranberries

300g (9½ ounces) plain sweet biscuits

150g (4½ ounces) butter, melted

¾ cup (180ml) thickened (heavy) cream

360g (11½ ounces) white chocolate,
   chopped coarsely

1kg (2 pounds) cream cheese, softened

1½ cups (330g) caster (superfine) sugar

3 eggs

1½ teaspoons vanilla bean paste

FROSTED CRANBERRIES

½ cup (110g) white (granulated) sugar

300g (9½ ounces) frozen cranberries,
   thawed on a paper towel, kept cold in
   the refrigerator

1 Preheat oven to 150°C/300°F. Grease a 12-hole ¾-cup (180ml) cheesecake pan with removable bases (or line two 6-hole (¾-cup/180ml) texas muffin pans with paper cases).
2 Process biscuits until fine. Add butter; process to combine. Place 2 tablespoons of crumb mixture into each pan hole, pressing down firmly over bases. Refrigerate for 30 minutes.
3 Combine cream and chocolate in a small saucepan; stir over low heat until smooth. Cool.
4 Beat cream cheese, sugar, eggs and vanilla paste with an electric mixer until smooth. Beat in the chocolate mixture. Place ½ cup of cream cheese mixture into each pan hole (mixture will reach the top of the pan); place pan on an oven tray.
5 Bake cheesecakes for 30 minutes or until almost set. Cool in oven with the door ajar. Refrigerate cheesecakes for at least 1 hour.
6 Just before serving, make frosted cranberries. Serve cheesecakes topped with cranberries.
FROSTED CRANBERRIES Spread sugar on a tray. Roll cranberries in sugar to lightly coat.

CHOCOLATE BLANCMANGE
with Vanilla Cherries

¼ cup (35g) cornflour (cornstarch)

2 tablespoons cocoa powder

2 tablespoons caster (superfine) sugar

1¼ cups (310ml) milk

300ml pouring cream

1 teaspoon vanilla extract

1 vanilla bean

½ cup (110g) caster (superfine) sugar, extra

¾ cup (180ml) water

500g (1 pound) fresh cherries

1 Sift cornflour, cocoa and sugar into a medium saucepan; gradually stir in milk and cream. Cook, stirring, over medium heat, until mixture boils and thickens. Reduce heat; simmer, stirring, for 2 minutes. Remove from heat; stir in extract.

2 Spoon mixture into six serving glasses; cover surface directly with plastic wrap. Refrigerate for 3 hours.

3 Split vanilla bean in half lengthways, scrape seeds into a medium saucepan; add pod, extra sugar and the water. Stir over high heat, without boiling, until sugar dissolves. Bring to the boil. Reduce heat; simmer, uncovered, for 10 minutes or until syrup is slightly thickened.

4 Transfer syrup to a medium heatproof bowl, add cherries. Cover; refrigerate for 1 hour.

5 Serve blancmange topped with cherries and syrup.

AMARETTO AND CARAMEL
Ice-cream Cake

You will need to start this recipe the day before.

3 cups (750ml) milk

3 cups (750ml) pouring cream

18 egg yolks (see notes)

2 cups (440g) caster (superfine) sugar

2½ tablespoons amaretto

220g (7 ounces) amaretti biscuits, crushed roughly

1 tablespoon amaretto, extra

CARAMEL SAUCE

2 cups (440g) caster (superfine) sugar

1½ tablespoons liquid glucose

½ cup (125ml) water

1 cup (250ml) pouring cream

120g (4 ounces) butter, softened, chopped

1 Heat milk and cream in a large saucepan until almost boiling. Whisk egg yolks and sugar in a large bowl until combined. Gradually whisk milk mixture into yolk mixture. Return mixture to pan; stir constantly over low heat for 7 minutes or until custard thickens. Do not boil. Strain mixture into a large bowl; stir in liqueur. Cover surface with plastic wrap; refrigerate for 4 hours or until chilled.

2 Meanwhile, make caramel sauce.

3 Grease a 22cm (9-inch) springform pan; line base and side with baking paper. Reserve 1 tablespoon amaretti crumbs to serve. Sprinkle one-third of the remaining amaretti crumbs on base of the pan. Place pan in freezer to chill.

4 Churn half the chilled custard in an ice-cream machine according to manufacturer's instructions. Working quickly, spoon ice-cream into chilled pan; smooth surface. Using a quarter of the caramel sauce, dollop four tablespoons onto the ice-cream layer. Using a knife, gently swirl the caramel through ice-cream. Sprinkle with half the remaining amaretti crumbs. Cover with plastic wrap; freeze for 1 hour or until firm.

5 Repeat step 4 with remaining chilled custard, another quarter of the caramel sauce and remaining amaretti crumbs. Cover with plastic wrap; freeze overnight until firm. Stir extra amaretto into caramel sauce; refrigerate until required.

6 Before serving, reheat remaining caramel sauce in a microwave oven on low. Drizzle sauce over ice-cream cake; sprinkle with reserved amaretti.

CARAMEL SAUCE Stir sugar, glucose and the water in a medium saucepan over medium heat until sugar dissolves, brushing down side of pan occasionally with a wet pastry brush. Bring to the boil. Reduce heat; simmer, without stirring, for 7 minutes or until a deep caramel colour. Remove pan from heat. Carefully add cream, taking care as mixture will splutter. Return to heat; stir until smooth. Cool caramel until just warm. Gradually whisk in butter until combined. Transfer sauce to a jug, cover; set aside at room temperature until required.

Notes

This recipe only uses egg
yolks, which of course means
you will have 18 egg whites
left over. The good news is
that you can freeze them for
later use. As you separate
the eggs, place each white
into the hole of an ice-cube
tray. Once frozen transfer
them to a small container or
resealable plastic bag, and
note the date; they will keep
for up to 1 year. Thaw in the
fridge before use.

RHUBARB AND WHITE CHOCOLATE
Bread and Butter Pudding

470g (15 ounces) trimmed rhubarb stalks

¾ cup (165g) raw caster (superfine) sugar

450g (14½ ounce) loaf brioche

90g (3 ounces) butter, softened

1 teaspoon ground cardamom

180g (5½ ounces) white chocolate,
   chopped finely

1 vanilla bean

5 eggs

2 cups (500ml) pouring cream

1½ cups (375ml) milk

2 teaspoons icing (confectioners') sugar

1 Preheat oven to 180°C/350°F.

2 Cut rhubarb into 6cm (2½-inch) lengths. Place rhubarb in a 4-litre (16-cup) ovenproof dish; sprinkle with ¼ cup of the raw caster sugar. Roast, covered, for 25 minutes or until just tender. Transfer half the rhubarb to a medium bowl.

3 Meanwhile, trim brioche; cut into 1.5cm (¾-inch) thick slices. Combine 70g (2½ ounces) of the butter and cardamom in a small bowl; spread butter mixture onto each brioche slice. Sprinkle three-quarters of the chocolate over buttered brioche; sandwich together. Layer brioche on top of rhubarb in dish. Top with remaining rhubarb and chocolate.

4 Split vanilla bean in half lengthways; scrape out seeds. Combine seeds with eggs, ¼ cup of the raw caster sugar, cream and milk in a jug. Pour half the cream mixture over brioche; stand until mixture has soaked into brioche. Pour remaining mixture over brioche; dot with remaining butter, sprinkle with remaining raw caster sugar.

5 Place ovenproof dish in a large baking dish; add enough boiling water to come halfway up side of ovenproof dish.

6 Bake pudding for 30 minutes or until just set. Remove pudding from baking dish; stand for 10 minutes. Serve dusted with sifted icing sugar.

SERVING SUGGESTION Serve with fresh or poached fruit.

BANOFFEE MERINGUE
with Honeycomb

4 egg whites

¼ teaspoon cream of tartar

¼ cup (55g) caster (superfine) sugar

¾ cup (165g) firmly packed light brown sugar

2 teaspoons cornflour (cornstarch)

1 teaspoon white vinegar

¼ teaspoon vanilla extract

2 medium bananas (400g), sliced

1 tablespoon caster (superfine) sugar, extra

300ml thick (double) cream

100g (3 ounces) honeycomb, chopped coarsely

DULCE DE LECHE

395g (12½ ounces) canned sweetened
   condensed milk

1 Make dulce de leche.

2 Preheat oven to 120°C/250°F. Line two large oven trays with baking paper. Mark a 12.5cm x 30cm (5-inch x 12-inch) rectangle on each sheet of paper; turn paper, marked-side down, on trays.

3 Beat egg whites, cream of tartar and sugars in a medium bowl with an electric mixer on high speed for 8 minutes or until thick and glossy and sugar is dissolved. Beat in cornflour, vinegar and extract on low speed. Divide mixture between trays, spreading to cover just inside marked rectangles; swirl surface of meringue.

4 Bake meringue for 1 hour or until dry to touch. Cool in oven with door ajar.

5 Place banana slices, in a single layer, on an oven tray; sprinkle with extra caster sugar. Using a blowtorch, caramelise sugar.

6 Whisk dulce de leche in a medium bowl until smooth. Whisk cream in a small bowl until soft peaks form.

7 Break meringue into pieces; divide half among 12 x 1½ cup (375ml) glasses or bowls. Top with half the whipped cream and half the dulce de leche. Repeat layering with remaining meringue, cream and dulce de leche. Top with banana slices and honeycomb.

DULCE DE LECHE Preheat oven to 220°C/425°F. Pour condensed milk into a 1.5-litre (6-cup) ceramic ovenproof dish. Cover dish tightly with foil; crush excess foil upwards. Place ceramic dish in a medium baking dish; add enough boiling water to come halfway up the side of the ceramic dish. Bake for 1 hour. Whisk mixture; cover, bake for a further 30 minutes or until a golden caramel colour, adding extra boiling water to baking dish as needed to maintain water level during baking. Remove dish from water; cool. Whisk mixture until smooth. Transfer to a medium bowl; cover, refrigerate until chilled.

DO-AHEAD Dulce de leche can be made a day ahead. Meringue is best made on day of serving. Store in an airtight container and assemble close to serving.

Notes

Dulce de leche is a caramel sauce. If you prefer, you can use ready-made dulce de leche sold in jars from delis, gourmet food stores and supermarkets. Plain honeycomb is available from some specialty sweet stores or greengrocers. Blowtorches are available from homeware and hardware stores. Alternatively, you can place the bananas under a hot grill (broiler) to caramelise the sugar.

BAKED RICOTTA
Tartlets

⅓ cup (55g) whole blanched almonds, roasted

¼ cup (35g) sesame seeds, roasted

1¼ cups (185g) plain (all-purpose) flour

125g (4 ounces) chilled butter, chopped

¼ cup (55g) caster (superfine) sugar

1 egg yolk

1 teaspoon vanilla extract

1 tablespoon water, approximately

1 tablespoon pine nuts, chopped finely

2 teaspoons icing (confectioners') sugar

½ cup (170g) fine-cut orange marmalade, warmed

1 medium orange (240g), rind removed, cut into thin strips

RICOTTA FILLING

1¼ cups (300g) soft ricotta

¼ cup (55g) caster (superfine) sugar

1 egg, beaten lightly

1 egg yolk

1 tablespoon finely grated orange rind

1 Process almonds and seeds until finely chopped. Add flour, butter and caster sugar; process until mixture resembles breadcrumbs. Add egg yolk, extract and the water; process until ingredients just come together. Wrap dough in plastic wrap; refrigerate for 30 minutes.

2 Meanwhile, make ricotta filling.

3 Preheat oven to 190°C/375°F. Grease 10 small fluted brioche tins, 8cm (3¼ inches) top measure and 3.5cm (1½ inches) deep. Place on an oven tray.

4 Roll pastry between sheets of baking paper until 3mm (⅛ inch) thick. Using a 9cm (3¾-inch) round cutter, cut 10 rounds from pastry. Lift pastry into tins, press into base and side, trim edges. Cover; refrigerate for 10 minutes.

5 Meanwhile, re-roll pastry scraps until 3mm (⅛ inch) thick; cut pastry into 1cm (½-inch) wide strips.

6 Spoon ricotta filling into tart shells; decorate with pastry strips. Sprinkle with pine nuts.

7 Bake tartlets for 35 minutes or until pastry is golden and filling cooked through. Leave tartlets in tins for 5 minutes before turning, top-side up, onto a wire rack to cool. Serve warm, dusted with icing sugar, topped with marmalade and strips of rind.

RICOTTA FILLING Process ingredients until just smooth and combined.

Dessert SAUCES

SPICED RUM BUTTER

PREP TIME 10 MINUTES **MAKES** 2½ CUPS

Beat 250g (8oz) softened unsalted butter in a small
bowl with an electric mixer until as white as possible.
Beat in ½ cup (110g) firmly packed light brown sugar,
2 teaspoons mixed spice, 1½ teaspoons each ground
cinnamon and ground ginger, a large pinch each
ground nutmeg and ground cloves, and 2 tablespoons
dark rum until mixture is light and fluffy.

STRAWBERRY COULIS

PREP TIME 10 MINUTES **MAKES** 1 CUP

Push 300g (9½oz) thawed, frozen strawberries
through a fine sieve into a small bowl; discard seeds.
Stir 1 tablespoon sifted icing (confectioners') sugar
into sauce.

TIPS Any berries, fresh or frozen, can be used; blend or
process berries until smooth, then continue as above.
Other fruits such as mango, passionfruit, kiwifruit, and
even guava or pineapple, are also suitable. Adjust the
amount of sugar according to the fruit used.

HAZELNUT HARD SAUCE

PREP TIME 10 MINUTES **MAKES** 1¾ CUPS

Beat 125g (4oz) softened unsalted butter and 1 cup (160g) sifted icing (confectioners') sugar in a small bowl with an electric mixer until as white as possible. Beat in 2 tablespoons pouring cream, 2 tablespoons hazelnut-flavoured liqueur and 1 tablespoon orange-flavoured liqueur. Serve topped with zested strips of orange rind.

RICH CARAMEL SAUCE

PREP + COOK TIME 25 MINUTES
MAKES 1½ CUPS

Stir 1 cup (220g) caster (superfine) sugar and ½ cup water in a small saucepan over low heat until sugar dissolves. Boil, uncovered, without stirring, 15 minutes or until mixture turns a caramel colour. Remove from heat; allow bubbles to subside. Gradually add 300ml thickened (heavy) cream, stirring constantly, over low heat, until sauce is smooth. Cool for 10 minutes.

Traditional DESSERTS

Notes

To crush ginger nuts,
place in a metal or plastic
bowl and use the end of a
rolling pin to crush them; sift
to remove any fine crumbs.
Avoid eating whole spices
as these are left in the syrup
as a garnish only, the figs
however will be delicious.

CHAI PARFAIT WITH
Fig and Whole Spice Syrup

You will need an empty 1 litre cardboard milk carton to mould the parfait in. Alternatively you can use a 1 litre (4-cup) terrine tin.

1½ cups (375ml) milk

2½ tablespoons good-quality loose-leaf black tea

2 star anise

10 cloves

1 cinnamon stick, broken in half

2 cardamon pods, bruised

1½ teaspoons finely grated fresh ginger

300ml pouring cream

8 egg yolks

½ cup (110g) caster (superfine) sugar

2 ginger nut biscuits (30g), crushed coarsely

2 tablespoons roasted unsalted shelled
  pistachios, chopped coarsely

¼ cup (35g) glacé ginger, chopped coarsely

FIG & WHOLE SPICE SYRUP

½ cup (110g) firmly packed light brown sugar

½ cup (125ml) water

3 cardamom pods

4 black peppercorns

6 cloves

6 allspice

1 star anise

1 cinnamon stick, broken in half

100g (3 ounces) dried wild figs

2 teaspoons freshly squeezed orange juice

1 Heat milk in a large heavy-based saucepan until almost boiling. Remove from heat; stir in tea, spices and ginger until combined. Stand for 15 minutes. Pour through a sieve; discard solids.
2 Return strained milk to pan, stir in cream; bring almost to the boil. Meanwhile, whisk egg yolks and sugar in a medium bowl until pale. Gradually whisk hot milk mixture into egg yolk mixture until combined. Return mixture to pan; stir continuously over low heat until custard thickens enough to coat the back of a spoon (do not allow to boil).
3 Pour custard into a medium stainless steel bowl, place bowl over a second larger bowl filled with ice; whisk custard for a few minutes to cool slightly. Cover surface with plastic wrap; refrigerate until chilled.
4 Churn chilled custard in an ice-cream machine, following manufacturer's directions. Five minutes before end of churning, add biscuits, nuts and glacé ginger; churn for a further 5 minutes or until incorporated.
5 Pour ice-cream into a clean 1 litre (4 cup) cardboard milk carton; seal top. Freeze, standing carton upright, for 6 hours or overnight.
6 Make fig and whole spice syrup.
7 To serve, remove parfait from freezer and tear away cardboard milk carton. Place on a platter with a lip; spoon over fig and whole spice syrup.
FIG & WHOLE SPICE SYRUP Place ingredients, except juice, in a small heavy-based saucepan over low heat; stir for 1 minute until sugar dissolves. Bring to the boil. Reduce heat; simmer for about 12 minutes or until figs have softened and syrup thickened slightly. Cool, then stir in juice. Cut half the figs in half.

DO-AHEAD Parfait can be made a day ahead.

Traditional DESSERTS

PLUM AND GINGER *Crostata*

7 large yellow-fleshed black plums (1.2kg),
    cut into thin wedges

1 egg, beaten lightly

¼ cup (55g) demerara sugar

2 tablespoons glacé ginger,
    chopped coarsely

PASTRY

1⅔ cups (250g) plain (all-purpose) flour

⅓ cup (55g) icing (confectioners') sugar

½ teaspoon salt

150g (4½ ounces) cold unsalted butter,
    chopped finely

¼ cup (60ml) iced water

WALNUT & GINGER PASTE

¾ cup (75g) walnuts, roasted

½ cup (115g) glacé ginger

50g (1½ ounces) butter, softened

2 tablespoons instant polenta (cornmeal)

1 tablespoon plain (all-purpose) flour

1 egg yolk

1 Make pastry.

2 Make walnut and ginger paste.

3 Preheat oven to 190°C/375°F.

4 Roll out pastry between two pieces of floured baking paper into a 35cm (14-inch) round. Remove top piece of baking paper; carefully lift baking paper with pastry onto a large oven tray. Using a 26cm (10-inch) bowl or plate as a guide, mark a round in the centre of the pastry. Spread walnut and ginger paste inside the marked round.

5 Starting at the edge of the filled round, place plum wedges in concentric circles. Carefully fold pastry edge in, pleating it as you go to partially cover the outside circle of plums. Brush folded edge with egg. Sprinkle sugar over plums and pastry.

6 Bake crostata for 40 minutes or until pastry is golden and filling cooked. Stand on tray for 20 minutes. Just before serving, top with glacé ginger.

PASTRY Process flour, sugar and salt until combined. Add butter; process until mixture resembles breadcrumbs. Add the iced water; pulse until mixture almost comes together. Turn dough onto a work surface and form into a thin disc. Warp dough in plastic wrap; freeze for 30 minutes only.

WALNUT & GINGER PASTE Process ingredients until mixture forms a smooth paste.

SERVING SUGGESTION Serve with thick (double) cream or ice-cream.

SPICED APPLE *Stack*

You will need to start this recipe a day ahead.

600g (1¼ pounds) dried apple slices

1.5 litres (6 cups) water

1 cup (220g) firmly packed light brown sugar

2 teaspoons ground cinnamon

½ teaspoon ground nutmeg

½ teaspoon ground allspice

¼ teaspoon ground cloves

250g (8 ounces) butter, softened

2 cups (440g) caster (superfine) sugar

2 teaspoons vanilla extract

2 eggs

2 cups (300g) plain (all-purpose) flour

4 cups (600g) self-raising flour

1 teaspoon bicarbonate of (baking) soda

¼ teaspoon salt

⅔ cup (160ml) buttermilk

1½ tablespoons icing (confectioners') sugar

3 cinnamon sticks

1 Place dried apples and the water in a large saucepan; cover surface with a round of baking paper, then a small plate to weight down. Bring to the boil over high heat. Reduce heat; simmer, for 20 minutes or until apple is soft. Drain. Cool. Blend or process apple mixture, in batches, until smooth; transfer to a large bowl. Stir in brown sugar and spices.

2 Preheat oven to 180°C/350°F. Grease and line two oven trays with baking paper.

3 Beat butter, caster sugar and extract in a small bowl with an electric mixer until pale and fluffy. Beat in eggs, one at a time, until just combined. Transfer mixture to a large bowl. Sift flours, soda and salt into another large bowl. Stir flour mixture into creamed mixture alternately with buttermilk, in three batches, until combined (mixture will be stiff; you may need to finish combining with your hands). Knead dough on a floured surface until smooth and combined.

4 Divide dough into eight equal portions. Roll one portion of dough between sheets of baking paper into a 23cm (9¼-inch) round. Using a 22cm (9-inch) plate or cake pan as a guide, cut round from dough. Transfer to one tray. Repeat with another portion of dough and second tray.

5 Bake for 12 minutes, swapping trays from top to bottom halfway through cooking time or until golden. Stand dough on trays for 5 minutes before transferring to wire racks to cool. Repeat steps 4 and 5 with remaining dough portions, in batches, to make eight rounds in total.

6 Place a cake round on a platter or cake stand; spread with a slightly rounded ½ cup of apple filling. Repeat layering with remaining cake rounds and apple filling, finishing with a cake round. Cover cake with plastic wrap; refrigerate overnight. Just before serving, dust cake with icing sugar; decorate with cinnamon sticks.

DO-AHEAD This cake needs to be made at least a day ahead. Or, up to 2 days ahead; store, covered, in the fridge.

Cakes
AND
Puddings

THREE-IN-ONE
Basic Fruit Mix

This basic fruit mix is enough to make a regular-sized fruit cake (see page 169), a pudding (boiled or steamed) large enough to serve 10 (see page 177), and 12 mince pies (see page 174).

2⅓ cups (375g) sultanas

2 cups (320g) dried currants

2⅓ cups (375g) coarsely chopped raisins

1 cup (150g) finely chopped pitted dates

⅔ cup (120g) finely chopped pitted
   prunes

1 cup (200g) finely chopped dried figs

2 large apples (400g), grated coarsely

¼ cup (90g) golden syrup or treacle

2¼ cups (500g) firmly packed
   dark brown sugar

2 cups (500ml) brandy

2 teaspoons ground ginger

1 teaspoon ground nutmeg

1 teaspoon ground cinnamon

1 Combine ingredients in a large bowl; cover tightly with plastic wrap.
2 Store fruit mixture in a cool, dark place for a month (or longer, if desired) before using. Stir mixture every 2 or 3 days.

Notes

This cake could also be baked in a deep 18cm (7¼-inch) square cake pan. The oven temperature and baking times are the same.

THREE-IN-ONE MIX
Fruit Cake

See pages 170 & 171 for step-by-step images and information on how to prepare and cook this fruit cake.

4¼ cups three-in-one basic fruit mix
  (recipe page 166)

185g (6 ounces) butter, melted

3 eggs, beaten lightly

1½ cups (225g) plain (all-purpose) flour

½ teaspoon bicarbonate of (baking) soda

¼ cup (60ml) brandy

1 Preheat oven to 140°C/280°F. Line base and side of a deep 20cm (8-inch) round cake pan with one layer of brown paper and two layers of baking paper, extending the papers 5cm (2 inches) above side of pan.

2 Place basic fruit mix in a large bowl. Stir in butter, eggs, and sifted flour and soda. Spread mixture into pan; level the surface.

3 Bake cake for 2½ hours or until cooked when tested. Brush hot cake with brandy. Cover hot cake with foil, wrap in a clean towel; cool cake in pan overnight.

Fruit Cake

LINING A ROUND CAKE PAN [1]
Cut strips of baking or brown paper to line side of the pan, overlapping ends slightly. Make a 2cm (¾in) fold; snip the paper up to the fold and fit around the pan.

LINING A ROUND CAKE PAN [2]
Lightly grease the pan to hold paper in place; position paper around the side of the pan, with the snipped fold at the base. Two or more layers of paper are often used.

LINING A ROUND CAKE PAN [3]
Trace the base of the pan onto the paper; cut out the paper slightly inside the marked circle. Position in the pan to cover the snipped paper and line the base.

FILLING THE CAKE PAN [1]
Fruit cakes often end up with air pockets because the mixture is heavy and doesn't flow. Push mixture in the pan to eliminate any air pockets; level with a spatula.

Fruit Cake

FILLING THE CAKE PAN [2]

Hold the pan with both hands and bang it down hard on the bench (or drop it from about 20cm/8in). Repeat twice to settle the mixture, and get rid of air bubbles.

TESTING IF THE CAKE IS COOKED

Push the blade of a sharp-pointed knife straight down the centre to the base. Withdraw it slowly; if you feel uncooked mixture on the knife, return cake to oven.

BRUSHING THE CAKE WITH ALCOHOL

Most recipes suggest brushing the cake with alcohol; this softens the crust and imparts a little more flavour. Brush the cake immediately it comes out of the oven.

COOLING THE CAKE

Snip around the lining paper level with the cake top; fold paper over the cake. Cover cake, still in the pan, tightly with foil; wrap in a towel and cool overnight.

Traditional CAKES AND PUDDINGS

ORANGE PUDDING
with Rum Syrup Sauce

See page 199 for helpful step-by-step images and information on how to prepare and cook a steamed pudding.

10g (½ ounce) butter, melted

2 tablespoons light brown sugar

1 large orange (300g), unpeeled

90g (3 ounces) butter, extra, softened

¾ cup (165g) caster (superfine) sugar

2 teaspoons finely grated orange rind

2 eggs

1¼ cups (185g) self-raising flour

⅓ cup (50g) plain (all-purpose) flour

½ cup (125ml) milk

RUM SYRUP SAUCE

50g (1½ ounces) butter

⅓ cup (115g) golden syrup or treacle

¼ cup (55g) firmly packed light
   brown sugar

2 tablespoons dark rum

1 Place a large sheet of foil on the bench; top with a sheet of baking paper the same size. Fold a 5cm (2-inch) pleat lengthways through the centre of both sheets. Brush a 2-litre (8-cup) pudding steamer with the melted butter. Sift brown sugar into the steamer; shake steamer to coat the sides evenly with sugar.

2 Thinly slice unpeeled orange using a mandoline, V-slicer or sharp knife into 3mm (⅛-inch) slices. Arrange orange slices on the base and around the side of the steamer, ensuring that the slices around the side touch the slices on the base.

3 Beat extra butter, the caster sugar and rind in a small bowl with an electric mixer until light and fluffy; beat in eggs, one at a time. Transfer mixture to a medium bowl; stir in sifted flours and milk, in two batches.

4 Spoon mixture into steamer, level surface. Place pleated foil and paper, paper-side down, on top of pudding, with pleat running through the centre. Secure with kitchen string or a lid. If using string, make a handle with string to make it easier to lift the steamer from the water.

5 Place pudding steamer in a large saucepan with enough boiling water to come halfway up the side of the steamer; cover pan with a tight fitting lid. Simmer for 1 hour, replenishing with boiling water as necessary to maintain water level. Stand pudding in steamer for 5 minutes before turning out.

6 Make rum syrup sauce. Serve pudding with sauce.

RUM SYRUP SAUCE Stir butter, syrup and sugar in a small saucepan over low heat until sugar dissolves; bring to the boil. Reduce heat; simmer, uncovered, for 3 minutes or until thickened slightly. Remove from heat; stir in rum.

THREE-IN-ONE MIX
Fruit Mince Pies

You will need a 7.5cm (3-inch) round cutter and a 4.5cm (1¾-inch) star cutter, or you can cut the stars out freehand using a sharp pointed knife.

1 cup (150g) plain (all-purpose) flour

1 tablespoon icing (confectioners') sugar

1 tablespoon custard powder
   (instant pudding mix)

90g (3 ounces) cold butter, chopped

1 egg, separated

1 tablespoon iced water, approximately

1 cup three-in-one basic fruit mix
   (recipe page 166)

1 teaspoon finely grated lemon rind

1 tablespoon white (granulated) sugar

1 Grease a 12-hole (2-tablespoon/40ml) round-based patty pan tray.
2 Process flour, icing sugar, custard powder and butter until crumbly. Add egg yolk and enough of the water to make ingredients just come together. Knead dough on a lightly floured surface until smooth. Wrap dough with plastic wrap; refrigerate for 30 minutes.
3 Preheat oven to 200°C/400°F.
4 Roll two-thirds of the dough between sheets of baking paper until 3mm (⅛ inch) thick. Using the round cutter, cut out 12 rounds from the pastry (re-roll pastry scraps if necessary to make a total of 12 rounds). Press rounds into tray; reserve pastry scraps.
5 Combine basic fruit mix and rind in a medium bowl. Drop level tablespoons of fruit mixture into pastry cases.
6 Roll remaining dough between sheets of baking paper until 3mm (⅛ inch) thick. Using the star cutter, cut out 12 stars. Place stars in centre of pies; brush with egg white, sprinkle with white sugar.
7 Bake pies for 20 minutes or until pies are browned lightly. Stand for 5 minutes before transferring to a wire rack to cool.

STORAGE Fruit mince pies will keep in an airtight container for up to 1 week. Freeze pies for up to 3 months; thaw overnight in the fridge.

Notes

Make a double batch of these mince pies and top one batch with stars and the other batch with a lattice pattern. Roll reserved pastry as directed in step 6; cut pastry into 3mm wide strips. Arrange strips on tarts in a lattice pattern.

THREE-IN-ONE MIX
Boiled Christmas Pudding

See page 178 for step-by-step images and information on how to prepare and cook this boiled pudding. This pudding mixture can also be steamed; for helpful step-by-step images and information, see page 199.

4¼ cups three-in-one basic fruit mix (recipe page 166)

185g (6 ounces) butter, melted

2 eggs, beaten lightly

2 cups (140g) lightly packed stale breadcrumbs

¾ cup (110g) plain (all-purpose) flour

1 Place basic fruit mix in a large bowl. Stir in butter, eggs, breadcrumbs and sifted flour.

2 Fill a boiler three-quarters full with hot water; cover, bring to the boil.

3 Have ready 2.5 metres (8 feet) of kitchen string and an extra ¾ cup (110g) plain flour. Wearing thick rubber gloves, dip prepared pudding cloth (see notes) into boiling water; boil for 1 minute. Using tongs, and wearing thick rubber gloves, remove cloth from water, squeeze excess water from cloth. Working quickly, spread hot cloth on bench, rub extra flour into centre of cloth to cover an area of about 40cm (16 inches) in diameter; leave flour a little thicker in centre of cloth where the 'skin' on the pudding will need to be thickest.

4 Place pudding mixture in centre of cloth; gather cloth evenly around pudding, avoiding any deep pleats, pat into a round shape. Tie cloth tightly with kitchen string as close to mixture as possible. Knot corners of cloth together to make pudding easier to remove from the boiler.

5 Gently lower pudding into boiling water. Tie the free ends of the string to handles of the boiler to suspend the pudding. Cover boiler with a tight-fitting lid; boil rapidly for 6 hours. Replenish the boiling water as needed to maintain the boil and water level; there must be enough boiling water for the pudding to be immersed at all times.

6 Untie pudding from the handles. Place the handle of a wooden spoon through the knotted cloth loops to lift the pudding from the water. Don't put the pudding on the bench; suspend it from the spoon on rungs of an upturned stool. The pudding must be suspended freely. If the pudding has been cooked correctly, the cloth will start to dry in patches within a few minutes; hang the pudding for 10 minutes.

7 Place the pudding in a bowl, cut string; gently peel away cloth to uncover about half the pudding. Scrape the 'skin' back onto the pudding with a palette knife if necessary. Invert pudding onto a plate and continue to peel off the cloth completely. Stand the pudding for at least 20 minutes or until the 'skin' darkens and the pudding becomes firm before cutting to serve.

Boiled Christmas Pudding

WRAPPING THE PUDDING MIX [1]

Spread hot cloth on the bench; rub ½ cup plain flour into centre of cloth to cover an area about 40cm (16in) in diameter. Leave flour a little thicker in the centre.

WRAPPING THE PUDDING MIX [2]

Place pudding mixture in a mound in the centre of the cloth, within the floured area. Gather the cloth evenly around the mixture, avoiding any deep pleats.

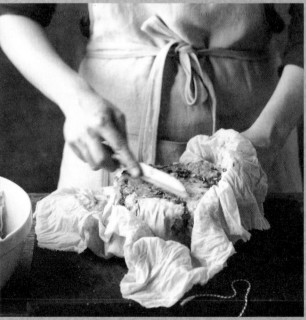

BOILING THE PUDDING

Lower pudding into boiling water, tie string to pan handles; there must be enough water for the pudding to float freely at all times. Weight the lid down.

UNWRAPPING THE PUDDING

Suspend pudding for 10 minutes so it begins to dry. Place it on a board; cut string, carefully peel back most of the cloth. Turn pudding right-way up; remove cloth.

Traditional CAKES AND PUDDINGS

It wouldn't be Christmas without a pudding full of boozy-soaked fruit and spices. Boiled or steamed it's up to you, just don't skimp on the custard and cream.

THE GREAT AUSTRALIAN
Christmas Pudding

1 cup (240g) mixed glacé fruit

¼ cup (60g) glacé cherries

¼ cup (40g) sultanas

¼ cup (60ml) brandy

4 large eggs, separated

½ cup (80g) icing (confectioners') sugar

¼ cup (25g) cocoa powder

60g (2 ounces) dark (semi-sweet) chocolate

⅓ cup (45g) roasted hazelnuts, chopped coarsely

45g (1½ ounces) chocolate honeycomb bar,
   chopped coarsely

2 teaspoons powdered gelatine

1 tablespoon hot water

1 cup (250ml) pouring cream

180g (5½ ounces) white chocolate

¼ cup (35g) hazelnuts, extra, chopped coarsely

1 Place mixed glacé fruit into a food processor fitted with a metal blade. Process for 3 seconds. Add cherries, process for 2 seconds. Place fruit mixture in a medium bowl, add sultanas; stir in brandy. Cover, store in a cool, dark place overnight (fruit chunks should not be too large or they will tear the pudding when cutting).

2 Line a 2-litre (8-cup) pudding steamer with plastic wrap, smoothing the wrap to remove as many wrinkles as possible.

3 Beat egg whites in a small bowl with an electric mixer until firm peaks form; gradually beat in combined sifted icing sugar and cocoa. Gradually beat in lightly beaten egg yolks.

4 Place dark chocolate in a medium heatproof bowl over a medium saucepan of simmering water (don't let water touch the base of the bowl); stir until smooth. Cool for 5 minutes.

5 Stir melted chocolate into egg mixture. Pour chocolate mixture over fruit, mix well. Stir in nuts and honeycomb.

6 Sprinkle gelatine over the hot water in a small heatproof jug; stand jug in a small saucepan of simmering water, stir until gelatine dissolves. Cool slightly. Stir gelatine into chocolate mixture.

7 Beat cream in a small bowl with electric mixer until firm peaks form; fold into chocolate mixture. Pour mixture into pudding steamer; smooth surface. Cover; freeze overnight.

8 Invert pudding onto a chilled serving plate; remove steamer, peel away plastic wrap. Return to the freezer.

9 Place white chocolate in a medium heatproof bowl over a medium saucepan of simmering water (don't let the water touch the base of the bowl); stir until smooth. Cool for 5 minutes, then spoon chocolate gently over top of pudding. Return pudding to freezer immediately to allow chocolate to set. Serve topped with extra hazelnuts.

Notes

If you prefer, instead of using a food processor to chop the fruit, you can chop it finely by hand. Use a warm knife to cut the pudding if the white chocolate is hard to cut through neatly.

Notes

Use a zesting tool to create the long thin strips of rind. If you don't have one, remove wide strips of rind with a vegetable peeler, then cut into thin strips with a sharp knife.

CHEAT'S FROZEN
Christmas Puddings

2 litres (8 cups) vanilla ice-cream,
   softened
800g (1½ pounds) golden fruit cake,
   crumbled
⅓ cup (80ml) brandy or rum
chopped pecans, orange rind strips (see
   notes) and chocolate curls, to decorate

CHOCOLATE SAUCE
180g (5½ ounces) dark (semi-sweet)
   chocolate, chopped
1 cup (250ml) thickened (heavy) cream

1 Line eight ¾ cup (180ml) moulds with plastic wrap, extending the plastic about 3cm (1¼ inches) over edge of moulds.
2 Process ice-cream, cake and brandy, in batches, until combined. Spoon ice-cream mixture into moulds. Cover with plastic wrap then foil; freeze overnight.
3 Make chocolate sauce.
4 Just before serving, turn puddings onto a baking-paper-lined tray; gently peel away plastic wrap, transfer puddings to serving plates. Drizzle sauce over puddings; decorate with nuts, rind and chocolate curls.
CHOCOLATE SAUCE Stir ingredients in a small saucepan over low heat until smooth.

CITRUS BRANDY
Steamed Fruit Pudding

See page 199 for helpful step-by-step images and information on how to prepare and cook a steamed pudding. This pudding mixture can also be boiled; see notes.

250g (8 ounces) butter, softened

1 cup (220g) firmly packed brown sugar

1 tablespoon finely grated orange rind

1 tablespoon finely grated lemon rind

4 eggs

1¾ cups (250g) coarsely chopped pitted dates

1½ cups (240g) coarsely chopped raisins

1½ cups (240g) sultanas

1 small apple (130g), peeled, grated

1 small carrot (70g), grated coarsely

¾ cup (125g) mixed peel

2 cups (140g) stale breadcrumbs

1½ cups (225g) plain (all-purpose) flour

pinch salt

½ teaspoon ground nutmeg

1 teaspoon mixed spice

½ teaspoon bicarbonate of (baking) soda

¼ cup (60ml) brandy

1 Grease a 3-litre (12-cup) pudding steamer well; line the base with baking paper. Place a large sheet of foil on the bench; top with a sheet of baking paper the same size. Fold a 5cm (2-inch) pleat lengthways through the centre of both sheets.
2 Beat butter, sugar and rinds in a large bowl with an electric mixer until light and fluffy. Add eggs, one at a time, beating well after each addition. Stir in fruit, carrot, mixed peel and breadcrumbs. Fold in sifted dry ingredients, then stir in brandy.
3 Spoon mixture into steamer, level surface. Place pleated foil and paper, paper-side down, on top of pudding, with pleat running through the centre. Secure with kitchen string or a lid. If using string, make a handle with string to make it easier to lift the steamer from the water.
4 Place steamer in a large saucepan with enough boiling water to come halfway up the side of the steamer; cover pan with a tight fitting lid. Simmer, covered, for 4 hours, replenishing with boiling water as necessary to maintain the water level. Stand the pudding for 5 minutes before turning out.

SERVING SUGGESTION Make the rum syrup sauce from page 173, using brandy instead of rum, and adding long thin strips of rind from one orange and one lemon into the syrup while it's simmering until thickened. Spoon over pudding just before serving.

Notes

This recipe can be turned into a boiled pudding following the instructions on pages 177 & 178. Boil rapidly for 4 hours; replenish with boiling water every 20 minutes (the water must not go off the boil). Re-boil the pudding for 2 hours on the day of serving.

INDIVIDUAL BOILED
Christmas Puddings

See page 178 for helpful step-by-step images and information on how to prepare and cook a boiled pudding. This mixture can also be steamd in eight 1-cup (250ml) pudding steamers; for step-by-step images and information on steamed puddings, see page 199.

500g (1 pound) mixed dried fruit

¾ cup (125g) coarsely chopped
  pitted dates

¾ cup (120g) chopped raisins

1 cup (250ml) water

1 cup (220g) lightly packed dark
  brown sugar

125g (4 ounces) butter, chopped

1 teaspoon bicarbonate of (baking) soda

2 eggs

1 cup (150g) plain (all-purpose) flour

1 cup (150g) self-raising flour

1 teaspoon mixed spice

2 tablespoons dark rum

2 cups (300g) plain (all-purpose) flour,
  extra

1 Place fruit, the water, sugar and butter in a large saucepan over medium heat; stir constantly until butter is melted and sugar is dissolved. Increase heat to high; bring to the boil. Reduce heat; simmer, uncovered, for 8 minutes. Stir in soda. Cool to room temperature.

2 Transfer cooled mixture to a large bowl; stir in eggs, sifted flours and spice and rum.

3 Fill a boiler three-quarters full with hot water, cover with a tight-fitting lid; bring to the boil. Prepare one cloth at a time: wearing thick rubber gloves and using tongs, dip pudding cloth into boiling water, then boil for 1 minute. Remove cloth, squeeze out excess water. Quickly spread hot cloth on the bench; rub ¼ cup of the extra plain flour into the centre of the cloth, leaving the flour a little thicker in the centre.

4 Divide pudding mixture evenly between pudding cloths; place the mixture in a mound in the centre, keeping it within the floured area. Gather the cloth evenly around the mixture, avoiding any deep pleats. Tie cloth tightly with kitchen string as close to the mixture as possible.

5 Fill the boiler three-quarters full with hot water; bring to the boil. Lower puddings into boiling water, tie string to pan handles; boil rapidly for 4 hours, replenishing with boiling water as required (the water must not go off the boil).

PROCESSOR
Fruit Cake

500g (1 pound) mixed dried fruit

185g (6 ounces) butter, chopped

¼ cup (90g) golden syrup or treacle

1 cup (220g) firmly packed light
  brown sugar

¾ cup (180ml) sweet sherry

½ teaspoon bicarbonate of (baking) soda

2 eggs, beaten lightly

1 cup (150g) plain (all-purpose) flour

1 cup (150g) self-raising flour

1 teaspoon mixed spice

⅓ cup (55g) blanched almonds

¼ cup (60ml) sweet sherry, extra

1 Wash dried fruit under cold water; drain well. Place fruit in a medium saucepan with butter, golden syrup, sugar and sherry; stir over medium heat, without boiling, until sugar dissolves. Bring to the boil. Remove from heat; stir in soda. Cool.

2 Preheat oven to 150°C/300°F. Grease a deep 20cm (8-inch) round cake pan; line base and side with baking paper.

3 Blend or process cooled fruit mixture, in several batches, until smooth; transfer to a large bowl. Stir in egg, sifted flours and spice. Pour mixture into pan; smooth surface. Decorate cake with nuts.

4 Bake cake for 2 hours. Brush hot cake with extra sherry, cover with foil; leave cake in pan to cool.

STORAGE This cake will keep in an airtight container at room temperature for up to 10 days. Freeze for up to 3 months.

Notes

You can turn this into an 'eggless processor fruit cake', if you like; omit the eggs, and increase the golden syrup to ⅓ cup (155g). The cake doesn't keep quite as well without eggs, about 5 days, but will freeze for 3 months.

Golden
FRUIT CAKE

250g (8 ounces) butter, chopped coarsely

1 teaspoon grated lemon rind

1 cup (220g) caster (superfine) sugar

4 eggs

1½ cups (240g) sultanas

¾ cup (125g) mixed peel

½ cup (70g) slivered almonds

⅔ cup (140g) glacé cherries, quartered

½ cup (115g) coarsely chopped
glacé pineapple

½ cup (125g) coarsely chopped
glacé apricots

½ cup (115g) coarsely chopped
glacé ginger

1½ cups (225g) plain (all-purpose) flour

1 Preheat oven to 150°C/300°F. Line a deep 20cm (8-inch) round cake pan with three layers of baking paper, extending the paper 5cm (2 inches) above side of pan.

2 Beat butter, rind and sugar in a small bowl with an electric mixer until light and fluffy. Beat in eggs one at a time. Transfer to a large bowl; stir in fruit, then sifted flour.

3 Spread mixture evenly into pan. Bake about 2¾ hours or until cooked when tested.

4 Cover hot cake with foil, wrap in a clean towel; cool in pan overnight.

TIP You can also make this cake in an 18cm (7¼-inch) square cake pan.

DO-AHEAD The cake can be made 2 weeks ahead; store in an airtight container in the fridge.

BUTTERY LIGHT FRUIT CAKE
with Almond Crumble

1 cup (160g) sultanas

½ cup (85g) chopped raisins

½ cup (125g) chopped glacé peach

½ cup (125g) chopped glacé apricot

¼ cup (60g) chopped glacé orange rind

¼ cup (50g) chopped red glacé cherries

½ cup (125ml) orange-flavoured liqueur

185g (6 ounces) butter

2 teaspoons vanilla extract

1 cup (220g) caster (superfine) sugar

2 eggs

⅓ cup (80g) sour cream

¾ cup (90g) almond meal

¾ cup (110g) plain (all-purpose) flour

⅓ cup (50g) self-raising flour

ALMOND CRUMBLE

½ cup (75g) plain (all-purpose) flour

60g (2 ounces) butter

2 tablespoons firmly packed light
   brown sugar

90g (3 ounces) marzipan or almond paste

½ cup (40g) natural sliced almonds

1 Combine fruit and liqueur in a large bowl. Cover; stand for 1 hour or until most of the liquid is absorbed. Stir well.

2 Make almond crumble.

3 Preheat oven to 150°C/300°F. Grease a deep 14cm x 23cm (5½-inch x 9¼-inch) loaf pan; line base and sides with two thicknesses of baking paper, extending the papers 5cm (2 inches) above sides.

4 Beat butter, extract and sugar in a small bowl with an electric mixer until combined. Beat in eggs, one at a time; beat in sour cream. Stir butter mixture into fruit mixture, then stir in almond meal and sifted flours. Spoon mixture into pan; smooth surface. Sprinkle with almond crumble.

5 Bake cake for 1¾ hours. Cover with foil; cool cake in pan.

ALMOND CRUMBLE Place flour in a medium bowl; rub in butter until crumbly. Stir in sugar, crumbled marzipan and nuts.

TIP Cointreau, Curaçao or Grand Marnier are orange-flavoured liqueurs; use your favourite.

STORAGE This cake will keep in an airtight container at room temperature for 4 weeks.

RICH EGGLESS
Fruit Cakes

4 cups (750g) mixed dried fruit

1 cup (250ml) water

½ cup (110g) firmly packed dark
   brown sugar

90g (3 ounces) butter

1 cup (150g) plain (all-purpose) flour

½ cup (75g) self-raising flour

½ teaspoon bicarbonate of (baking) soda

1 teaspoon mixed spice

¼ cup (60ml) sweet sherry, rum or brandy

2 tablespoons sweet sherry, rum or
   brandy extra

1 Combine fruit, the water, sugar and butter in a large saucepan; stir over medium heat until sugar dissolves. Cover; simmer for 3 minutes. Remove from heat; stand until cold.

2 Preheat oven to 150°C/300°F. Place two paper cases in each hole of a 6-hole (¾-cup) texas muffin pan (double cases protect the mixture from drying out during the long baking time).

3 Stir sifted dry ingredients alternately with sherry into the cold fruit mixture; mix well. Divide mixture between pan holes.

4 Bake cakes about 1¼ hours. Brush hot cakes evenly with extra sherry. Turn cakes, top-side up, onto a wire rack to cool.

GLUTEN-FREE
Steamed Pudding

See page 199 for step-by-step images and information on how to prepare and cook this steamed pudding.

2¼ cups (360g) sultanas

1½ cups (240g) coarsely chopped raisins

½ cup (80g) dried currants

1½ cups (210g) chopped pitted dates

1 cup (220g) firmly packed dark
   brown sugar

2 tablespoons honey

185g (6 ounces) butter

1½ cups (375ml) water

½ cup (125ml) orange juice

1 cup (125g) soya flour

1 cup (180g) rice flour

1 teaspoon cream of tartar

½ teaspoon bicarbonate of (baking) soda

2 teaspoons mixed spice

1 cup (120g) almond meal

1 Place fruit, sugar, honey, butter, the water and juice in a large saucepan; stir over medium heat, without boiling, until butter melts. Transfer mixture to a large heatproof bowl. Cool.

2 Grease a 2.25-litre (9-cup) pudding steamer well; line base with baking paper. Place a large sheet of foil on the bench; top with a sheet of baking paper the same size. Fold a 5cm (2-inch) pleat lengthways through the centre of both sheets.

3 Stir sifted dry ingredients into cold fruit mixture.

4 Spoon mixture into steamer, level surface. Place pleated foil and paper, paper-side down, on top of pudding, with pleat running through the centre. Secure with kitchen string or lid. If using string, make a handle with string to make it easier to lift the steamer from the water.

5 Place steamer in a large saucepan with enough boiling water to come halfway up side of steamer; cover pan with a tight fitting lid. Simmer, covered, for 6 hours, replenishing the pan with boiling water as necessary to maintain water level. Stand pudding for 10 minutes before turning out.

SERVING SUGGESTION Serve with cream or gluten-free vanilla custard.

Notes

Both soya and rice flour can be found in the supermarket or health food shops. To store pudding, wrap in plastic wrap and seal tightly in a freezer bag or airtight container; store in the fridge or freezer.

Gluten-free Steamed Pudding

PREPARING THE PUDDING STEAMER

Grease the pudding steamer by brushing generously with melted butter (cooking oil spray won't coat the steamer thickly enough). Line base with baking paper.

PREPARING TO STEAM THE PUDDING [1]

Place a sheet of baking paper on a sheet of foil; fold a 5cm (2in) pleat through the centre, then cover pudding. This allows for expansion during steaming.

PREPARING TO STEAM THE PUDDING [2]

Spoon mixture into steamer, cover with pleated foil and baking paper; secure with kitchen string under the rim of the steamer, and/or a tight-fitting lid.

STEAMING THE PUDDING

Place pudding in a boiler with enough boiling water to come halfway up side of the steamer. Cover pan with a tight-fitting lid; weight lid down with something heavy.

Traditional CAKES AND PUDDINGS

NIGHT BEFORE
Fruit Cake

1½ cups (240g) mixed dried fruit

⅓ cup (60g) finely chopped glacé ginger

410g (13 ounces) bottled fruit mince

175g (5½ ounces) butter, chopped coarsely

⅔ cup (150g) firmly packed dark
   brown sugar

1 teaspoon finely grated lemon rind

2 tablespoons lemon juice

½ cup (125ml) brandy

½ teaspoon bicarbonate of (baking) soda

3 eggs, beaten lightly

½ cup (120g) mashed banana

1½ cups (225g) plain (all-purpose) flour

½ cup (75g) self-raising flour

½ cup (70g) slivered almonds

1 Combine fruit, ginger, fruit mince, butter, sugar, rind, juice and ⅓ cup of the brandy in a medium saucepan; stir over medium heat until butter is melted and sugar dissolved. Bring mixture to the boil, remove from heat; stir in soda. Transfer to a large bowl; cool.
2 Preheat oven to 160°C/325°F. Grease a 20cm x 30cm (8-inch x 12-inch) rectangular pan; line base and two long sides with baking paper, extending paper 5cm (2 inches) above sides.
3 Stir egg and banana into fruit mixture, then stir in sifted flours. Spread mixture into pan; sprinkle with nuts.
4 Bake cake for 45 minutes or until cooked when tested. Brush hot cake with remaining brandy, cover with foil, wrap in a clean towel; cool in pan overnight.
5 Cut cake into 24 squares. Dust with sifted icing (confectioners') sugar to serve, if you like.

Notes

You need 1 large (230g) overripe banana to get the amount of mashed banana required here. The cake can be made a week ahead; store, covered, in an airtight container in the fridge or freeze for up to 3 months.

WHISKY CARAMEL
Christmas Cake

1½ cups (240g) sultanas

1½ cups (240g) dried currants

⅓ cup (60g) mixed peel

1½ cups (240g) chopped raisins

⅔ cup (120g) chopped pitted prunes

¾ cup (125g) chopped pitted dates

¼ cup (60g) chopped glacé figs

⅓ cup (55g) chopped glacé ginger

250g (8 ounces) butter, chopped

1 cup (220g) firmly packed dark
   brown sugar

5 eggs

1½ cups (225g) plain (all-purpose) flour

½ cup (75g) self-raising flour

2 tablespoons whisky

WHISKY CARAMEL

1 tablespoon white (granulated) sugar

15g (½ ounce) butter

¼ cup (60ml) whisky

1 Make whisky caramel.

2 Preheat oven to 150°C/300°F. Line a deep 20cm (8-inch) square cake pan with one layer of brown paper, then three layers of baking paper, extending the papers 5cm (2 inches) above sides.

3 Combine fruit and ginger in a large heatproof bowl with the hot whisky caramel.

4 Beat butter in a small bowl with an electric mixer until soft; add sifted sugar, beat only until combined. Add eggs, one at a time, beating well after each addition. Stir butter mixture into fruit mixture, stirring well to break up any large clumps of fruit. Stir in sifted flours until well combined.

5 Spread mixture into pan. Bake for 3½ hours or until cooked when tested. Brush hot cake with whisky. Cover hot cake with foil, wrap in a clean towel; cool in pan overnight.

WHISKY CARAMEL Place sugar in a small heavy-based pan; place over medium heat, leave until sugar is melted and a light golden brown – do not stir. Remove from heat, add butter and whisky. Return to a low heat; stir until any pieces of toffee have melted, do not allow to boil.

Traditional CAKES AND PUDDINGS

GLUTEN-FREE
Christmas Fruit Cake

See pages 170 & 171 for helpful step-by-step images and information on how to prepare and cook a fruit cake.

1kg (2 pounds) mixed dried fruit

½ cup (125ml) sweet sherry

250g (8 ounces) dairy-free spread

½ cup (125ml) soy milk

1¼ cups (250g) firmly packed
  brown sugar

1¼ cups (170g) gluten-free plain
  (all-purpose) flour

1 cup (65g) gluten-free baby rice cereal
  (see notes)

½ cup (75g) 100% corn (maize) cornflour
  (cornstarch)

½ teaspoon bicarbonate of (baking) soda

1 teaspoon ground cinnamon

3 eggs, beaten lightly

1 Preheat oven to 150°C/300°F. Grease a deep 20cm (8-inch) round cake pan; line base and side with three layers of baking paper, extending the papers 5cm (2 inches) above side.
2 Combine fruit and ¼ cup sherry in a large bowl.
3 Combine dairy-free spread, milk and sugar in a medium saucepan; cook, stirring, over low heat until sugar is dissolved and spread is melted; pour over fruit mixture.
4 Stir sifted dry ingredients into fruit mixture, in two batches, until combined. Add eggs, stir until combined. Spread mixture evenly into pan.
5 Bake cake for about 2½ hours or until cooked when tested. (Cover cake during cooking if over-browning.) Cover hot cake with foil, wrap in a clean towel; cool in pan overnight.

DO-AHEAD Cake can be made up to 2 weeks ahead; store in an airtight container in the fridge, or freeze for up to 3 months.

EGGNOG APPLE CAKE
with Brown Butter Frosting

4 small green apples (520g), peeled, chopped finely

¼ cup (60ml) brandy

¼ cup (55g) caster (superfine) sugar

170g (5½ ounces) butter, softened

80g (2½ ounces) cream cheese, softened

1¼ cups (275g) caster (superfine) sugar, extra

2 teaspoons vanilla extract

4 eggs

1½ cups (225g) plain (all-purpose) flour

1 teaspoon baking powder

1 teaspoon ground nutmeg

½ teaspoon salt

¼ teaspoon ground nutmeg, extra

BROWN BUTTER FROSTING

80g (2½ ounces) butter

125g (4 ounces) butter, extra, softened

1½ cups (350g) icing (confectioners') sugar

1 teaspoon vanilla extract

1 Preheat oven to 160°C/325°F. Grease a 20cm (8-inch) round cake pan; line base and side with baking paper.

2 Combine apple, brandy and sugar in a large saucepan; cook, stirring, over medium heat until sugar dissolves. Reduce heat to low; cook, uncovered, stirring occasionally, for 10 minutes or until apple is tender. Cool.

3 Beat butter, cream cheese, extra sugar and extract in a medium bowl with an electric mixer until pale and creamy. Beat in eggs, one at a time, until just combined. Add sifted flour, baking powder, nutmeg and salt; stir until just combined. Fold apple through cake mixture. Spoon mixture into pan.

4 Bake cake for 1 hour 35 minutes or until a skewer inserted into the centre comes out clean. Stand cake in pan for 15 minutes before turning, top-side down, onto a baking-paper-covered wire rack to cool.

5 Make brown butter frosting.

6 Spread frosting on cooled cake. Drizzle with reserved browned butter; dust with extra nutmeg.

BROWN BUTTER FROSTING Melt butter in a small frying pan over medium heat; cook for 2 minutes or until butter is nut brown. Cool slightly. Beat extra butter in a small bowl with an electric mixer until pale and creamy. Add sifted icing sugar, in three batches, beating until light and fluffy. Add extract and 2 tablespoons of the browned butter; beat until combined. Reserve remaining browned butter.

DO-AHEAD Uniced cake can be made a day ahead; store in an airtight container at room temperature.

Sweet SAUCES

ORANGE LIQUEUR CUSTARD

PREP + COOK TIME 20 MINUTES
MAKES ABOUT 1⅓ CUPS

Combine 2 tablespoons custard powder and ¼ cup caster (superfine) sugar in a small saucepan; gradually stir in ½ cup orange juice and 1 cup water. Stir mixture constantly over medium-high heat until it boils and thickens (or microwave on HIGH for 5 minutes). Stir in ¼ cup sour cream, 1 teaspoon finely grated orange rind and 1 tablespoon orange-flavoured liqueur. Serve custard hot.

TIP Cointreau and Grand Marnier are citrus-flavoured liqueurs; use your favourite brand.
DO-AHEAD The custard can be made the day before; store, covered, in the fridge. Reheat custard gently when required. This recipe is not suitable to freeze.

CREAMY CUSTARD SAUCE

PREP + COOK TIME 25 MINUTES
MAKES ABOUT 1 CUP

Combine ¼ cup caster (superfine) sugar and ½ cup water in a small saucepan. Stir constantly over medium-high heat, without boiling, until sugar is dissolved. Bring to the boil; reduce heat, simmer, uncovered, for 7 minutes or until sugar syrup is reduced to about ¼ cup. Beat 2 egg yolks in a small bowl with an electric mixer until thick and creamy; gradually beat in hot sugar syrup in a thin steady stream, beat until mixture is thick and creamy. Fold in ½ cup lightly whipped thickened (heavy) cream. Refrigerate until ready to serve.

TIP Flavour the sauce with 2 tablespoons of your favourite liqueur, folded in with the cream.
DO-AHEAD This sauce can be made 2 days ahead; store, covered, in the fridge. This recipe is not suitable to freeze.

RUM CREAM SAUCE

PREP TIME 10 MINUTES (+ REFRIGERATION)
MAKES ABOUT 3 CUPS

Beat 125g (4oz) softened cream cheese and 30g (1oz) softened butter in a small bowl with an electric mixer until mixture is light and creamy. Beat in 2 cups sifted icing (confectioners') sugar, 1 egg and 1 teaspoon lemon juice. Transfer mixture to a large bowl; fold in 300ml whipped thickened (heavy) cream and 2 tablespoons rum. Refrigerate for several hours before serving.

DO-AHEAD This sauce can be made up to 2 days ahead; store, covered, in the fridge. This recipe is not suitable to freeze.

CINNAMON BRANDY SAUCE

PREP + COOK TIME 20 MINUTES
MAKES ABOUT 2¼ CUPS

Combine 2 teaspoons ground cinnamon, 3 teaspoons arrowroot and ¼ cup caster (superfine) sugar in a small saucepan; gradually stir in 1½ cups water until smooth. Stir constantly over medium-high heat until sauce boils and thickens; reduce heat, simmer, uncovered for 2 minutes (or microwave on HIGH for 2 minutes). Stir ¼ cup brandy and 15g (½oz) butter into sauce until combined. Serve sauce hot.

TIP Arrowroot is a thickening agent; it is available in the baking aisle in supermarkets.
DO-AHEAD This sauce is best made on the day of serving. This recipe is not suitable to freeze.

ORANGE LIQUEUR CUSTARD

CREAMY CUSTARD SAUCE

RUM CREAM SAUCE

CINNAMON BRANDY SAUCE

Edible Gifts

Almond
CARAMEL BARS

45g (1½ ounces) butter

⅓ cup (55g) blanched almonds, chopped coarsely

200g (6½ ounces) soft caramels, chopped coarsely (see tips)

2 tablespoons pouring cream

200g (6½ ounces) dark (semi-sweet) chocolate, chopped coarsely

1 Grease a 20cm x 30cm (8-inch x 12-inch) slice pan; line base and sides with baking paper, extending the paper 5cm (2 inches) above long sides.

2 Melt butter in a small saucepan over low heat, add almonds; cook for 5 minutes or until a light golden brown colour. Add caramels, stir over low heat until melted; pour off any excess butter.

3 Return nut mixture to heat, add cream; cook, stirring, over medium-low heat, for 4 minutes or until thickened slightly. Spread mixture evenly into pan. Refrigerate until set.

4 Place chocolate in a medium heatproof bowl over a medium saucepan of simmering water (don't let the water touch base of bowl); stir until melted and smooth. Spread evenly over caramel. Refrigerate until set.

5 Cut caramel with a warm knife into 2cm x 10cm (¾-inch x 4-inch) bars. Sandwich two pieces together, chocolate-side out, to make 15 bars.

TIPS You can use slivered almonds instead of blanched, if you prefer. We used Jersey Caramels, available in the confectionary aisle of the supermarket.
STORAGE Bars will keep in an airtight container in the fridge for up to 2 weeks.

Notes

Not actually a pepper,
but a berry from a rose
plant, pink peppercorns
have an interesting mild
peppery flavour. They
are available from delis,
as are slivered pistachios
and dried rose petals.

PISTACHIO, PINK PEPPER
and Rose Petal Bark

125g (4 ounces) Sao biscuits

150g (4½ ounces) butter, chopped

150g (4½ ounces) caster (superfine) sugar

100g (3 ounces) dark (semi-sweet) chocolate, chopped finely

2 tablespoons slivered pistachios or other nuts

2 tablespoons dried organic rose petals (see notes)

1 teaspoon pink peppercorns

1 Preheat oven to 200°C/400°F. Grease a 25cm x 35cm (10-inch x 14-inch) swiss roll pan; line with baking paper.

2 Place biscuits in a single layer in pan (trim to fit if necessary).

3 Place butter and sugar in a medium saucepan over low heat. Cook, stirring, for 2 minutes or until butter melts. Increase heat to high; cook, stirring, for 5 minutes or until sugar dissolves and mixture is well combined and bubbling. Pour evenly over biscuits; spread to cover.

4 Bake for 12 minutes or until golden. Remove from oven; sprinkle evenly with chocolate. Return to oven for 1 minute or until chocolate melts.

5 Using a palette knife or the back of a spoon, smooth chocolate. Immediately sprinkle with nuts, rose petals and peppercorns. Stand for 1 hour or until the chocolate is set. Using a large kitchen knife, cut bark into large shards to serve.

STORAGE Bark will keep in an airtight container for up to 1 week.

Chocolate fig PANFORTE

100g (3 ounces) dark (semi-sweet) chocolate, chopped

¾ cup (110g) plain (all-purpose) flour

2 tablespoons cocoa powder

2 teaspoons ground cinnamon

¾ cup (150g) coarsely chopped semi-dried figs

¼ cup (40g) finely chopped glacé orange

1 cup (160g) blanched almonds, roasted

1 cup (140g) hazelnuts, roasted

1 cup (120g) pecans, roasted

⅓ cup (115g) honey

⅓ cup (75g) caster (superfine) sugar

⅓ cup (75g) firmly packed brown sugar

2 tablespoons water

1 Preheat oven to 150°C/300°F. Grease a deep 20cm (8-inch) round cake pan; line base with baking paper.

2 Place chocolate in a small heatproof bowl over a small saucepan of simmering water (don't let water touch base of bowl); stir until chocolate is melted. Remove from heat.

3 Sift flour, cocoa and cinnamon into a large bowl; stir in fruit and nuts. Combine honey, sugars and the water in a small saucepan; stir over low heat until sugar dissolves. Simmer, uncovered, without stirring, for 5 minutes. Pour hot syrup then melted chocolate into nut mixture; mix well.

4 Press mixture firmly into pan; press a 20cm (8-inch) round of baking paper on top.

5 Bake for 40 minutes; cool in pan. Remove panforte from pan, discard baking paper; wrap in foil. Stand overnight before cutting into thin wedges to serve.

STORAGE Panforte will keep for up to 2 months, wrapped in baking paper, then foil, in an airtight containter.

ALMOND AND CRANBERRY
Toffee Wreaths

You need fluted cutters in two different sizes for these wreaths: we used 7cm (2¾-inch) and 3.5cm (1½-inch) cutters.

90g (3 ounces) butter

1 egg

⅓ cup (55g) icing (confectioners') sugar

½ teaspoon almond extract

½ cup (60g) almond meal

1 cup (150g) plain (all-purpose) flour

⅓ cup (100g) cranberry sauce

¼ cup ranberries

2 tablespoons slivered almonds

TOFFEE

¼ cup (55g) caster (superfine) sugar

2 tablespoons water

1 Beat butter, egg, sifted icing sugar and extract in a small bowl with an electric mixer until combined. Stir in almond meal and sifted flour. Divide dough in half; wrap each half in plastic wrap. Refrigerate for 30 minutes.

2 Preheat oven to 180°C/350°F. Grease and line oven trays with baking paper.

3 Roll each dough half between sheets of baking paper until 5mm (¼-inch) thick. Using a 7cm (2¾-inch) fluted cutter, cut 12 rounds from dough, re-rolling scraps as necessary. Using a 3.5cm (1½-inch) fluted cutter, cut rounds from centre of each round. Place wreaths about 2.5cm (1 inch) apart on trays.

4 Bake wreaths about 8 minutes. Cool on trays.

5 Meanwhile, warm cranberry sauce in microwave; strain through a fine sieve. Cool. Chop dried cranberries and nuts coarsely.

6 Spread cold wreaths with warmed sauce; sprinkle with combined cranberries and nuts.

7 Make toffee; drizzle over wreaths. Stand until set.

TOFFEE Stir sugar and the water in a small saucepan over high heat, without boiling, until sugar dissolves. Bring to the boil; boil, uncovered, without stirring, for 5 minutes or until caramel in colour. Remove from heat; allow bubbles to subside.

DO-AHEAD The biscuits can be made up to 4 weeks ahead; store in an airtight container. Top the wreaths with the fruit mixture and toffee up to 1 day ahead of serving.

Traditional EDIBLE GIFTS

HAZELNUT & IRISH CREAM TRUFFLES

PREP + COOK TIME 45 MINUTES
(+ REFRIGERATION) **MAKES** ABOUT 35

½ cup (125ml) pouring cream
250g (8 ounces) dark (semi-sweet) chocolate, chopped finely
3 teaspoons irish cream liqueur
⅓ cup (40g) finely chopped roasted hazelnuts
250g (8 ounces) dark chocolate Melts

1 Bring cream to the boil in a small saucepan over medium heat; pour over dark chocolate in a small heatproof bowl, stirring until chocolate melts. Stir in liqueur and nuts. Cover; refrigerate, stirring occasionally, for 30 minutes or until mixture starts to thicken but does not set.
2 Roll rounded teaspoons of mixture into balls; place, in a single layer, on a baking-paper-lined tray. Refrigerate truffles until firm.
3 Place chocolate Melts in a medium heatproof bowl over a medium saucepan of simmering water (don't let water touch base of bowl); stir until smooth. Dip truffles in chocolate then quickly and gently roll between the palms of your hands to coat evenly. Return to tray; refrigerate for 4 hours or until firm.

CHRISTMAS PUDDING TRUFFLES

PREP + COOK TIME 1 HOUR
(+ FREEZING & STANDING) **MAKES** 36

180g (5½ ounces) dark (semi-sweet) chocolate, chopped coarsely
800g (1½ pounds) fruit cake
½ cup (125ml) brandy
½ cup (80g) icing (confectioners') sugar
250g (8 ounces) dark chocolate Melts
150g (4½ ounces) white Candy Melts (see tip)
36 red mini M&Ms

1 Place chocolate in a small heatproof bowl over a small saucepan of simmering water (don't let water touch base of bowl); stir until melted and smooth.
2 Crumble cake into a large bowl; stir in melted chocolate, brandy and sifted icing sugar. Using wet hands, shape level tablespoons of mixture into balls, squeezing firmly, place on a baking-paper-lined tray; refrigerate until firm.
3 Melt dark chocolate Melts.
4 Dip cake balls in melted chocolate, then quickly and gently roll between the palms of your hands to coat evenly. Refrigerate until set.
5 Melt Candy Melts; drizzle over cake balls, top each with an M&M. Stand truffles on tray to set.

TIP If white Candy Melts are not available, you can use white chocolate Melts or royal icing instead.

Rum and raisin
SHORTBREAD

¼ cup (60ml) dark underproof rum

⅔ cup (110g) finely chopped raisins

250g (8 ounces) butter

1 cup (220g) caster (superfine) sugar

2½ cups (375g) plain (all-purpose) flour

½ cup (90g) rice flour

1 tablespoon caster (superfine) sugar,
  extra

1 Combine rum and raisins in a small bowl. Cover; stand for 1 hour or until rum is absorbed.
2 Preheat oven to 150°C/300°F.
3 Beat butter and sugar in a small bowl with an electric mixer until light and fluffy. Transfer mixture to a large bowl; stir in half the sifted flours, the raisin mixture, then remaining sifted flours. Knead dough on a floured surface until smooth. Divide dough in half.
4 Roll one portion of dough between sheets of baking paper into a 23cm (9¼-inch) round. Pinch edges with floured fingertips. Mark round into wedges; prick wedges with a fork. Sprinkle with extra sugar. Slide round, still on baking paper, onto an oven tray. Repeat with remaining dough and a second oven tray.
5 Bake shortbread for about 20 minutes. Cool on trays before cutting into wedges.

STORAGE Shortbread will keep in an airtight container at room temperature for up to 2 weeks.

COFFEE AND CHOCOLATE
Christmas Wreath

You need three or four different sized star cutters to make these wreaths: we used 8cm (3¼-inch), 6cm (2½-inch), 5cm (2-inch) and 3cm (1¼-inch) cutters.

1 teaspoon instant coffee granules

2 teaspoons boiling water

250g (8 ounces) butter, softened, chopped

2 eggs

1½ cups (330g) firmly packed dark brown sugar

¼ cup (25g) dutch cocoa powder, plus extra to serve

3½ cups (525g) plain (all-purpose) flour
    (measure flour in two equal amounts)

CHOCOLATE SAUCE

¼ cup (60ml) pouring cream

100g (3 ounces) dark (semi-sweet) chocolate, chopped coarsely

1½ tablespoons hazelnut-flavoured liqueur

1 Combine coffee with the water in a small bowl; stir until coffee dissolves.

2 Beat butter, eggs and sugar in a small bowl with an electric mixer until combined. Divide mixture into two medium bowls. Stir coffee mixture and cocoa into one bowl; keep the other bowl plain. Stir one amount of the sifted flour into the coffee mixture. Stir the remaining flour into the plain mixture.

3 Turn coffee dough onto a lightly floured surface; knead until smooth, wrap in plastic wrap. Knead plain dough until smooth, wrap in plastic wrap. Refrigerate doughs for 30 minutes.

4 Roll each dough half between sheets of baking paper until 5mm (¼-inch) thick; place on oven trays, refrigerate for 15 minutes.

5 Preheat oven to 180°C/350°F. Line two oven trays with baking paper. Draw a 25cm (10-inch) circle on each piece of baking paper; turn paper, marked-side down, on trays. (Use circles as a guide to position stars for wreath.)

6 Using the largest star cutter, cut out 40 stars. Use remaining cutters to cut out different-sized stars, re-rolling scraps as necessary. (Refrigerate dough for 10 minutes to firm if it becomes too soft.) Following the shape of the circle, place stars on trays, slightly overlapping to make two wreaths.

7 Bake wreaths for 15 minutes. Cool wreaths on trays for at least 1 hour before carefully transferring to the storage container.

8 Before serving, make chocolate sauce.

9 Dust wreaths with extra cocoa, serve with sauce.

CHOCOLATE SAUCE Bring cream almost to the boil in a small saucepan; remove from heat. Add chocolate then liqueur to pan; stir until smooth. Stand for 30 minutes or until thick.

STORAGE The wreaths are extremely fragile; slide the wreaths, on the baking paper, onto the upside-down lid of an airtight container, and secure the container, upside down, to the lid. The wreaths will keep in an airtight container for up to 2 weeks.

Joyeux Noël

Notes

You can use any colour
you like to tint the dough;
choose a matching lolly,
or coloured sugar, to coat
the pinwheel edges.

Candy Cane PINWHEELS

150g (4½ ounces) butter, softened

¾ cup (165g) caster (superfine) sugar

1 egg

1½ cups (225g) plain (all-purpose) flour

red food colouring (see notes)

½ cup (80g) icing (confectioners') sugar

2½ teaspoons water

100g (3 ounces) peppermint candy canes, chopped finely (see notes)

1 Beat butter and sugar in a small bowl with an electric mixer until pale and creamy. Add egg, beat until just combined. Add sifted flour; stir to combine.

2 Gently knead on a lightly floured surface until smooth. Divide dough in half. Tint one half red. Shape dough halves into separate discs; wrap in plastic wrap. Refrigerate for 15 minutes.

3 Preheat oven to 180°C/350°F. Grease an oven tray; line with baking paper.

4 Roll each dough half between sheets of baking paper into a 20cm x 30cm (8-inch x 12-inch) rectangle; remove top sheet of baking paper.

5 With one long side of the dough facing you, place the red dough on top of the plain dough, leaving a 1cm (½-inch) border on the long side closest to you; starting at this end, and using paper as a guide, roll dough to form a log. Wrap with plastic wrap; refrigerate for 30 minutes or until firm.

6 Using a small sharp knife, cut log into 1cm (½-inch) thick slices; place on oven tray. Bake for 10 minutes or until lightly golden and a pinwheel can be pushed gently without breaking. Cool pinwheels on trays.

7 Mix sifted icing sugar and the water in a small bowl to form a smooth paste. Place the candy cane on a small plate. Spread a little icing around the edge of a biscuit, then roll edge in candy cane; repeat with remaining biscuits. Stand biscuits until set.

STORAGE Uniced biscuits will keep in an airtight container for up to 1 week; decorated biscuits will keep for up to 3 days.

Gourmet
ROCKY ROAD

450g (14½ ounces) good-quality
  white chocolate

300g (9½ ounces) white marshmallows,
  chopped coarsely

¼ cup (20g) shredded coconut, toasted

400g (12½ ounces) turkish delight,
  chopped coarsely

¼ cup (40g) almonds, toasted,
  chopped coarsely

½ cup (75g) roasted pistachios

1 Grease two 8cm x 26cm (3¼-inch x 10½-inch) bar cake pans; line base and sides
with baking paper, extending the paper 5cm (2 inches) above long sides.
2 Place chocolate in a medium heatproof bowl over a medium saucepan of simmering
water (don't let water touch base of bowl); stir until smooth.
3 Combine marshmallow, coconut, turkish delight and nuts in a large bowl. Working
quickly, stir in the melted chocolate; spread mixture into pans, pressing down to flatten.
Refrigerate until set, then cut into slices.

DO-AHEAD Rocky road can be made up to 1 week ahead; keep refrigerated in an
airtight container.

Notes

If you're making the rocky road for children, swap the turkish delight for raspberry jubes; instead of almonds and pistachios, use the same quantity of chocolate-coated Clinkers.

HAZELNUT
Chocolate Drops

125g (4 ounces) butter, softened

1 teaspoon vanilla extract

½ cup (110g) caster (superfine) sugar

1 egg

1 cup (100g) ground hazelnuts

1 cup (150g) plain (all-purpose) flour

⅓ cup (110g) chocolate-hazelnut spread

2 teaspoons cocoa powder

1 Preheat oven to 160°C/325°F. Line oven trays with baking paper.

2 Beat butter, extract and sugar in a small bowl with an electric mixer until light and fluffy. Beat in egg; stir in ground hazelnuts and sifted flour.

3 Flour hands, roll level tablespoons of mixture into balls; place about 5cm (2 inches) apart on trays, flatten slightly. Using the end of a wooden spoon, press a hole into the centre of each biscuit; fill each hole with chocolate-hazelnut spread.

4 Bake biscuits for 20 minutes. Cool on trays. Before serving, dust biscuits with sifted cocoa.

STORAGE Biscuits will keep in an airtight container at room temperature for up to 1 week.

GIANT MACADAMIA, WHITE CHOCOLATE AND
Cranberry Cookies

185g (6 ounces) unsalted butter

¾ cup (105g) unsalted macadamias, chopped coarsely

1½ cups (225g) self-raising flour

½ cup (75g) plain (all-purpose) flour

1 cup (220g) firmly packed light brown sugar

½ cup (110g) caster (superfine) sugar

1 egg

1 egg yolk

150g (4½ ounces) white chocolate, chopped coarsely

¾ cup (100g) dried cranberries

1 Preheat oven to 180°C/350°F. Line three oven trays with baking paper.

2 Melt butter in a small saucepan over low heat. Cool.

3 Toast nuts in a large frying pan over low heat until browned lightly. Remove from pan.

4 Sift flours and sugars into a large bowl; add toasted nuts. Lightly beat egg, egg yolk and melted butter with a fork in a small bowl until combined; stir into flour mixture until it forms a soft dough. Stir in chocolate and cranberries.

5 Roll rounded tablespoons of mixture into balls. Place balls, about 8cm (3¼ inches) apart, on trays; flatten to about 8cm (3¼ inches) wide.

6 Bake cookies for 12 minutes; cool on trays.

STORAGE Cookies will keep in an airtight container at room temperature for up to 1 week.

Nibbles and Drinks

Fig, Prosciutto and Antipasti Salad

12 slices prosciutto (180g), trimmed,
    cut into two or three pieces

6 medium ripe figs (360g), quartered

¼ cup (40g) sicilian green olives

¼ cup (40g) drained caperberries, rinsed

300g (10½ ounces) marinated artichoke
    hearts, halved

1 tablespoon red wine vinegar

1 tablespoon extra virgin olive oil

1 tablespoon fresh micro red radish leaves

grilled bread, to serve

1 Arrange prosciutto, figs, olives, caperberries and artichokes on a serving platter.
2 Combine vinegar and oil in a small bowl; drizzle over salad.
3 Serve salad topped with radish leaves, and with grilled bread.

Notes

Marinated artichoke hearts with the stems are available from delicatessens. You can use bottled artichoke hearts in oil instead, available from most supermarkets.

Ham, Mustard and Parsley Terrine

2 medium brown onions (300g),
chopped coarsely

2 medium carrots (240g),
chopped coarsely

2 trimmed sticks celery (200g),
chopped coarsely

2 cups (500ml) apple juice

6 fresh thyme sprigs

½ teaspoon black peppercorns

2 ham hocks (2kg)

250g (8-ounce) piece speck

1 tablespoon wholegrain mustard

2 teaspoons dijon mustard

½ cup chopped fresh flat-leaf parsley

3 teaspoons powdered gelatine

1 tablespoon extra virgin olive oil

⅓ cup (55g) caperberries

grilled bread, to serve

1 Place vegetables, juice, thyme, peppercorns, ham hocks and speck in a large saucepan; cover with cold water. Bring to the boil over high heat. Reduce heat; simmer, covered, for 2 hours or until meat is falling off the bone, skimming the surface occasionally to remove the foam.
2 Oil a 7cm (2¾-inch) deep, 9cm x 22.5cm (3¾-inch x 9-inch) base terrine mould or loaf pan. Line base and sides with plastic wrap, extending the plastic 5cm (2 inches) over all sides.
3 Remove ham hocks and speck from stock; cool. Strain stock through a fine sieve over a large saucepan or bowl. Place 2 cups of stock in a medium jug. Discard remaining stock or reserve for another use.
4 Coarsely shred ham from bones and speck, removing as much fat and sinew as possible. Place shredded ham and speck in a large bowl with mustards and parsley; mix to combine. Press ham mixture into the pan.
5 Sprinkle gelatine over warm stock; stir with a fork until dissolved. Pour over ham mixture. Cover; refrigerate 3 hours or overnight until set.
6 Unmould terrine onto a serving platter; remove and discard plastic wrap. Drizzle oil over terrine, scatter with caperberries.

Lemon and Rosemary Salt-cured Beef Canapés

You will need to start this recipe at least a day ahead.

500g (1-pound) piece beef eye fillet

36 thin slices sourdough bread stick

¼ cup (60ml) olive oil

⅓ cup (80g) sour cream

⅓ cup (15g) mustard cress

LEMON & ROSEMARY SALT CURE

1 cup (125g) salt flakes

1 cup (220g) raw sugar

⅓ cup loosely packed fresh rosemary sprigs, chopped coarsely

2 tablespoons finely chopped lemon rind

1 teaspoon black peppercorns

½ cup (125ml) vermouth or vodka

1 Make lemon and rosemary salt cure.

2 Place two sheets of plastic wrap, long enough to enclose beef, overlapping by half on the bench; spread with half the salt cure. Place beef on top, cover beef with remaining salt cure; wrap beef tightly in plastic wrap. Place beef on a large deep tray; top with a smaller tray or board and weigh down with cans of food. Refrigerate for 12 hours. Remove weights, turn beef over; replace tray and weights. Refrigerate for a further 12 hours.

3 Preheat grill (broiler).

4 Place bread slices on oven trays; brush with oil. Grill until both sides are lightly toasted.

5 Unwrap beef, wipe salt cure away; thinly slice beef. Spread sour cream on toasts, top with beef slices and cress.

LEMON & ROSEMARY SALT CURE Using a mortar and pestle, pound ¼ cup of the salt and ¼ cup of the sugar with the rosemary, rind and pepper to a fine powder. Transfer to a medium bowl; stir in vermouth and remaining salt and sugar.

Notes

You need the freshest, best quality beef for this recipe. Use a vegetable peeler to remove strips of rind from the lemon before chopping. Beef will keep, in an airtight container, in the fridge for up to 1 week.

APPLE PIMM'S

MULLED "WINE" MOCKTAIL

SPARKLING RASPBERRY

LYCHEE & LIME MUDDLE

Christmas Eve Cocktails

APPLE PIMM'S

PREP TIME 15 MINUTES **SERVES** 8

Combine 2 cups cucumber juice (see tips), 1⅓ cups Pimm's, 1.5 litres (6 cups) chilled sparkling apple juice, 1 cup ginger wine, 1 thinly sliced lebanese cucumber, 1 quartered and thinly sliced medium red apple and 1 cup loosely packed fresh mint leaves in large jug. Serve over ice.

TIPS Juice about 800g (1½lbs) peeled cucumbers in a juicer separator. Or, puree peeled cucumber in blender or processor. Strain into a jug and discard the solids. Pimm's is a gin-based alcohol flavoured with herbs.

MULLED "WINE" MOCKTAIL

PREP + COOK TIME 20 MINUTES
(+ REFRIGERATION) **SERVES** 8

Combine 2 litres (8 cups) red grape juice, 4 pieces orange rind, 2 tablespoons light brown sugar, 2 cinnamon sticks, 12 cloves, 3 fresh bay leaves and 2 sprigs fresh thyme in a large saucepan. Simmer, uncovered, for 10 minutes (do not boil). Cool; refrigerate until cold. Strain mixture into a large jug; discard solids. Add 1 thinly sliced small orange, extra fresh bay leaves and fresh sprigs of thyme to mixture. Serve with ice.

SPARKLING RASPBERRY

PREP TIME 25 MINUTES
(+ REFRIGERATION) **SERVES** 8

Combine 180g (6oz) fresh or frozen raspberries, ⅓ cup strawberry-flavoured liqueur, ⅓ cup orange-flavoured liqueur, 1 tablespoon caster (superfine) sugar and the rind of ½ small orange cut into long thin strips in a small bowl. Refrigerate for 20 minutes, stirring occasionally, until sugar dissolves. Divide mixture into eight glasses; top with 3 cups (750ml) chilled sparkling white wine.

TIP Use a zesting tool to cut the orange into long thin strips.

LYCHEE & LIME MUDDLE

PREP + COOK TIME 30 MINUTES
(+ REFRIGERATION) **SERVES** 8

Thinly slice 12 fresh kaffir lime leaves and a 30g (1-oz) piece fresh ginger; place in a small saucepan with 2 cups water and ¼ cup grated palm sugar. Stir over medium heat until sugar dissolves; bring to the boil. Reduce heat; simmer, uncovered, until reduced to 1½ cups. Strain syrup into medium heatproof jug; discard solids. Cool; refrigerate until cold. Divide 1kg (2lbs) seeded lychees, 1 quartered and thinly sliced lime, 1⅓ cups white rum, ⅓ cup lime juice and the syrup into eight glasses; gently crush and mix with muddling stick (or the handle of a thick wooden spoon or a pestle). Top with ice and 2 cups chilled soda water.

TIP A muddling stick is a bartender's tool used to crush or mash fruits, herbs and spices in the bottom of a glass or cocktail shaker to release their flavour.

Spiced Eggplant and Haloumi Tarts

1 medium eggplant (300g), peeled, chopped coarsely

1 teaspoon ground coriander

1 teaspoon ground cumin

2 tablespoons olive oil

¼ cup (55g) firmly packed light brown sugar

¼ cup (60ml) water

¼ cup (60ml) lime juice (see tips)

2 tablespoons finely chopped fresh flat-leaf parsley

100g (3 ounces) haloumi cheese, sliced thickly

2 tablespoons lemon juice

1 teaspoon finely cracked black pepper

30 baked mini shortcrust or puff pastry tart shells

1 Preheat oven to 200°C/400°F.

2 Toss eggplant, spices and oil in a small baking dish; season. Cover dish; roast for 20 minutes. Remove cover; roast for a further 10 minutes or until eggplant is tender.

3 Combine sugar and the water in a small saucepan; stir over heat until sugar dissolves.

4 Blend or process eggplant mixture, sugar syrup and lime juice until eggplant is coarsely chopped. Stir in parsley; cover to keep warm.

5 Sprinkle haloumi with lemon juice and pepper; cook on a heated barbecue (or grill plate) until browned both sides. Cut haloumi into 30 pieces.

6 Fill tart shells with warm eggplant mixture; top with haloumi, and fine shreds of lime rind.

TIPS Before juicing the lime, use a zester to remove the rind into long thin strips, to garnish the tarts. Mini shortcrust and puff pastry tart shells are available from major supermarkets and delicatessens. Tarts are best assembled just before serving.

Notes

For a smokier flavour, cook the unpeeled eggplant whole on the barbecue. Prick the skin all over with a fork, then cook for 30 minutes (depending on its size and the heat of the barbecue) or until the eggplant collapses. Cool; peel away skin, then continue with the recipe.

Oysters with Three Toppings

We used pacific oysters in this recipe, because their full-bodied flavour teams well with these robust toppings.

36 oysters (900g), on the half shell

coarse rock salt, to serve

PONZU DRESSING

2 tablespoons light soy sauce

2 teaspoons peanut oil

2 teaspoons mirin

1 tablespoon brown sugar

2 tablespoons lime juice

SHALLOT DRESSING

⅓ cup (80ml) white wine vinegar

3 shallots (75g), chopped finely

GREEN MANGO & CUCUMBER SALSA

½ lebanese cucumber (65g), seeded, chopped finely

1 tablespoon finely shredded green mango

1 tablespoon finely chopped red onion

1 teaspoon finely grated lime rind

1 teaspoon lime juice

1 teaspoon fish sauce

1 tablespoon vegetable oil

1 Make ponzu dressing, shallot dressing and green mango and cucumber salsa.

2 Place oysters on a bed of rock salt; serve with the dressings.

PONZU DRESSING Combine sauce, oil, mirin and sugar in a medium saucepan; stir over low heat until sugar dissolves. Add juice; season to taste, cool.

SHALLOT DRESSING Bring vinegar to the boil in a small saucepan; remove from heat. Add shallot; cool.

GREEN MANGO & CUCUMBER SALSA Combine ingredients in a small bowl; season.

DO-AHEAD Ponzu dressing will keep for up to 2 weeks in the fridge; shallot dressing and the salsa are best made on the day of serving.

SERVING SUGGESTION Serve oysters on a bed of crushed ice, instead of coarse rock salt.

Christmas Day Cocktails

CLASSIC MARGARITA

PREP TIME 5 MINUTES **SERVES** 1

Combine 45ml dark tequila, 30ml orange-flavoured liqueur, 30ml lime juice, 30ml sugar syrup and 1 cup ice cubes in a cocktail shaker; shake vigorously. Rub lime slice around rim of a margarita glass; turn glass upside-down and dip wet rim into saucer of salt. Strain margarita into salt-rimmed glass. Garnish with lime slice.

TIP You can buy sugar syrup from liquor stores. To make your own: stir 1 cup caster (superfine) sugar with 1 cup water in a small saucepan over heat, until sugar dissolves; bring to the boil. Reduce heat; simmer, uncovered, for 5 minutes. Cool. Refrigerate in an airtight container for up to 1 month (Makes 350ml).

BELLINI

PREP TIME 5 MINUTES **SERVES** 1

Place 45ml peach nectar, 15ml peach schnapps and 5ml lime juice in a chilled champagne flute glass; stir gently. Top with 150ml chilled sparkling white wine. Garnish with a peach wedge.

TOM COLLINS

PREP TIME 5 MINUTES **SERVES** 1

Place ¼ cup gin, ⅓ cup lemon juice, 2 teaspoons pure icing (confectioners') sugar and ⅓ cup soda water into a chilled ice-filled highball glass; stir gently. Garnish with maraschino cherries and curls of lemon rind.

POMEGRANATE CAIPIROSKA

PREP TIME 5 MINUTES **SERVES** 1

Cut ½ lime into 4 wedges. Crush 2 lime wedges in a cocktail shaker with ¼ cup vodka, 30ml sugar syrup and 20ml pomegranate juice. Add 1 cup ice cubes; shake vigorously. Strain into an ice-filled old-fashioned glass; stir in 1 tablespoon pomegranate seeds. Garnish with remaining lime wedges.

TIP You can buy sugar syrup from liquor stores. To make your own: stir 1 cup caster (superfine) sugar with 1 cup water in small saucepan over heat, until sugar dissolves; bring to the boil. Reduce heat; simmer, uncovered, for 5 minutes. Cool. Refrigerate in an airtight container for up to 1 month (Makes 350ml).

CLASSIC MARGARITA

BELLINI

TOM COLLINS

POMEGRANATE CAIPROSKA

Grilled Prawns with Lemon Grass and Lime

60g (2 ounces) butter, softened

10cm (4-inch) stick fresh lemon grass (20g), chopped finely

1 tablespoon finely grated lime rind

2 tablespoons lime juice

16 shelled uncooked medium king prawns (shrimp) (500g)

2 tablespoons fresh micro coriander (cilantro)

1 Beat butter, lemon grass, half the rind and the juice in a small bowl until combined.

2 Melt half the butter mixture in a small saucepan; remove from heat. Thread two prawns onto each of eight skewers; brush with half the butter mixture.

3 Cook prawns on a heated oiled barbecue (or grill pan) until changed in colour.

4 Serve prawns topped with remaining butter mixture; top with remaining rind and coriander.

TIPS You will need to buy about 1kg (2 pounds) prawns in the shell for this recipe. Shell and devein the prawns, leaving the tails intact. You will need eight 25cm (10-inch) bamboo skewers. Soak them in water for at least 1 hour before use to prevent them splintering and scorching during cooking.

CHICKEN SKEWERS WITH OLIVE DRESSING

PREP + COOK TIME 30 MINUTES
(+ REFRIGERATION) **MAKES** 24

4 large chicken thigh fillets (800g)

3 cloves garlic, crushed

2 tablespoons finely chopped fresh oregano

2 teaspoons finely grated lemon rind

2 tablespoons strained lemon juice

2 tablespoons olive oil

lemon wedges, to serve

OLIVE DRESSING

½ cup (60g) pitted green olives

2 tablespoons fresh oregano leaves

⅓ cup (80ml) olive oil

1 Cut each thigh fillet into 6 long strips;
combine with garlic, oregano, rind, juice and
oil in a medium bowl. Cover with plastic wrap;
refrigerate 2 hours.

2 Make olive dressing.

3 Thread one strip of chicken onto each of 24
skewers. Cook chicken skewers, in batches,
on a heated oiled grill plate (or barbecue) for
2 minutes each side or until cooked through.

4 Serve chicken skewers with olive dressing
and lemon wedges.

OLIVE DRESSING Coarsely chop 4 olives;
reserve. Blend or process remaining olives
with oregano and oil until almost smooth.
Spoon dressing into a serving bowl; top with
reserved olives.

TIP Soak bamboo skewers in water for at least
1 hour before use to prevent them splintering
and scorching during cooking.

VIETNAMESE-STYLE MINI PORK ROLLS

PREP + COOK TIME 25 MINUTES
MAKES 12

12 mini panini rolls (300g)

1 lebanese cucumber (130g)

¼ cup (75g) whole-egg mayonnaise

¾ cup (45g) shredded iceberg lettuce

125g (4 ounces) shaved seasoned roast pork

½ medium carrot (60g), cut into matchsticks

¼ cup (60ml) sweet chilli sauce

⅓ cup loosely packed fresh coriander
  (cilantro) leaves

1 Preheat oven to 220°C/425°F.
2 Place rolls on oven tray. Bake for 5 minutes
or until golden and heated through. Cool.
3 Halve cucumber lengthways, remove seeds.
Cut cucumber into matchsticks.
4 Split bread rolls in half; spread bases with
mayonnaise. Top with lettuce, pork, cucumber
and carrot. Drizzle with sauce; top with
coriander and tops of rolls. Secure rolls with
decorative toothpicks or skewers.

DO-AHEAD These rolls are best assembled
close to serving.

A beautifully decorated
table really sets the scene for
a special gathering.

Gravlax with Herb Salad

You will need to start this recipe at least 2 days ahead.

½ cup (150g) rock salt

½ cup (110g) white (granulated) sugar

⅔ cup coarsely chopped fresh dill

2 teaspoons finely grated lime rind

2 teaspoons white peppercorns, crushed

1 tablespoon juniper berries, crushed

⅓ cup (80ml) gin

750g (1½-pound) centre-cut piece
    salmon fillet, skin-on, bones removed

2 tablespoons lime juice

2 tablespoons olive oil

HERB SALAD

2 punnets micro herbs, trimmed

¼ cup fresh dill sprigs

1 Combine salt, sugar, dill, rind, pepper, berries and gin in a medium bowl.

2 Spread half the salt mixture over the base of a shallow 20cm x 28cm (8-inch x 11¼-inch) ceramic or glass dish. Place salmon, skin-side down, on mixture; cover salmon with remaining salt mixture. Cover with plastic wrap. Place another dish on top, weigh down with cans of food. Refrigerate for 24-36 hours, turning salmon every 12 hours.

3 Remove salmon from dish; scrape away any loose salt mixture. Discard salt mixture. Pat salmon dry with paper towel. Holding a knife at a 45 degree angle, and using long strokes, slice salmon across the grain as thinly as possible. Arrange slices on a large platter.

4 Just before serving, make herb salad.

5 Drizzle salmon with juice and oil; top with herb salad.

HERB SALAD Combine herbs in a small bowl.

SERVING SUGGESTION Serve with toasted sliced french bread and crème fraîche, or pumpernickel bread or crackers.

Notes

Juniper berries
are available from
delicatessens, spice
shops and specialty
greengrocers.

KUMARA, MINT & GOAT'S
CHEESE TARTLETS

PECORINO & NIGELLA
SEED BISCUITS

WARM ORANGE &
FENNEL OLIVES

BLINIS WITH GOAT'S
CHEESE & CRANBERRY

KUMARA, MINT & GOAT'S CHEESE TARTLETS

PREP + COOK TIME 35 MINUTES
MAKES 24

Preheat oven to 200°C/400°F. Grease two 12-hole (1-tablespoon/20ml) mini muffin pans. Layer 4 sheets fillo pastry, brushing each with 50g (1½oz) melted butter. Cut pastry stack into 24 x 7cm (2¾-in) squares; line pan holes with squares. Bake for 5 minutes or until browned lightly; cool in pans. Meanwhile, boil, steam or microwave 1 small (300g) coarsely chopped kumara (orange sweet potato) until tender; drain. Cool. Mash kumara in a medium bowl with ¼ cup finely chopped fresh mint until smooth; season to taste. Spoon mash between tartlet shells. Top with 100g (3oz) crumbled soft goat's cheese and 24 small fresh mint leaves.

TIP Tartlet shells will keep in an airtight container for up to 1 week.

PECORINO & NIGELLA SEED BISCUITS

PREP + COOK TIME 1 HOUR
(+ REFRIGERATION) **MAKES** 70

Sift 1½ cups (225g) plain (all-purpose) flour into a large bowl, add 1 teaspoon nigella seeds; rub in 150g (5oz) coarsely chopped butter and 1¼ cups (100g) coarsely grated pecorino romano cheese. Add 1 egg yolk; mix to a firm dough. Wrap dough in plastic wrap; refrigerate for 1 hour. Divide dough into two portions, roll each portion on a floured surface until 5mm (¼in) thick. Cut out stars using a 5cm (2in) star cutter; place shapes on greased oven trays. Refrigerate for 30 minutes. Preheat oven to 180°C/350°F. Bake biscuits for 20 minutes; cool on trays.

TIPS Nigella seeds are available in most Asian and Middle Eastern food shops. Store biscuits in an airtight container for up to 1 week. The biscuit dough can be shaped into a log, wrapped tightly in plastic wrap and frozen. When you're ready, defrost dough in the fridge. Slice dough into 1cm (½-in) rounds and place on a greased oven tray; bake as directed.

WARM ORANGE & FENNEL OLIVES

PREP + COOK TIME 10 MINUTES **SERVES** 10

Using a vegetable peeler, peel thin pieces of rind from 1 medium (240g) orange. Place rind pieces, 400g (12½oz) mixed marinated pitted olives, ½ cup (125ml) dry red wine, 1 teaspoon coarsely cracked black pepper and ½ teaspoon fennel seeds in a medium saucepan; bring to a simmer. Remove from heat; stand for 10 minutes before serving warm.

SERVING SUGGESTION Serve with grissini breadsticks and cheese.

BLINIS WITH GOAT'S CHEESE & CRANBERRY

PREP + COOK TIME 40 MINUTES **MAKES** 48

Sift ¼ cup (35g) buckwheat flour, ½ cup (100g) plain (all-purpose) flour and 1½ teaspoons baking powder into a large bowl. Whisk in ¾ cup (180ml) milk, 1 egg and 25g (¾oz) melted butter until smooth. Whisk ⅓ cup (80g) soft goat's cheese and 2 tablespoons light sour cream together in a small bowl; season. Heat large frying pan on medium heat; grease with a little melted butter. Cook heaped teaspoon measures of batter, in batches, for 1 minute each side or until golden. Top warm blinis with cheese mixture, 1½ tablespoons cranberry sauce and ⅔ cup small fresh mint leaves.

TIP Remove goat's cheese from the fridge 30 minutes before using to soften it.
DO-AHEAD Blinis can be made a few hours ahead; reheat, covered with foil, in a 100°C/210°F oven for 5 minutes. Assemble just before serving.

Crushed Broad Bean and Pea Bruschetta

3⅓ cups (500g) frozen broad (fava) beans

1 cup (120g) frozen baby peas

⅓ cup firmly packed fresh mint leaves, shredded

2 cloves garlic, crushed

4 oval bread rolls

¼ cup (60ml) olive oil

½ cup (125ml) white vinegar

8 cold eggs

180g (5½ ounces) marinated persian fetta, drained

100g (3 ounces) semi-dried tomatoes in oil, drained, chopped finely

1 cup micro mint

1 Place broad beans and peas in separate heatproof bowls; cover each with boiling water. Stand for 5 minutes; drain. Peel broad beans. Place broad beans and peas in a large bowl; crush coarsely with a potato masher. Stir in mint and garlic; season to taste.

2 Preheat grill (broiler) to high. Split bread rolls in half. Brush cut side with half the oil. Place bread under grill, cut-side up, for 2 minutes or until lightly toasted. Turn, grill for 1 minute or until browned lightly.

3 Half-fill a large frying pan with water; bring to the boil, stir in vinegar. Break one egg into a cup, then slide into pan; repeat with another 3 eggs. Return water to the boil. Cover pan, turn off heat; stand for 2 minutes or until egg white is set and yolks are soft. Remove eggs, one at a time, with a slotted spoon; drain on paper towel. Cover to keep warm. Repeat with remaining eggs.

4 Spoon broad bean mixture on bread rolls; top with crumbled fetta, semi-dried tomato, eggs and micro mint. Drizzle with remaining oil; season with freshly ground black pepper.

Mains

Tomato and Spinach Stuffed Lamb Roasts

½ cup (75g) drained, coarsely chopped sun-dried tomatoes

100g (3 ounces) fetta, crumbled

40g (1½ ounces) baby spinach leaves, chopped coarsely

2 mini lamb roasts (700g)

800g (1½ pounds) kumara (orange sweet potato), cut into wedges

2 tablespoons olive oil

6 sprigs fresh thyme

¼ teaspoon dried chilli flakes

1 Preheat oven to 200°C/400°F.

2 Combine sun-dried tomato, fetta and spinach in a medium bowl.

3 Cut a horizontal pocket in each roast; do not cut all the way through. Press half the filling mixture into each pocket; secure with toothpicks.

4 Heat an oiled large ovenproof frying pan over high heat; cook lamb roasts, turning, until browned all over.

5 Meanwhile, place kumara in a roasting pan, drizzle with oil and sprinkle with thyme and chilli; toss to coat. Season.

6 Place frying pan and roasting pan in oven; roast, uncovered, for 20 minutes or until lamb is cooked as desired and kumara is golden and tender. Cover lamb; rest for 10 minutes.

7 Serve lamb sliced with kumara wedges.

DO-AHEAD The tomato and spinach filling can be prepared ahead of time; store, covered, in the fridge until ready to use. The lamb mini roasts are best stuffed just before roasting.

Rare Roast Beef with Anchovy Butter

½ cup (125ml) barbecue sauce

2 cloves garlic, crushed

1 tablespoon finely chopped fresh rosemary

⅓ cup (80ml) olive oil

2kg (4-pound) boneless beef sirloin

300g (9½ ounces) butter beans

300g (9½ ounces) green beans

800g (1½ pounds) button mushrooms

2 tablespoons finely chopped fresh chives

ANCHOVY BUTTER

200g (6½ ounces) butter, softened

4 shallots (100g), chopped finely

1 tablespoon dijon mustard

1 tablespoon finely chopped fresh
  tarragon

5 drained anchovy fillets, chopped finely

1 teaspoon ground sumac

1 Preheat oven to 220°C/425°F. Make anchovy butter.

2 Combine sauce, garlic, rosemary and 2 tablespoons of the oil in a small bowl; rub all over beef. Place beef on oiled wire rack over baking dish; pour in enough water to half fill the dish. Roast beef for 45 minutes or until done as desired. Remove beef from heat, cover loosely with foil; stand for 10 minutes before slicing thickly.

3 Boil, steam or microwave beans until tender; drain. Heat remaining oil in a large frying pan; cook mushrooms, stirring, over medium heat until tender. Combine mushrooms and beans in a large bowl; stir in chives, season to taste.

4 Serve beef and vegetable mixture topped with slices of anchovy butter.

ANCHOVY BUTTER Beat butter in a medium bowl with an electric mixer until soft; beat in remaining ingredients. Season to taste. Form mixture into a log on a large piece of plastic wrap; roll in wrap, twist ends to seal. Refrigerate or freeze until firm.

Modern MAINS

Barbecued Prawns with Witlof and Beetroot Salad

24 large uncooked king prawns (shrimp)
   (1.5kg)

2 tablespoons finely grated lemon rind

2 cloves garlic, crushed

2 teaspoons dried chilli flakes

¾ cup (180ml) olive oil

100g (3 ounces) beetroot (beets), scrubbed

4 witlof (belgian endive), leaves separated

1 small ruby grapefruit (350g),
   segmented (see notes)

1½ tablespoons red wine vinegar

1 cup loosely packed fresh baby
   flat-leaf parsley leaves

1 Cut unpeeled prawns in half lengthways on the underside.

2 Combine rind, garlic, chilli and ½ cup of the oil in a medium bowl; season. Add prawns; toss well to coat. Cover; refrigerate for 1 hour.

3 Using a mandoline or V-slicer, cut beetroot into thin slices. Place beetroot in a medium bowl with witlof, grapefruit segments and combined vinegar and remaining oil; toss gently to combine. Season.

4 Heat a barbecue (or grill plate) to medium-high heat; cook prawns, cut-side down, pressing to flatten slightly, for 1 minute. Turn; cook other side for 1 minute or until changed in colour and just cooked through.

5 Serve prawns with salad, topped with parsley.

DO AHEAD Prawns can be prepared a day ahead. Marinate for 1 hour before cooking.

Notes

To segment grapefruit,
cut off the rind along with
the white pith, following
the curve of the fruit.
Cut down both sides of
the white membrane to
release each segment.
Segment over a small bowl
to catch the juices.

Glazed Ham

See page 274 for step-by-step images and information on how to prepare and carve this glazed ham. For a smaller leg or half leg of ham, halve the glaze recipe.

8kg (16-pound) cooked leg of ham

2 cups (500ml) water

sprigs of fresh herbs (rosemary and
   bay leaves), to decorate (optional)

DOUBLE ORANGE GLAZE

300g (9½ ounces) orange marmalade
   (or blood orange marmalade)

¼ cup dark brown sugar

¼ cup freshly squeezed orange juice
   (or blood orange juice)

1 Preheat oven to 180°C/350°F. Score through the rind about 10cm (4 inches) from the shank end of the leg.

2 To remove the rind, run your thumb around the edge of the rind just under the skin. Start pulling the rind from the widest edge of the ham; continue to pull the rind carefully away from the fat up to the score line. Remove the rind completely. (Rind can be reserved and used to cover the cut surface of the ham and keep it moist during storage.)

3 Using a large sharp knife, score across the fat at 3cm (1¼-inch) intervals, cutting just through the surface of the top fat. Do not cut too deeply or the fat will spread apart during cooking.

4 Make double orange glaze.

5 Place the ham on a wire rack in a large roasting pan; pour 1½ cups of the water into the dish. Brush the ham well with the glaze. Cover the shank end with foil.

6 Bake ham for 1 hour 20 minutes or until browned all over, brushing occasionally with the glaze during cooking, and adding the remaining water if needed.

DOUBLE ORANGE GLAZE Stir ingredients in a small bowl until combined. Season.

TIPS Rind will remove more easily from ham if warmed in a 150°C/300°F oven for 30 minutes. If the glaze becomes too thick to brush on, microwave until it reaches the correct consistency. Use a microwave-safe glass or ceramic container; don't use plastic as the glaze will get very hot.

DO-AHEAD The glaze can be made up to 1 week ahead; store in the fridge. Ham can be glazed a day ahead and served cold.

STORAGE Store cold leftover ham in the fridge in a calico ham bag. Ham bags are available from kitchenware stores and major supermarkets. The ham will keep for up to 1 week.

GLAZING THE HAM

Place the scored ham on a rack. Brush glaze mixture all over ham. Cover shank end with foil. Bake as directed, brushing occasionally with the glaze during cooking.

CARVING THE HAM [1]

Place ham on a board and steady it with a carving fork. Using a large sharp knife, make a vertical cut toward the bone at the shank end; cut out a small wedge of ham.

CARVING THE HAM [2]

Carve towards the bone, taking long sweeps with the knife; the slices will increase in size as you carve. Carve only as much ham as you need at a time, or it will dry out.

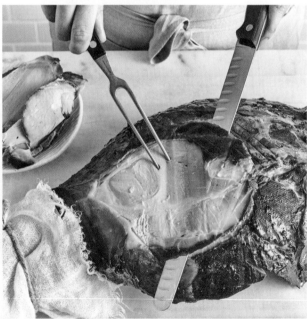

CARVING THE HAM [3]

Turn ham over; carve parallel to the bone. Freeze bone for up to 3 months; use for stock or soup. It will add quite a bit of salt to a recipe so you won't need to add more.

Notes

It is important that both fish fillets are similar in length and thickness as this will ensure the fish will cook evenly. Combine the dressing ingredients close to serving to preserve the colour of the herbs.

Fennel Roast Fish

3 baby fennel bulbs (390g), trimmed,
   sliced thinly, reserve ½ cup of fronds

2 green onions (scallions), chopped

2 tablespoons olive oil

2 x 750g (1½-pound) boneless, skinless
   firm white fish fillets

100g (3 ounces) pitted sicilian olives,
   sliced thickly

⅓ cup fresh mint leaves

¼ cup micro radish leaves

HERB DRESSING

1 clove garlic, crushed

1 teaspoon finely grated lemon rind

⅓ cup (80ml) lemon juice

⅓ cup finely chopped fresh mint

½ cup finely chopped fresh
   flat-leaf parsley

½ cup (125ml) olive oil

1 Preheat oven to 200°C/400°F. Line a large oven tray with baking paper.

2 Combine fennel, green onion and half the oil in a large bowl; season.
Place fennel mixture on tray; top with fish, drizzle with remaining oil. Season.

3 Bake for 20 minutes or until fish is tender. Stand for 5 minutes.

4 Meanwhile, make herb dressing.

5 Serve fish topped with olives, reserved fennel fronds, mint and micro radish;
drizzle with herb dressing.

HERB DRESSING Combine ingredients in a medium bowl; season.

SERVING SUGGESTION Serve with a green salad and steamed baby potatoes.

Red Braised Duck with Plums

1.8kg (3¾-pound) whole duck

9 small blood plums (675g), halved

10cm (4-inch) strip orange rind, sliced thinly

2 tablespoons peanut oil

RED BRAISING LIQUID

3 litres (12 cups) water

1½ cups (375ml) chinese cooking wine
   (shao hsing)

1 cup (250ml) dark soy sauce

½ cup (110g) finely ground yellow rock sugar

6 cloves garlic, crushed

3 teaspoons thinly sliced fresh ginger

4 green onions (scallions), chopped coarsely

1 teaspoon sesame oil

5 star anise

2 cinnamon sticks

SPROUT SALAD

6 green onions (scallions), sliced thinly

2 cups loosely packed fresh coriander
   (cilantro) leaves

1 cup (80g) bean sprouts

1⅓ cups (100g) trimmed snow pea sprouts

2 teaspoons sesame oil

1 teaspoon sesame seeds

1 Make red braising liquid.

2 Rinse duck under cold water, remove neck. Place duck, breast-side down, in a boiler or flameproof dish large enough to hold the duck. Pour braising liquid over duck; weigh down with a plate. Bring to the boil; boil, uncovered, for 40 minutes. Cover; simmer for 15 minutes. Carefully turn duck without piercing the skin. Cover; simmer for a further 15 minutes. Remove from heat; leave duck in liquid for 45 minutes or until duck is cooked through.

3 Remove duck from braising liquid; place on a wire rack over tray. Cool. Strain liquid into a large jug; refrigerate. Pat duck dry with paper towel; cut into serving-sized pieces.

4 Remove fat from surface of braising liquid. Heat 2 cups of the liquid in a medium saucepan; bring to the boil. Reduce heat; simmer gently, uncovered, for 20 minutes or until liquid is reduced by half. Add plums and rind; simmer for 5 minutes or until plums are tender.

5 Meanwhile, make sprout salad.

6 Heat oil in a wok; cook duck, in batches, until crisp and browned.

7 Serve duck with plum mixture and sprout salad.

RED BRAISING LIQUID Place ingredients in a large saucepan; bring to the boil, stirring, until sugar is dissolved. Cool.

SPROUT SALAD Place ingredients in a medium bowl; toss gently to combine.

TIPS If fresh plums are not available, use drained canned plums. Yellow rock sugar is available in Asian supermarkets; it has a richer, subtler flavour than granulated white sugar. It is used mainly for braises and sauces as it gives them a beautiful lustre and glaze.

SERVING SUGGESTION Serve with steamed jasmine rice.

Barbecue Salmon with Yoghurt Dressing

2 medium lemons (280g), sliced thinly

1.3kg (2¾-pound) side of salmon, skin off, bones removed (see notes)

2 tablespoons finely grated lemon rind

2 tablespoons finely chopped fresh flat-leaf parsley

1 cup (250ml) dry white wine

FENNEL SALAD

3 baby fennel bulbs (390g), trimmed, sliced thinly

2 tablespoons olive oil

2 teaspoons finely grated lemon rind

2 tablespoons lemon juice

400g (12½ ounces) canned chickpeas (garbanzo beans), drained, rinsed

1 medium red onion (170g), sliced thinly

200g (6½ ounces) fetta, diced

1 cup (115g) firmly packed trimmed watercress

YOGHURT DRESSING

1 tablespoon olive oil

2 teaspoons mild harissa paste

2 tablespoons finely chopped fresh chives

¾ cup (200g) yoghurt

1 Make fennel salad.

2 Place lemon slices in a 45cm x 34cm (18-inch x 13½-inch) deep disposable aluminium barbecue dish or shallow baking dish; top with salmon. Combine rind, parsley and wine; pour over salmon, cover with foil. Cook, in covered barbecue, using indirect heat, following manufacturer's instructions, for 20 minutes or until done as desired. Remove salmon from barbecue, cover with foil; stand for 10 minutes before serving.

3 Make yoghurt dressing. Serve salmon with salad and dressing.

FENNEL SALAD Combine fennel, oil, rind and juice; cook on a heated barbecue (or grill plate), turning, until fennel is tender, cool for 5 minutes. Combine remaining ingredients in a large bowl; stir in fennel mixture. Season to taste.

YOGHURT DRESSING Whisk ingredients in a small bowl; season to taste.

Notes

For even cooking, fold the tail of the fish under so that both ends of the salmon are roughly the same thickness. The fish can be cooked in the oven at 180°C/350°F for about the same time.

Poached Duck and Cashew Salad with Duck Crackling

3 duck breasts (450g)

2 cups (500ml) chicken stock

½ cup (125ml) salt-reduced soy sauce

2 star anise

½ cup (125ml) vegetable oil

¼ cup (65g) grated palm sugar

½ cup (75g) roasted unsalted cashews

150g (4½ ounces) dried rice
   vermicelli noodles

2 lebanese cucumbers (260g)

1 large carrot (180g), cut into matchsticks

2 purple shallots (50g), sliced thinly

1 fresh long red chilli, sliced thinly

1 cup (80g) bean sprouts

⅓ cup fresh mint leaves

⅓ cup fresh coriander (cilantro) leaves

⅓ cup fresh thai basil leaves

LIME DRESSING

1 clove garlic, crushed

1½ tablespoons grated palm sugar

1½ tablespoons fish sauce

⅓ cup (80ml) lime juice

¼ cup (60ml) peanut oil

1 Remove skin from duck breasts. Place duck breast, stock, soy and star anise in a medium saucepan; bring to the boil. Reduce heat; simmer, uncovered, for 3 minutes. Remove from heat. Cool duck in poaching liquid.

2 Meanwhile, heat oil in a small frying pan; cook duck skin until crisp. Remove with a slotted spoon; drain on paper towel. Drain fat from pan.

3 Heat a cleaned frying pan over medium heat; cook sugar and nuts, stirring, for 5 minutes or until caramelised. Pour onto a baking-paper-lined oven tray. Cool.

4 Make lime dressing.

5 Place noodles in a large heatproof bowl, cover with boiling water; stand until just tender. Drain; return noodles to bowl.

6 Halve cucumber lengthways; remove seeds. Cut cucumber into matchsticks. Add cucumber to noodles with carrot, shallots, chilli, sprouts and ½ cup of the dressing; toss to combine.

7 Thinly slice duck and duck skin. Coarsely chop nuts.

8 Add herbs to salad; toss gently to combine.

9 Serve salad topped with duck; sprinkle with skin and nuts, drizzle with remaining dressing.

LIME DRESSING Stir ingredients in a small bowl until sugar dissolves.

Rolled Lamb Shoulder with Harissa Couscous Stuffing

⅓ cup (65g) couscous

⅓ cup (80ml) boiling water

2 x 750g (3-pound) boned lamb shoulders

¼ cup (40g) pine nuts, roasted

½ cup coarsely chopped fresh mint

1 tablespoon olive oil

HARISSA

2 medium red capsicum (bell peppers) (400g)

1 tablespoon olive oil

1 small red onion (100g), chopped coarsely

4 cloves garlic, chopped coarsely

1 tablespoon ground coriander

1 tablespoon caraway seeds

2 teaspoons ground cumin

1 fresh red thai (serrano) chilli, chopped coarsely

1 tablespoon finely chopped preserved lemon rind

2 tablespoons finely chopped fresh mint

1 Preheat oven to 200°C/400°F.

2 Make harissa.

3 Combine couscous and the water in a medium bowl; stand for 5 minutes. Stir in harissa.

4 Place lamb, fat-side down, on a board. Spread couscous mixture over lamb; top with pine nuts and mint. Roll tightly to enclose filling; secure with kitchen string at 2cm (¾-inch) intervals.

5 Heat oil in a large flameproof baking dish; cook lamb, turning, until browned all over.

6 Transfer dish to oven; roast lamb, uncovered, for 45 minutes. Cover with foil; stand for 10 minutes before serving.

HARISSA Place capsicum on an oven tray; roast for 20 minutes or until skin blisters and blackens (leave the oven on). Cover capsicum with plastic wrap for 5 minutes; peel away skin, discard stems and seeds. Meanwhile, heat oil in a small frying pan; cook onion and garlic, stirring, until softened. Add spices; cook, stirring, until fragrant. Process capsicum and onion mixture with remaining ingredients until smooth.

SERVING SUGGESTION Serve with rocket, grilled flatbread and Greek-style yoghurt.

Lobster with Green Olive and Currant Salsa

1 medium fennel bulb (300g), trimmed,
  fronds reserved

150g (5 ounces) curly endive

3 cooked lobsters (1.8kg), halved
  lengthways

GREEN OLIVE & CURRANT SALSA

3 medium lemons (420g)

⅓ cup (70g) pitted small green olives,
  chopped coarsely

2 tablespoons drained baby capers

2 tablespoons dried currants

⅓ cup finely chopped fresh flat-leaf parsley

2 tablespoons olive oil

1 Make green olive and currant salsa.

2 Slice fennel thinly with a mandoline or V-slicer. Place in a medium bowl with endive
and half the salsa; toss gently to combine.

3 Divide lobster and fennel salad among serving plates. Drizzle with remaining salsa;
top with reserved fronds.

GREEN OLIVE & CURRANT SALSA Finely grate rind from one lemon. Cut off the rind from
all lemons along with the white pith, following the curve of the fruit. Segment lemons over a
medium bowl to catch the juices, by cutting down both sides of the white membrane to release
each segment. Chop segments finely; add to bowl with grated rind and remaining ingredients.
Stand for 20 minutes; season to taste.

Turkey Roll with Pork and Fennel Sausage Stuffing

1.5kg (3-pound) single turkey breast,
  skin on

1 tablespoon olive oil

6 baby fennel bulbs (780g), halved

1 medium lemon (140g), quartered

½ cup (125ml) dry white wine

PORK & FENNEL SAUSAGE STUFFING

½ cup (35g) fresh breadcrumbs

⅓ cup (80ml) milk

1 tablespoon olive oil

1 medium brown onion (150g),
  chopped finely

2 cloves garlic, crushed

70g (2½ ounces) rocket (arugula),
  chopped finely

7 pork and fennel sausages (560g),
  cases removed

1 Preheat oven to 200°C/400°F.

2 Make pork and fennel sausage stuffing.

3 Pat turkey dry with paper towel; place skin-side down on board. Starting from one long edge, slice through centre, horizontally, not quite through to other side, to open up flat. Spread with stuffing mixture. Roll tightly to enclose stuffing; secure with kitchen string at 2.5cm (1-inch) intervals.

4 Heat oil in a large baking dish in the oven for 5 minutes. Add turkey roll; turn to coat. Place fennel and lemon around turkey; add wine to dish. Roast, uncovered, for 50 minutes, basting turkey frequently. Cover turkey loosely with foil; stand for 10 minutes before slicing.

5 Serve sliced turkey with fennel and lemon.

PORK & FENNEL SAUSAGE STUFFING Combine breadcrumbs and milk in a small bowl. Heat oil in a medium frying pan; cook onion, stirring occasionally, until tender. Stir in garlic, then stir in rocket until wilted. Transfer to a medium bowl; cool for 20 minutes. Stir in sausage mince and breadcrumb mixture; season.

Notes

It's important not to overcrowd the turkey, fennel and lemon in the baking dish so they cook evenly and caramelise. When the roll is cooked, juices should run clear when tested with a skewer.

Roast Beef with Tuna Aïoli

¼ cup (60ml) olive oil

800g (1½-pound) piece centre-cut
   beef eye fillet

1 small french bread stick (150g),
   sliced thinly

½ cup (150g) aïoli

95g (3 ounces) canned tuna in oil, drained

5 drained anchovy fillets

1 tablespoon lemon juice

2 cloves garlic, sliced thinly

2 teaspoons drained baby capers

½ cup loosely packed small fresh
   flat-leaf parsley leaves

1 Preheat oven to 180°C/350°F.

2 Heat 1 tablespoon of the oil in a medium flameproof baking dish over high heat;
cook beef, turning, until browned all over. Season. Roast beef for 30 minutes for medium.
Transfer beef to a plate; cool. Cover; refrigerate 3 hours or overnight.

3 Place bread slices on a large baking-paper-lined oven tray; brush with another tablespoon
of the oil. Bake for 10 minutes or until golden and crisp.

4 Meanwhile, blend or process aïoli, tuna, anchovies and juice until smooth. Season.

5 Heat remaining oil in a small frying pan; cook garlic slices until lightly golden.
Drain on paper towel.

6 Thinly slice beef; arrange on a serving platter. Top with garlic, capers and parsley;
drizzle with tuna aïoli. Serve with crisp bread.

Eat, drink and be merry with family and friends. There is much to celebrate at Christmas.

Turkey Roll with Cherry and Almond Stuffing

3kg (6-pound) double turkey breasts, boned, skin on

20g (¾ ounce) butter, melted

1 tablespoon plain (all-purpose) flour

⅓ cup (80ml) tawny port

¾ cup (180ml) dry white wine

1 cup (250ml) chicken stock

2½ cups (375g) fresh cherries, pitted, quartered

CHERRY & ALMOND STUFFING

30g (1 ounce) butter

7 shallots (175g), chopped finely

4 cloves garlic, chopped finely

½ cup coarsely chopped fresh marjoram

2 cups (330g) cooked brown rice

1 cup (150g) fresh cherries, pitted, quartered

¼ cup (35g) dried cherries

½ cup (80g) almond kernels, roasted, chopped coarsely

2 eggs

1 Preheat oven to 200°C/400°F.

2 Make cherry and almond stuffing.

3 To butterfly turkey, place breasts, skin-side down, on chopping board; starting from centre of breasts, split one breast in half horizontally, stopping about 1cm (½ inch) from the end, open out flap. Repeat on other side; you should now have one long piece of turkey. Use hands to flatten turkey meat.

4 Place cherry and almond stuffing at one end of turkey; roll up tightly from short side. Use kitchen string to secure at 2.5cm (1-inch) intervals along roll. Brush with butter; season. Place turkey in flameproof dish with enough water to barely cover base of dish. Roast for 1½ hours or until cooked through. Add more water to dish as necessary during cooking to prevent juices burning. To test if turkey is cooked, insert a skewer into the thickest part of the roll; remove skewer and press the flesh. Juices should run clear. Cover roll with foil; stand for 20 minutes.

5 Meanwhile, pour pan juices into medium jug; skim fat, return 1 tablespoon of fat to baking dish. Place dish over medium heat; stir in flour, cook, stirring, until well browned. Add port; bring to the boil. Add wine, stock and reserved pan juices; stir until gravy boils and thickens. Add cherries; simmer, uncovered, for 2 minutes or until softened. Season to taste.

6 Serve sliced turkey with gravy.

CHERRY & ALMOND STUFFING Melt butter in small frying pan; cook shallot and garlic until browned lightly. Place shallot mixture in large bowl with remaining ingredients; stir to combine. Season well.

Notes

Order turkey breasts from your butcher and ask him to bone and butterfly them for you. Dried cherries are available from specialty food stores. If unavailable, use dried cranberries. To make shallots easier to peel, pour boiling water over shallots in a heatproof bowl; stand for 1 minute. Skins will slip off easily. You need to cook ⅔ cup brown rice for this recipe.

Notes

To remove seeds from pomegranate, cut pomegranate in half crossways; hold it, cut-side down, in the palm of your hand over a large bowl, then hit the outside firmly with a wooden spoon. The seeds should fall out easily; discard any white pith that falls out with them. We used pacific dory in this recipe, but any thin white fish fillet will be fine.

Fish with Fennel and Pomegranate Salad

3 baby fennel bulbs (390g), shaved,
  fronds reserved

¼ cup loosely packed small
  fresh flat-leaf parsley leaves

¼ cup loosely packed small
  fresh basil leaves

¼ cup loosely packed small
  fresh mint leaves

1 medium pomegranate (320g),
  seeds removed (see notes)

1 tablespoon lemon juice

¼ cup (60ml) olive oil

4 x 300g (9½ ounces) white fish fillets
  (see notes)

30g (1 ounce) butter

AÏOLI DRESSING

¼ cup (75g) mayonnaise

1 clove garlic, crushed

2 tablespoons lemon juice

1 Make aïoli dressing.

2 Place fennel and herbs in a large bowl with 2 tablespoons of the pomegranate seeds,
the juice and 1 tablespoon of the oil; toss gently to combine.

3 Heat remaining oil in a large frying pan over high heat. Season fish. Cook fish, skin-side
down first, for 1 minute or until golden brown. Turn over, add butter; cook until butter turns
nut brown. Cook fish for 30 seconds or until just cooked through.

4 Divide fennel salad between plates. Top with fish; sprinkle with fennel fronds and remaining
pomegranate seeds. Serve with dressing.

AÏOLI DRESSING Whisk ingredients in a small jug until well combined. Season to taste.

DO AHEAD Aïoli dressing can be made 2 days ahead; keep covered in the fridge.

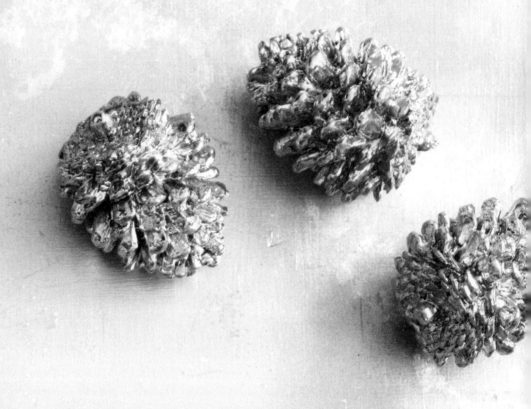

Nothing says
Christmas like the
smell of a plump
roast turkey wafting
through the house.

ROAST TURKEY WITH
BACON AND SAGE STUFFING
(RECIPE PAGE 303)

STUFFING THE TURKEY
After rinsing turkey inside and out under cold water, pat dry with paper towel. Spoon the stuffing mixture into the large cavity, pressing in with your fingers.

TRUSSING THE TURKEY
Tie the legs together with kitchen string, fill the neck cavity with stuffing, securing with toothpicks, then tuck the wing tips underneath the turkey.

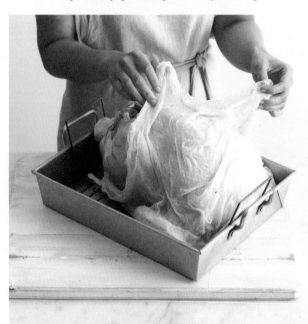

COVERING WITH MUSLIN
Place turkey on an oiled rack in a flameproof baking dish. Dip a 50cm (20-inch) square of muslin in melted butter, place over turkey; cover with foil before roasting.

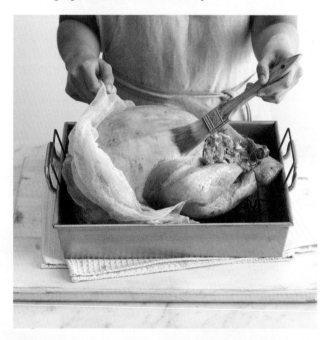

BASTING WITH PAN JUICES
Roast turkey for 2 hours, then remove foil and muslin. Baste with combined pan juices and oil, then continue roasting turkey, uncovered, for another hour.

Roast Turkey with Bacon and Sage Stuffing

5kg (10-pound) turkey

50cm (20-inch) square muslin

125g (4 ounces) butter, melted

1 tablespoon olive oil

2 tablespoons sea salt

2 tablespoons fresh thyme leaves

BACON & SAGE STUFFING

50g (1½ ounces) butter

4 rindless bacon slices (260g), chopped finely

1 medium brown onion (150g), chopped finely

2 trimmed sticks celery (200g), chopped finely

1 tablespoon finely chopped fresh sage

2 teaspoons fresh thyme leaves

4 cups (280g) stale breadcrumbs

1 egg, beaten lightly

PORT GRAVY

40g (1½ ounces) butter

1 medium brown onion (150g), chopped finely

1 trimmed stick celery (100g), chopped finely

2 cloves garlic, crushed

¼ cup (35g) plain (all-purpose) flour

¼ cup (60ml) port

2¼ cups (560ml) chicken stock, approximately

1 Preheat oven to 180°C/350°F.

2 Make bacon and sage stuffing.

3 Rinse turkey inside and out under cold water; pat dry with paper towel. Fill large cavity with stuffing. Tie legs together with kitchen string. Fill the neck cavity with stuffing; secure opening with toothpicks. Tuck wing tips under the turkey.

4 Place turkey on an oiled wire rack in a flameproof baking dish. Dip the muslin in melted butter, then place over turkey. Cover dish tightly with foil. Roast for 2 hours.

5 Remove foil and muslin from turkey; brush turkey with combined pan juices and oil. Roast, uncovered, for a further 1 hour or until browned and cooked through. To test, insert a skewer into the thickest part of the thigh. Remove the skewer, press the flesh to release the juices; if the juices are clear, the turkey is cooked. (Or, insert a thermometer into the thickest part of turkey thigh, without touching the bone; it should read 90°C/180°F. Test the stuffing as well – it should read at least 75°C/150°F.) Remove turkey from dish, sprinkle with salt and thyme. Cover with foil; stand for 20 minutes.

6 Meanwhile, make port gravy.

7 Serve turkey with port gravy, roasted potatoes and steamed greens, if desired.

BACON & SAGE STUFFING Heat butter in a large frying pan; cook bacon, stirring, for 3 minutes or until browned. Add onion and celery; cook, stirring for 5 minutes or until soft. Cool 10 minutes. Combine bacon mixture with remaining ingredients.

PORT GRAVY Drain turkey pan juices from baking dish into a large jug, skim fat from the top; reserve juices, discard fat. Place dish over medium heat, melt butter in dish; cook onion, celery and garlic, stirring, for 5 minutes or until soft. Add flour; cook, stirring, for 5 minutes or until flour is well browned. Remove from heat, stir in port; return to heat. Gradually stir in combined reserved pan juices and stock. Cook, stirring, until mixture boils and thickens. Strain gravy into a large jug.

Modern MAINS

Roast Pork Loin with Cranberry Sauce

2kg (4-pound) boneless pork loin, rind on

60g (2 ounces) butter

1 tablespoon olive oil

1 medium red onion (170g), chopped finely

1 clove garlic, crushed

100g (3 ounces) mild salami, chopped finely

¼ cup (35g) roasted unsalted shelled pistachios

¼ cup (35g) dried cranberries

1 tablespoon finely chopped fresh sage

½ cup (25g) fresh breadcrumbs

2 tablespoons fine table salt

1½ cups (375ml) chicken stock

½ cup (125ml) port

¼ cup (80g) cranberry sauce

ROASTED VEGETABLES

500g (1 pound) pumpkin, cut into wedges

2 medium parsnips (500g), quartered

2 medium red onions (340g), quartered

500g (1 pound) baby carrots, trimmed

12 baby new potatoes (480g), halved

¼ cup (60ml) olive oil

2 tablespoons fresh thyme leaves

1 Preheat oven to 200°C/400°F.

2 Using a sharp knife, score pork skin by making shallow cuts at 1cm (½-inch) intervals. Place pork on a board, fat-side down; slice through thickest part of pork horizontally, without cutting through other side. Open pork out to form one large piece. Trim pork; reserve 150g (5 ounces) trimmings for seasoning. Blend or process pork trimmings with 20g (¾ ounce) of the butter; place in a large bowl.

3 Heat oil in a medium frying pan; stir onion and garlic, over heat until onion softens. Add remaining butter, salami, nuts, cranberries and sage; cook for 2 minutes. Transfer mixture to a medium bowl; cool. Stir in breadcrumbs and minced trimmings.

4 Press seasoning mixture along one long side of the pork; roll pork to enclose filling, secure with kitchen string at 2cm (¾-inch) intervals. Rub pork skin with salt; place on a wire rack in a large shallow baking dish. Roast pork, uncovered, for 1¼ hours or until pork is cooked through.

5 Meanwhile, make roasted vegetables.

6 Remove pork from dish; cover loosely with foil, stand for 15 minutes. Drain excess fat from dish, add stock, port and sauce to dish; stir over heat until sauce is reduced by half. Season to taste; cover to keep warm.

7 Serve sliced pork with vegetables and sauce.

ROASTED VEGETABLES Combine vegetables in a large baking dish with oil and thyme. Roast, uncovered, for last 30 minutes of pork cooking time, turning once. Season to taste.

Notes

Ask your butcher to leave a flap measuring about 20cm (8 inches) in length to help make rolling the loin easier. The secret to exceptional crackling is to ensure the pork skin is dry and well-seasoned with fine salt before cooking. Pat the pork dry with paper towel; refrigerate, uncovered, for a few hours or overnight for the skin to dry out.

Crispy Pork Rack with Sticky Bourbon Apples

2.2kg (4½-pound) rack of pork, rind on

2 tablespoons olive oil

1 tablespoon coarse cooking (kosher) salt

½ cup (110g) firmly packed light brown sugar

½ cup (125ml) bourbon

4 medium pink lady apples (600g), quartered

4 medium red onions (680g), root ends intact, cut into eighths

1 Preheat oven to 250°C/500°F.

2 Pat pork rind dry with paper towel. Using a very sharp knife or Stanley knife, score the rind at 1cm (½-inch) intervals, cutting into the fat but not deep enough to cut through to the flesh. Place pork on a wire rack in a large baking dish. Rub rind with oil, then rub in salt.

3 Roast pork for 40 minutes or until skin blisters. (Your oven will smoke, but don't worry – you need this strong heat for really great crackling; the rind will not blister after this stage.)

4 Reduce oven to 180°C/350°F; roast pork for a further 40 minutes or until pork is just cooked through.

5 Meanwhile, combine sugar and bourbon in a medium baking dish. Add apple and onion; stir to coat. Roast in oven for the last 25 minutes of pork cooking time.

6 Serve pork with sticky apple mixture.

SERVING SUGGESTION Serve with steamed asparagus and zucchini topped with chopped, roasted unsalted pistachios.

Cold Seafood Platter with Three Sauces

2 cooked lobsters (2.4kg)

4 cooked balmain bugs (rock lobster) (800g)

2 cooked blue swimmer crabs (650g)

1kg (2 pounds) cooked medium
  king prawns (shrimp)

18 oysters, on half shell

3 medium lemons (420g), cut into wedges

SAFFRON AÏOLI

pinch saffron threads

1 tablespoon boiling water

1 clove garlic, crushed

2 egg yolks

1 teaspoon dijon mustard

½ cup (125ml) grape seed or rice bran oil

¼ cup (60ml) extra virgin olive oil

2 tablespoons lemon juice

HORSERADISH COCKTAIL SAUCE

2 tablespoons tomato sauce (ketchup)

2 teaspoons horseradish cream

1 tablespoon lemon juice

1½ teaspoons worcestershire sauce

2 tablespoons pouring cream

CITRUS & SHALLOT VINEGAR

1 shallot (25g), chopped finely

1½ tablespoons sherry vinegar

2 teaspoons finely grated lemon rind

1 tablespoon lemon juice

2 tablespoons orange juice

1½ tablespoons finely chopped fresh chives

1 Make saffron aïoli, horseradish cocktail sauce, then citrus and shallot vinegar. Cover separately; refrigerate until required.

2 Place a lobster upside-down on board. Cut through chest and tail; turn lobster over and cut through head. Pull halves apart. Using a small spoon, remove brain matter and liver. Rinse lobster carefully under cold water; repeat with remaining lobster.

3 Turn a bug upside-down; cut off head. Using a sharp knife, cut bug tail in half lengthways. Carefully lift out and discard centre vein from tail. Repeat with remaining bugs.

4 Lift crab tail flap, then with a peeling motion, lift off the back shell. Remove and discard the whitish gills, liver and brain matter. Rinse crab carefully under cold water. Repeat with remaining crab. Cut crab bodies into quarters; crack claws.

5 Shell and devein prawns, leaving heads and tails intact.

6 Arrange seafood on a large platter with lemon wedges. Serve with sauces.

SAFFRON AÏOLI Place saffron and the water in a small heatproof bowl; stand for 5 minutes. Whisk garlic, egg yolks and mustard in a medium bowl. Gradually add oils in a thin, steady stream, whisking constantly until mixture thickens. Stir juice and saffron mixture into aïoli. Season to taste.

HORSERADISH COCKTAIL SAUCE Combine ingredients in a small bowl; season to taste.

CITRUS & SHALLOT VINEGAR Combine ingredients in a small bowl.

DO AHEAD Saffron aïoli and cocktail sauce can be made up to 4 days ahead; store, covered, in the fridge. Citrus and shallot vinegar can be made several hours before serving.

Modern MAINS

Pork Belly with Grilled Pineapple Salad

2.5kg (5-pound) piece boneless pork belly

2 cloves garlic, crushed

1 teaspoon chinese five-spice

2 tablespoons finely grated fresh ginger

1 tablespoon sea salt

⅓ cup (80ml) chinese cooking wine (shao hsing) or dry sherry

1 medium pineapple (1.25kg), peeled, cut into small wedges

2 medium red capsicums (bell peppers) (400g), sliced thickly

3 lebanese cucumbers (400g), cut into lengths on the diagonal

1 cup loosely packed fresh coriander (cilantro) leaves

1 teaspoon japanese soy sauce

2 tablespoons sweet chilli sauce

2 tablespoons lime juice

1 Preheat oven to 170°C/340°F. Line a large baking dish with baking paper.

2 Using a very sharp knife or Stanley knife, score pork belly skin at 5mm (¼-inch) intervals.

3 Place pork on a wire rack, skin-side up, over the sink. Pour boiling water over the skin, then pat dry with paper towel.

4 Combine garlic, five-spice, ginger and half the salt in a small bowl. Rub paste over pork flesh only, not the skin. Pour cooking wine into lined dish. Place pork in dish, skin-side up. Rub remaining salt into skin. Roast pork for 3 hours or until tender.

5 Increase oven to 250°C/500°F; roast pork for a further 30 minutes or until skin crackles.

6 Meanwhile, heat a grill plate (or barbecue) over high heat. Cook pineapple and capsicum until browned. Remove to a serving plate; cool. When cool, add cucumber and coriander.

7 Combine sauces and juice in a small bowl; spoon dressing over pineapple salad.

8 Serve pork belly cut into thick strips with pineapple salad.

Seared Tuna with Verjuice Dressing

Buy individual tuna steaks instead of the fillet, if you prefer. Cook steaks for about 5 minutes, depending on their thickness.

2 tablespoons hot english mustard

¼ cup (60ml) light soy sauce

1 tablespoon peanut oil

800g (1½-pound) piece tuna fillet

8 baby new potatoes (320g), halved

250g (8 ounces) green beans

1 cup (150g) pitted black olives

250g (8 ounces) cherry tomatoes, halved

1 small red onion (100g), cut into wedges

6 medium-boiled eggs, halved

VERJUICE DRESSING

2 tablespoons verjuice

1 tablespoon dijon mustard

¼ cup (60ml) walnut oil

1 tablespoon finely chopped
   fresh chervil

1 Combine mustard, sauce and oil in a large bowl, add tuna; turn to coat. Cover; refrigerate for 3 hours or overnight.

2 Make verjuice dressing.

3 Boil, steam or microwave potato and beans, separately, until tender; drain. Place potatoes and beans in a large bowl with olives, tomato, onion and dressing; toss gently to combine. Top with eggs; season to taste.

4 Remove tuna from marinade; discard marinade. Cook tuna on a hot barbecue (or grill plate) for 10 minutes, turning, until marked well on all sides and cooked to your liking. Remove from heat, cover loosely with foil; stand for 10 minutes.

5 Cut tuna into slices; serve with salad.

VERJUICE DRESSING Place ingredients in a screw-top jar; shake well. Season.

TIP Verjuice is an unfermented grape juice with a fresh lemony-vinegar flavour. It's available in supermarkets, usually in the vinegar section.

Rib Steaks with Roasted Capsicum and Almond Salsa

8 beef rib steaks (rib-eye), bone in,
  trimmed (2.7kg)

1 teaspoon paprika

ROASTED CAPSICUM & ALMOND SALSA

400g (12½ ounces) roasted red capsicum
  (bell pepper), chopped coarsely

½ cup (80g) almond kernels, roasted,
  chopped coarsely

1 small red onion (100g), chopped finely

1 cup (120g) pitted green olives,
  sliced thinly

1 cup coarsely chopped fresh
  flat-leaf parsley

½ cup coarsely chopped fresh oregano

2 long fresh red chillies, chopped finely

1 tablespoon extra virgin olive oil

1 tablespoon lemon juice

2 cloves garlic, crushed

1 Sprinkle beef, both sides, with paprika. Cook beef on a heated oiled grill plate (or barbecue) until done as desired. Remove from heat. Cover; stand for 10 minutes.

2 Meanwhile, make roasted capsicum and almond salsa.

3 Serve beef with salsa.

ROASTED CAPSICUM & ALMOND SALSA Combine capsicum, nuts, onion, olives, herbs and chilli in a medium bowl. Add combined oil, juice and garlic; toss gently to combine.

Hot Seafood Platter

500g (1 pound) white fish fillets
   (see notes)

500g (1 pound) calamari rings

1 cup (150g) plain (all-purpose) flour

¼ cup (60ml) milk

4 eggs, beaten lightly

2 cups (140g) stale breadcrumbs

⅓ cup finely chopped fresh
   flat-leaf parsley

½ cup (40g) finely grated parmesan

1 tablespoon finely grated lemon rind

1 medium tomato (150g), halved

1 tablespoon vodka

¼ teaspoon Tabasco sauce

2 teaspoons worcestershire sauce

1 teaspoon lemon juice

vegetable oil, for shallow-frying

12 oysters, on the half shell

1 trimmed celery stick (100g),
   chopped finely

3 slices pancetta (45g), chopped finely

8 uncooked large king prawns (shrimp)
   (560g)

watercress, red vein sorrel and lime
   wedges, to serve

1 Coat fish and calamari in flour. Dip in combined milk and egg, then toss in combined breadcrumbs, parsley, parmesan and rind. Cover; refrigerate for 15 minutes.
2 Meanwhile, using largest holes on a four-sided box grater, grate the tomato halves, from cut-side, into a small bowl; discard skin. Stir in vodka, sauces and juice.
3 Heat oil in a large deep frying pan; shallow-fry fish and calamari, in batches, until browned and cooked through. Drain on paper towel.
4 Meanwhile, preheat grill (broiler).
5 Place oysters on an oven tray. Spoon tomato mixture onto oysters; top with celery and pancetta. Place under hot grill for 5 minutes or until pancetta is crisp.
6 Cook prawns on a heated oiled grill plate (or barbecue) until browned lightly and cooked through. Arrange seafood on a large serving platter with watercress, sorrel and lime wedges.

SERVING SUGGESTION Serve with any or all of the three dipping sauces from the cold seafood platter (page 308).

Notes

We used king george whiting fillets in this recipe but you can use your favourite white fish fillets instead.

Sides

Tomato, Basil and Pine Nut Salad

Use an assortment of tomatoes in season to make a bright summery salad. We used a mixture of ox heart, roma (plum), cherry, yellow teardrop and black tomatoes.

1kg (2 pounds) mixed tomatoes

¼ cup lightly packed small
　fresh basil leaves

BASIL & PINE NUT DRESSING

½ cup firmly packed fresh basil leaves

¼ cup (40g) pine nuts, roasted

1 clove garlic, quartered

⅓ cup (80ml) olive oil

1½ teaspoons red wine vinegar

1 Make basil and pine nut dressing.

2 Roughly chop or halve tomatoes, combine in a serving bowl; season. Drizzle with dressing; sprinkle with basil leaves.

BASIL & PINE NUT DRESSING Blend or process basil, nuts and garlic until chopped coarsely. With motor operating, gradually add oil; process until chopped finely. Stir in vinegar.

GLAZED BABY CARROTS WITH HAZELNUTS

ROASTED CARAMELISED PARSNIPS

HASSELBACK POTATOES

CREAMED SPINACH

Vegetable sides

GLAZED BABY CARROTS WITH HAZELNUTS

PREP + COOK TIME 25 MINUTES
SERVES 4

Melt 30g (1oz) butter in a large frying pan; cook 800g (1½lbs) baby carrots, turning occasionally, until almost tender. Add 2 teaspoons finely grated orange rind, ¼ cup (60ml) orange juice, 2 tablespoons dry white wine and 2 tablespoons maple syrup; bring to the boil. Reduce heat; simmer, uncovered, until liquid has almost evaporated and carrots are tender and caramelised. Serve carrots sprinkled with ½ cup coarsely chopped roasted hazelnuts.

ROASTED CARAMELISED PARSNIPS

PREP + COOK TIME 1 HOUR 10 MINUTES
SERVES 4

Preheat oven to 220°C/425°F. Combine 1kg (2lbs) parsnips, halved lengthways, 2 tablespoons olive oil, ¼ cup (55g) firmly packed light brown sugar and 1 teaspoon ground nutmeg in a large shallow baking dish; roast, uncovered, for 1 hour or until parsnips are browned and tender. Serve sprinkled with 1 tablespoon finely chopped fresh flat-leaf parsley.

HASSELBACK POTATOES

PREP + COOK TIME 1 HOUR 30 MINUTES
SERVES 4

Preheat oven to 180°C/350°F. Place 4 medium (800g) desiree potatoes, halved, cut-side down, on a chopping board; working with one half at a time, place a chopstick on the board along each side of potato. Slice potato thinly, cutting through to chopsticks to prevent cutting all the way through. Repeat with remaining halves. Combine 40g (1½oz) melted butter and 2 tablespoons olive oil in a medium baking dish; add potatoes, turn to coat. Place, rounded-side up, in single layer; roast for 1 hour, brushing often with oil mixture. Combine ¼ cup (25g) packaged breadcrumbs and ½ cup (40g) finely grated parmesan in a small bowl; sprinkle over potatoes. Roast potatoes for a further 10 minutes or until browned.

CREAMED SPINACH

PREP + COOK TIME 15 MINUTES
SERVES 4

Melt 20g (¾oz) butter in a large frying pan; cook 600g (1¼lbs) spinach, stirring, until wilted. Add ½ cup (125ml) pouring cream; bring to the boil. Reduce heat; simmer, uncovered, until liquid reduces by half.

Mixed Bean Salad with Creamy Basil Dressing

400g (12½ ounces) canned butter beans, drained, rinsed

400g (12½ ounces) canned borlotti beans, drained, rinsed

250g (8 ounces) cherry tomatoes, quartered

12 cherry bocconcini cheese (180g), halved

60g (2 ounces) rocket (arugula) leaves

½ cup (80g) toasted pine nuts

CREAMY BASIL DRESSING

2 tablespoons olive oil

2 tablespoons white wine vinegar

2 teaspoons white balsamic vinegar

2 tablespoons coarsely chopped fresh basil

¼ cup (60ml) pouring cream

1 Make creamy basil dressing.

2 Place beans in a large bowl with remaining salad ingredients; toss to combine.

3 Just before serving, drizzle dressing over salad; toss gently to combine.

CREAMY BASIL DRESSING Whisk oil, vinegars and basil in a small bowl; whisk in cream.

DO-AHEAD The dressing and the salad mixture can be prepared a few hours ahead. Add the dressing just before serving.

Notes

If you want to cook the bugs yourself, you will need to buy about 3.5kg (8 pounds) of uncooked bugs. You can use prawns (shrimp), lobster, scampi or crab instead of the bugs.

Balmain Bug and Apple Salad

1kg (2 pounds) cooked balmain bug
  (rock lobster) meat (see notes)
2 lebanese cucumbers (260g),
  cut into ribbons
2 medium apples (300g), halved, sliced
2 cups loosely packed fresh vietnamese
  mint leaves
2 cups loosely packed fresh coriander
  (cilantro) leaves

PURPLE SHALLOT DRESSING

3 purple shallots (75g), sliced thinly
2 fresh small red thai (serrano) chillies,
  sliced thinly
1 tablespoon finely grated lime rind
⅓ cup (80ml) lime juice
2 tablespoons finely grated palm sugar
1 tablespoon fish sauce

1 Make purple shallot dressing.
2 Place bug meat in a large bowl with remaining ingredients and dressing; toss gently
to combine. Serve immediately.
PURPLE SHALLOT DRESSING Combine ingredients in a small bowl; stand for 10 minutes.

It doesn't have to be snowing outside for it to be a white Christmas.

Warm Kipfler and Cucumber Salad with Dill

1 medium red onion (170g), sliced thinly

4 lebanese cucumbers (520g), seeded, sliced thinly

¼ cup (60ml) white wine vinegar

1 tablespoon white (granulated) sugar

1 teaspoon salt

1kg (2 pounds) kipfler (fingerling) potatoes, unpeeled, sliced diagonally

¼ cup (60ml) olive oil

1 cup loosely packed fresh dill sprigs

¼ cup (50g) salted baby capers, rinsed

1 Combine onion and cucumber in a medium heatproof bowl.

2 Place vinegar, sugar and salt in a small saucepan over low heat; stir, without boiling, until sugar is dissolved. Bring to the boil; pour over onion mixture. Cool.

3 Meanwhile, boil, steam or microwave potato until tender; drain.

4 Place potato and onion mixture in a large bowl with oil, dill and capers; toss gently to combine. Season to taste. Serve warm.

Grilled Nectarine, Prosciutto and Pistachio Salad

1 tablespoon pomegranate molasses

2 tablespoons olive oil

4 medium nectarines (680g), halved,
  stone removed, cut into quarters

cooking-oil spray

3 balls buffalo mozzarella (390g), torn

100g (3 ounces) thinly sliced prosciutto

60g (2 ounces) rocket (arugula), trimmed

¼ cup (35g) coarsely chopped pistachios

2 tablespoons pomegranate seeds

1 Place molasses and oil in a screw-top jar; shake well. Season.

2 Heat a grill plate (or barbecue) over medium-high heat. Lightly spray nectarines with cooking oil; cook nectarines until charred on both sides.

3 Arrange nectarines, mozzarella, prosciutto and rocket on a large platter. Drizzle with dressing; sprinkle with pistachios and pomegranate seeds.

TIP You can use peaches or rockmelon wedges instead of nectarines, if you like.

DO AHEAD This recipe is best made close to serving.

Mixed Peas, Mint and Roasted Almond Salad

150g (5 ounces) snow peas, trimmed

150g (5 ounces) sugar snap peas, trimmed

125g (4 ounces) snow pea sprouts, trimmed

150g (5 ounces) young pea tendrils, trimmed

1 cup loosely packed fresh mint leaves

½ cup (70g) slivered almonds, roasted

MUSTARD & CIDER DRESSING

2 tablespoons olive oil

1 tablespoon cider vinegar

2 teaspoons wholegrain mustard

1 Cook snow peas and sugar snap peas in a saucepan of boiling salted water for 2 minutes or until barely tender; drain. Rinse under cold running water; drain.

2 Make mustard and cider dressing.

3 Place peas in a large bowl with remaining ingredients and dressing; toss gently to combine.

MUSTARD & CIDER DRESSING Whisk ingredients in a small bowl; season.

TIP Snow pea sprouts and pea tendrils can sometimes be hard to buy, use bean sprouts or any other type of sprouts instead.

Chickpea, Green Chilli and Walnut Salad

800g (1½ pounds) canned chickpeas (garbanzo beans), drained, rinsed

1 cup coarsely chopped fresh flat-leaf parsley

1 cup coarsely chopped fresh mint

1 cup (160g) pitted green olives, chopped coarsely

4 green onions (scallions), sliced thinly

2 fresh long green chillies, sliced thinly

1 medium red capsicum (bell pepper) (200g), chopped finely

1 cup (100g) roasted walnuts, chopped coarsely

LEMON DRESSING

¼ cup (60ml) olive oil

¼ cup (60ml) lemon juice

1 Make lemon dressing.

2 Place chickpeas in a large bowl with remaining ingredients.

3 Just before serving, drizzle dressing over salad; toss gently to combine.

LEMON DRESSING Place ingredients in a screw-top jar; shake well. Season to taste.

DO-AHEAD Prepare the dressing and the chickpea salad a few hours ahead. Add the dressing just before serving.

Fresh Cherry and Pistachio Tabbouleh

1½ cups (240g) burghul

2 cups (500ml) boiling water

500g (1 pound) fresh cherries,
   pitted, halved

1 cup (140g) roasted unsalted shelled
   pistachios, chopped coarsely

2 cups firmly packed fresh mint leaves,
   chopped finely

1 cup firmly packed fresh flat-leaf
   parsley leaves, chopped finely

1 small red onion (100g), chopped finely

½ cup loosely packed small
   mint leaves, extra

½ cup loosely packed small
   flat-leaf parsley leaves, extra

RED WINE VINEGAR DRESSING

½ cup (125ml) olive oil

⅓ cup (80ml) red wine vinegar

1 Combine burghul and the water in a large heatproof bowl. Stand for 15 minutes or until burghul is tender and the water absorbed.

2 Make red wine vinegar dressing.

3 Add cherries, nuts, chopped herbs and onion to burghul. Stir in dressing; season.

4 Serve tabbouleh topped with extra herbs.

RED WINE VINEGAR DRESSING Whisk ingredients in a small bowl; season to taste.

TIP You will need about 3 bunches of mint for this recipe.

Asparagus Salad with Spring Onion and Pea Vinaigrette

1 cup (250ml) dry white wine

1 teaspoon white (granulated) sugar

8 spring onions (200g), trimmed,
  sliced thinly

1½ cups (180g) frozen peas

500g (1 pound) asparagus

1 tablespoon olive oil

1 Bring wine and sugar to the boil in a medium frying pan. Reduce heat; simmer, uncovered until mixture is reduced to about ¼ cup.

2 Meanwhile, half-fill another medium frying pan with water, add a little salt; bring to the boil. Drop onion into boiling water, cook for 30 seconds; remove with a slotted spoon to a strainer. Rinse under cold water; drain.

3 Using the same boiling water, repeat with peas then asparagus. Place asparagus on a serving platter.

4 Add oil to wine mixture with onion and peas; heat gently over low heat, season. Pour vinaigrette over asparagus. Serve salad warm or at room temperature.

Chicken, Rocket and Date Salad

600g (1¼ pounds) chicken breast fillets

1.5 litres (6 cups) water

2 large oranges (600g)

¼ cup (60ml) lemon juice

1 tablespoon fresh lemon thyme leaves

1 tablespoon extra virgin olive oil

150g (4½ ounces) rocket (arugula) leaves

8 fresh dates (160g), pitted, quartered lengthways

1 medium pomegranate (380g), halved crossways, seeds removed (see notes)

24 dry roasted natural almonds (15g), chopped coarsely

1 Place chicken and the water in a medium saucepan over high heat; bring to the boil. Reduce heat to low; simmer, uncovered, for 10 minutes. Remove from heat; cool chicken in poaching liquid for 20 minutes.

2 Meanwhile, using a zester, remove rind from 1 orange into long thin strips. Cut off the rind from both oranges along with the white pith, following the curve of the fruit. Segment oranges over a medium bowl to catch the juices, by cutting down both sides of the white membrane to release each segment. Reserve ¼ cup (60ml) of juice.

3 To make dressing, stir reserved juice, lemon juice, rind, thyme and oil in a small jug. Season with pepper.

4 Remove chicken from poaching liquid; shred coarsely.

5 Arrange rocket on a large serving plate; drizzle with a little dressing. Top with chicken, orange segments, dates, pomegranate seeds and nuts. Serve drizzled with remaining dressing.

DO-AHEAD The chicken can be cooked a day ahead; refrigerate, covered, until required.

Notes

If you don't have a zester, use a peeler to cut strips of orange rind, then cut the rind into thin strips. To remove the seeds from the pomegranate, hold each half, cut-side down, in the palm of your hand over a bowl, then hit the outside firmly with a wooden spoon. The seeds should fall out easily; discard any white pith that falls out with them.

Salad sides

PRESERVED LEMON & MINT COUSCOUS

PREP + COOK TIME 15 MINUTES **SERVES** 4

Cook 250g (8oz) pearl couscous in a saucepan of boiling water until tender; drain. Place couscous in a large bowl with ½ cup currants, 1 teaspoon ground cumin, 2 tablespoons finely chopped preserved lemon rind, 1 cup fresh mint leaves and ¼ cup lemon juice; toss gently to combine. Season to taste.

ROASTED CORN & AVOCADO SALAD

PREP + COOK TIME 30 MINUTES **SERVES** 6

Cook 4 trimmed corn cobs on a heated oiled grill plate (or barbecue) until browned all over. When cool enough to handle, cut kernels from cobs. Place kernels in a bowl with 1 thinly sliced small red onion, 2 coarsely chopped large avocados, 250g (8oz) halved cherry tomatoes, 2 tablespoons lime juice and ¼ cup fresh micro coriander (cilantro) leaves; toss gently to combine. Season to taste.

GREEN APPLE
& MINT SLAW

PREP TIME 15 MINUTES **SERVES** 4

Cut 2 large unpeeled green apples into matchsticks.
Place in a large bowl with 1 cup finely shredded green
cabbage, 1 thinly sliced green onions (scallions), ¼ cup
small fresh mint leaves, 2 tablespoons extra virgin olive
oil and 2 tablespoons lemon juice; toss gently to combine.
Season to taste.

WILD RICE SALAD
WITH SPINACH & FIGS

PREP + COOK TIME 15 MINUTES **SERVES** 8

Cook 2 cups wild rice blend in a large saucepan of boiling
water until tender; drain. Rinse under cold water; drain. Place
in a large bowl. Place 2 teaspoons finely grated orange rind,
½ cup orange juice, 2 tablespoons olive oil and 1 tablespoon
white balsamic vinegar in a screw-top jar; shake well. Add
dressing to rice with ¾ cup coarsely chopped roasted pecans,
½ cup thinly sliced dried figs, 100g (3oz) baby spinach leaves
and 2 thinly sliced green onions (scallions); toss gently to
combine. Season to taste.

Modern SIDES

Pear and Blue Cheese Salad with Mustard Dressing

6 small witlof (belgian endive) (750g),
　leaves separated

350g (11 ounces) watercress, trimmed

2 small pears (360g), halved, cored,
　sliced thinly

1 cup (110g) chopped roasted walnuts

100g (3 ounces) creamy blue cheese,
　crumbled

MUSTARD DRESSING

2 tablespoons olive oil

1 tablespoon red wine vinegar

1 teaspoon dijon mustard

1 teaspoon light brown sugar

1　Make mustard dressing.

2　Place witlof, watercress and pear in a large bowl with nuts and dressing; toss to combine.

3　Serve salad sprinkled with blue cheese.

MUSTARD DRESSING Place ingredients in a screw-top jar; shake well. Season to taste.

Roasted Brussels Sprouts and Lentil Salad

1½ cup (300g) dried French-style
   green lentils
3 cups (750ml) water
16 brussels sprouts, trimmed, halved
olive-oil spray

⅓ cup (45g) slivered almonds, toasted
½ cup fresh mint leaves
¼ cup (60ml) balsamic vinaigrette
⅓ cup (25g) shaved parmesan

1 Preheat oven to 200°C/400°F. Line an oven tray with baking paper.
2 Place lentils and the water in a small saucepan; bring to the boil over high heat. Reduce heat to low; simmer, covered, for 45 minutes or until lentils are tender. Drain.
3 Meanwhile, cook sprouts in a medium saucepan of boiling water, uncovered, for 3 minutes; drain. Spread sprouts on oven tray; spray with oil. Roast for 20 minutes or until golden.
4 Place lentils and sprouts in a large bowl with remaining ingredients, season with pepper; toss gently to combine.

Desserts

Passionfruit Jelly with Poached Pineapple

12 passionfruit

¾ cup (180ml) fresh orange juice, strained

¼ cup (60ml) fresh lemon juice, strained

¾ cup (165g) caster (superfine) sugar

1 cup (250ml) water

1 tablespoon powdered gelatine

⅓ cup (80ml) boiling water

½ cup (40g) flaked coconut or shaved
   fresh coconut, toasted (see notes)

POACHED PINEAPPLE

1 small pineapple (900g)

1 cup (220g) caster (superfine) sugar

1 cup (250ml) water

10cm (4-inch) stick fresh lemon grass
   (20g), halved lengthways

4 fresh kaffir lime leaves, crushed

1 Halve passionfruit; scoop pulp into a fine sieve over a 2-cup (500ml) measuring jug.
Press to extract as much juice as possible; discard seeds. Add orange and lemon juices to
passionfruit juice; you should have 2 cups juice.
2 Place juice in a medium saucepan with sugar and the water; stir over high heat, without
boiling, until sugar dissolves. Bring to the boil; remove from heat.
3 Sprinkle gelatine over the boiling water in a small heatproof jug. Stand jug in a small
saucepan of simmering water; stir until gelatine dissolves. Stir gelatine mixture into
juice mixture.
4 Pour jelly mixture into six 1-cup (250ml) glasses. Cover; refrigerate for 4 hours or until set.
5 Meanwhile, make poached pineapple.
6 Serve jellies topped with poached pineapple and coconut.
POACHED PINEAPPLE Peel pineapple; cut in half lengthways. Slice each half into
very thin slices. Place sugar and the water in a medium saucepan; stir over high heat,
without boiling, until sugar dissolves. Add lemon grass and lime leaves; bring to the boil.
Reduce heat; simmer, uncovered, for 5 minutes. Add pineapple; simmer, uncovered, for
3 minutes or until pineapple is tender. Transfer pineapple mixture to a heatproof bowl.
Cover; refrigerate for 2 hours.

Notes

To toast the coconut, stir flaked
coconut in a medium frying
pan over low-medium heat
for 3 minutes or until golden.
Remove from pan immediately
to prevent over-browning.
Fresh coconut can be shaved
using a vegetable peeler.

Baklava Cheesecake

⅓ cup (35g) walnuts

⅔ cup (90g) roasted unsalted
shelled pistachios

2 teaspoons mixed spice

250g (8 ounces) butternut snap cookies

½ cup (70g) slivered almonds

125g (4 ounces) unsalted butter, melted

CHEESECAKE FILLING

3 teaspoons powdered gelatine

¼ cup (60ml) water

500g (1 pound) cream cheese, softened

½ cup (110g) caster (superfine) sugar

¼ cup (90g) honey

1½ cups (375ml) thickened (heavy) cream

1 Preheat oven to 220°C/425°F. Grease a 26cm (10½-inch) springform tin.

2 Roast walnuts and pistachios on an oven tray for 5 minutes. Sprinkle nuts with mixed spice; roast for a further 1 minute. Cool. Process spiced nuts with cookies until chopped finely; transfer to a medium bowl, stir in almonds.

3 Reserve one-third of the nut mixture in a small bowl. Stir butter into remaining nut mixture. Press mixture evenly over base of tin; refrigerate for 30 minutes.

4 Meanwhile, make cheesecake filling.

5 Pour cheesecake filling into tin; top with reserved nut mixture. Cover; refrigerate overnight.

CHEESECAKE FILLING Sprinkle gelatine over the water in a small heatproof jug; stand jug in a small saucepan of simmering water. Stir until gelatine dissolves; cool for 5 minutes. Beat cream cheese, sugar and honey in a medium bowl with an electric mixer until smooth; beat in cream, then stir in gelatine mixture.

DO-AHEAD Cheesecake can be made a day ahead; keep, covered, in the fridge.

Black Forest Trifle

200g (6½ ounces) dark (semi-sweet) chocolate, chopped coarsely

200g (6½ ounces) unsalted butter, chopped

4 eggs

⅔ cup (150g) caster (superfine) sugar

1 cup (150g) self-raising flour

fresh cherries with stems attached and chocolate shards, to decorate

POACHED CHERRIES

¾ cup (165g) caster (superfine) sugar

⅔ cup (160ml) water

1⅓ cups (330ml) dry red wine

1 cinnamon stick

500g (1 pound) cherries, pitted

¼ cup (60ml) orange-flavoured liqueur

MASCARPONE CREAM

4 eggs, separated

½ cup (110g) caster (superfine) sugar

500g (1-pound) mascarpone

1 teaspoon finely grated orange rind

1 Preheat oven to 180°C/350°F. Grease a 19cm x 29cm (7¾-inch x 11¾-inch) slice pan; line base with baking paper, extending the paper 5cm (2 inches) over long sides.

2 Place chocolate and butter in a medium heatproof bowl over a medium saucepan of simmering water (don't let water touch base of bowl); stir until melted. Remove from heat; cool.

3 Beat eggs, sugar and a pinch of salt in a small bowl with an electric mixer for 7 minutes or until thick and pale. Sift flour over mixture; fold in gently with a large metal spoon. Add melted chocolate; carefully fold through.

4 Spread mixture into pan; bake for 25 minutes or until firm to the touch and a skewer inserted into the centre comes out clean. Stand in pan for 10 minutes, before turning onto a wire rack to cool.

5 Meanwhile, make the poached cherries and the mascarpone cream.

6 To assemble the trifle, break sponge into small pieces. Place half the sponge into base of a large trifle bowl. Spoon over half the poached cherries and poaching liquid, then top with half the mascarpone cream. Repeat with a second layer of ingredients; cover. Refrigerate until required. Just before serving, decorate with cherries and chocolate shards.

POACHED CHERRIES Stir sugar and the water in a medium saucepan over high heat, without boiling, until sugar dissolves. Bring to the boil; boil uncovered, without stirring, for 10 minutes or until caramel in colour. Meanwhile, combine wine and cinnamon stick in a medium saucepan over medium heat. Remove caramel from the heat and carefully pour in warm wine mixture. Return to heat; stir until mixture is smooth. Bring to the boil; boil, uncovered, for 5 minutes or until mixture is reduced to about 1 cup (250ml); discard cinnamon. Add cherries and liqueur; stir until heated through. Transfer to a heatproof container; refrigerate until required.

MASCARPONE CREAM Beat egg whites and half the sugar in a medium bowl with an electric mixer until soft peaks form. Combine egg yolks, remaining sugar, mascarpone and rind in a medium bowl; whisk to combine. Lightly fold the egg whites into the mascarpone mixture.

DO-AHEAD The poached cherries and sponge cake an be made the day before.

Notes

If it is not too humid, meringue rounds can be made 3 days ahead; store in airtight containers in a cool, dark place. Assemble the cake close to serving. Use unsprayed roses that are pesticide and herbicide free.

Berry and Rose Meringue Cake

You will need to make the meringue rounds in three batches.

cornflour (cornstarch), for dusting

6 egg whites

1½ cups (330g) caster (superfine) sugar

3 teaspoons cornflour (cornstarch), extra

1½ teaspoons rosewater

600ml thickened (heavy) cream

¼ cup (40g) icing (confectioners') sugar

2 teaspoons rosewater, extra

500g (1 pound) strawberries, sliced thinly

125g (4 ounces) raspberries

SUGARED ROSE PETALS

1 unsprayed rose, petals separated (see notes)

1 egg white, beaten lightly

1½ cups (330g) white (granulated) sugar

1 Preheat oven to 120°C/250°F. Line two oven trays with baking paper. Draw a 20cm (8-inch) circle on each piece of paper; turn paper, marked-side down, on trays. Lightly grease paper; dust with a little cornflour, shaking away excess.

2 Place two of the egg whites and ½ cup of the caster sugar in a small bowl of an electric mixer; beat on high for 6 minutes or until thick and glossy. Fold in 1 teaspoon of the extra cornflour and ½ teaspoon of the rosewater.

3 Divide meringue mixture between the two trays, spreading just inside the marked circle. Bake for 1 hour or until firm, dry to the touch and crisp. Cool in oven with door ajar.

4 Repeat Steps 2 and 3 two more times with the remaining egg whites, caster sugar, cornflour and rosewater, to make six meringue rounds.

5 Meanwhile, make sugared rose petals.

6 Beat cream, sifted icing sugar and extra rosewater in a medium bowl with an electric mixer until firm peaks form.

7 Peel away lining paper from meringues. Place one meringue round on a serving plate. Spread with a layer of cream and sliced strawberries. Repeat with remaining meringue rounds, cream and strawberries, finishing with meringue. Serve topped with raspberries and sugared rose petals.

SUGARED ROSE PETALS Using an artist's paintbrush, paint petals, one at a time, with egg white, then sprinkle with sugar. Place sugared rose petals on a wire rack to dry.

Christmas is a time for snowflakes and sparkles. Create a winter wonderland with ribbon and baubles.

Pistachio Meringue with White Peaches and Berries

You will need to make this recipe at least a day ahead.

2 cups (500ml) thickened (heavy) cream

4 medium white peaches (600g),
  cut into thin wedges

125g (4 ounces) fresh blueberries

125g (4 ounces) fresh blackberries

2 tablespoons coarsely chopped roasted
  unsalted shelled pistachios

PISTACHIO MERINGUE

1 cup (140g) coarsely chopped roasted
  unsalted shelled pistachios

6 egg whites

1½ cups (330g) caster (superfine) sugar

2 teaspoons cornflour (cornstarch)

2 teaspoons vanilla extract

2 teaspoons white vinegar

1 Make pistachio meringue.

2 Beat cream in a small bowl with electric mixer until firm peaks form. Place a meringue round on serving plate; spread with half the cream, top with half the peaches and berries. Repeat layering with remaining meringue, cream, peaches and berries. Sprinkle with nuts.

PISTACHIO MERINGUE Preheat oven to 120°C/250°F. Line two oven trays with baking paper. Mark a 22cm (9-inch) circle on each piece of paper; turn paper, marked-side down, on trays. Process half the nuts until finely chopped. Beat egg whites in a medium bowl with an electric mixer until soft peaks form. Add sugar, a tablespoon at a time, beating until sugar dissolves between additions; beat until mixture is thick and glossy. Beat in cornflour, extract and vinegar; fold in ground nuts. Divide meringue mixture between trays, spreading just inside the circle. Sprinkle with remaining nuts. Bake for 1¼ hours. Cool meringues in oven with door ajar.

DO-AHEAD Make and assemble this recipe at least a day ahead; this makes slicing it so much easier.

Notes

Macaroons are available at bakeries or specialty food shops; if you can't find blood orange macaroons choose a plain orange or lemon flavour instead. You will need about 9 oranges for this recipe. Grate the rind from the oranges for the custard before juicing them for the jelly.

Champagne and Orange French Macaroon Trifle

7 vanilla french macaroons (112g)

7 blood orange french macaroons (112g)

2 tablespoons natural sliced almonds, toasted

CHAMPAGNE & ORANGE JELLY

6 teaspoons powdered gelatine

2 cups (500ml) fresh orange juice, strained

1 cup (250ml) champagne or sparkling wine

½ cup (110g) caster (superfine) sugar

2 medium oranges (480g)

CANDIED ORANGE RIND

2 medium oranges (480g)

1 cup (250ml) water

½ cup (110g) caster (superfine) sugar

ORANGE-SCENTED CUSTARD

1½ cups (375ml) thick custard

1½ cups (375g) mascarpone cheese

2 tablespoons finely grated orange rind

1 tablespoon orange-flavoured liqueur

VANILLA CREAM

1 vanilla bean, split lengthways

2 cups (500ml) thickened (heavy) cream

¼ cup (40g) icing (confectioners') sugar

1 Make champagne and orange jelly. Pour into a 3-litre (12-cup) deep glass dish. Cover; refrigerate for 3 hours or until set.

2 Make candied orange rind, orange-scented custard and vanilla cream.

3 Just before serving, top jelly with macaroons, custard and cream. Top with nuts, candied rind and any syrup from the rind.

CHAMPAGNE & ORANGE JELLY Stir gelatine into ½ cup of the juice in a small bowl until combined. Stand for 5 minutes. Place remaining juice, champagne and sugar in a medium saucepan over medium heat; stir until sugar is dissolved. Bring to the boil; boil for 1 minute. Remove from heat; stir in gelatine mixture until gelatine is dissolved. Segment oranges; add segments to juice mixture.

CANDIED ORANGE RIND Remove rind from oranges with a zester. Place the water in a small saucepan; bring to the boil. Add rind; simmer for 1 minute. Drain rind; reserve ½ cup of the liquid. Place reserved liquid and sugar in same pan over medium heat; stir until sugar is dissolved. Bring to the boil; simmer, uncovered, for 1 minute. Add rind; simmer, uncovered, for 5 minutes or until candied. Drain. Spread out on baking paper to cool.

ORANGE-SCENTED CUSTARD Whisk ingredients together in a large bowl.

VANILLA CREAM Scrape seeds from vanilla bean. Beat cream, seeds and sugar in a medium bowl with an electric mixer until soft peaks form.

DO-AHEAD You can make the jelly, candied rind, and orange custard a day ahead. Refrigerate jelly and custard separately until ready to assemble. Store rind in an airtight container at room temperature.

Strawberry and Apple Jelly

500g (1 pound) strawberries,
  chopped coarsely

1⅔ cups (410ml) water

½ cup (125ml) apple concentrate
  (see notes)

6 gold-strength gelatine leaves

fresh mixed berries (strawberries,
  blueberries, raspberries), to serve

1 Place strawberries, the water and apple concentrate into a medium saucepan; bring to the boil. Reduce heat; simmer, uncovered, for 3 minutes, then remove from heat. When cool, blend until smooth; pour liquid through a fine sieve into a large measuring jug. You will need 600ml (2⅓ cups) of the strawberry mixture for the jelly. Top up with water if there isn't enough of the strawberry mixture. Return to same pan and warm over low heat.

2 Soak gelatine leaves in cold water for a few minutes or until soft. Squeeze to remove any excess water.

3 Add softened gelatine to warm strawberry mixture; stir to combine. Pour into a bowl, cover; refrigerate for several hours or until firm.

4 Layer generous spoonfuls of jelly and mixed berries into six chilled glasses.

Notes

Apple concentrate is a thick syrup, made by reducing apple juice to a sweet syrup. It gives a lovely aromatic flavour to the strawberry jelly and can also be lightly drizzled over a fruit salad or used to sweeten smoothies. Apple concentrate is available from most health food stores.

Honey Panna Cotta with Apricots in Thyme Syrup

3 teaspoons powdered gelatine

¼ cup (60ml) water

2⅓ cups (580ml) buttermilk

½ cup (125ml) pouring cream

½ cup (175g) honey

APRICOTS IN THYME SYRUP

2 cups (500ml) water

½ cup (175g) honey

2 teaspoons fresh thyme leaves

12 small apricots (600g), halved, stones removed

1 tablespoon lemon juice

1 Sprinkle gelatine over the water in a small heatproof jug; stand jug in a small saucepan of simmering water, stir until gelatine dissolves.

2 Meanwhile, bring buttermilk and cream to the boil in a medium saucepan; remove from heat. Whisk in honey and gelatine mixture; strain into a large jug. Cool.

3 Divide buttermilk mixture among eight ⅔-cup (160ml) glasses. Refrigerate for 6 hours or overnight until set.

4 Make apricots in thyme syrup.

5 Serve panna cotta topped with apricots and syrup.

APRICOTS IN THYME SYRUP Bring the water, honey and thyme to the boil in a medium saucepan. Add apricots; simmer gently, uncovered, for 5 minutes or until almost tender. Remove from heat; add juice, cool. Refrigerate until cold.

Tropical Splice with Mojito Fruit Salad

1 litre (4 cups) mango sorbet (see notes)

1 litre (4 cups) good-quality vanilla bean ice-cream

1 lime, grated finely

½ cup (110g) caster (superfine) sugar

¾ cup (180ml) water

1 lime, cut into wedges, wedges halved

¼ cup (60ml) strained lime juice

½ cup (125ml) white rum

1 medium pineapple (1.4kg), peeled, quartered, cored, sliced thinly

1 medium mango (430g), sliced thinly

1 medium kiwifruit (85g), peeled, cut into wedges

⅓ cup (80ml) passionfruit pulp

½ cup baby or micro mint sprigs

1 Grease and line base and long sides of an 11cm x 25cm (4½-inch x 10-inch), 1.5-litre (6-cup) capacity, loaf pan with baking paper, extending the paper 5cm (2 inches) above edge. Grease paper; repeat, lining base and short sides.

2 Spoon sorbet into pan; smooth surface. Cover; freeze for 1 hour or until firm.

3 Scoop ice-cream over sorbet layer, scattering with lime rind as you go; smooth surface with the back of a spoon. Cover; freeze 2 hours or overnight or until firm.

4 Reserve 1 tablespoon of the sugar. Stir remaining sugar and the water in a medium saucepan over medium heat, without boiling, until sugar dissolves. Bring to the boil; boil, uncovered, for 1 minute.

5 Place lime wedges and remaining sugar in a large heatproof bowl, using the end of a rolling pin, crush lime wedges. Pour over warm sugar syrup, lime juice, rum. Add pineapple, mango, kiwi and passionfruit; toss gently to combine. Refrigerate until required.

6 Rub the outside of the loaf pan with a warm, damp cloth. Turn out onto a serving platter; remove lining paper. Serve topped with fruit salad and mint.

Notes

You can use any other sorbet
flavour instead of the mango,
if you prefer, such as lime,
raspberry or passionfruit. You
will need about 4 passionfruit
for this recipe. You can also
serve the splice topped with
toasted coconut flakes and
extra lime rind, if you like.

Notes

We used Grand Marnier in this recipe but you could use any citrus-flavoured liqueur you like. You can make it with all kinds of seasonal fruit such as a mixture of mixed berries, sliced peaches, plums, nectarines or mango. Store the reserved panettone in plastic wrap and toast for breakfast.

Panettone with Mascarpone and Raspberries

1 panettone (about 1.1kg)

¼ cup (60ml) orange-flavoured liqueur

750g (1½ pounds) fresh raspberries

2 teaspoons icing (confectioners') sugar

MASCARPONE FILLING

750g (1½ pounds) mascarpone cheese

¼ cup (40g) icing (confectioners') sugar

3 egg whites

1 Make mascarpone filling.

2 Using a serrated knife, cut domed top off the panettone; reserve for another use. Split remaining panettone into three layers.

3 Place base of panettone onto a serving plate. Sprinkle with 1 tablespoon of liqueur; spread with one-third of filling and scatter with one-third of the raspberries. Top with another layer of panettone. Repeat to make another two layers; finishing with mascarpone filling. Refrigerate, loosely covered.

4 Remove panettone from fridge 30 minutes before serving. Top with remaining raspberries; dust with sifted icing sugar.

MASCARPONE FILLING Combine mascarpone and sifted icing sugar in a large bowl. Beat egg whites in a small bowl with an electric mixer until soft peaks form. Fold egg whites into mascarpone mixture, in two batches.

DO-AHEAD This dessert is best made the day before or up to 5 hours before serving to allow the flavours to develop.

Chocolate, Honey and Red Berry Parfait

You will need to start this recipe at least a day ahead.

½ cup (80g) almond kernels

1 vanilla bean

400g (12½ ounces) ricotta

⅔ cup (230g) honey

2 cups (560g) Greek-style yoghurt

100g (3 ounces) dark chocolate (70% cocoa), chopped

100g (3 ounces) raspberries

100g (3 ounces) cherries, pitted, halved

2 tablespoons honey, extra

raspberries and pitted cherries, extra, to serve

1 Preheat oven to 180°C/350°F. Line the base of a 10.5cm x 23.5cm (4-inch x 9½-inch) terrine or loaf pan with baking paper, extending the paper 2cm (¾ inch) over two long sides.

2 Spread nuts in a single layer on an oven tray. Roast for 10 minutes or until skins begin to split. Remove from tray; cool. Chop coarsely.

3 Meanwhile, split vanilla bean lengthways; scrape seeds into a food processor. Add ricotta and honey; process until smooth. Transfer mixture to a large bowl.

4 Fold in chopped nuts, yoghurt, chocolate, raspberries and cherries. Spoon mixture into pan; smooth surface. Cover with foil. Freeze for 8 hours or overnight until firm.

5 Wipe base and sides of pan with a warm cloth. Turn parfait onto a chopping board; stand for 10 minutes before cutting into slices with a large straight-bladed knife. Divide slices among shallow serving dishes; drizzle with extra honey and top with extra berries.

Tiramisu Torte

3 eggs

½ cup (110g) caster (superfine) sugar

¼ cup (35g) plain (all-purpose) flour

¼ cup (35g) self-raising flour

¼ cup (35g) cornflour (cornstarch)

2 tablespoons instant coffee granules

¾ cup (180ml) boiling water

⅓ cup (80ml) marsala

2 tablespoons coffee-flavoured liqueur

500g (1 pound) mascarpone cheese

⅓ cup (55g) icing (confectioners') sugar

300ml thickened (heavy) cream

2 tablespoons coarsely chopped
    vienna almonds (see notes)

1 Preheat oven to 180°C/350°F. Grease a deep 22cm (9-inch) square cake pan with butter.
2 Beat eggs in a small bowl with an electric mixer for 10 minutes or until thick and creamy; gradually add caster sugar, 1 tablespoon at a time, beating until sugar dissolves after each addition. Transfer to a large bowl.
3 Sift flours twice. Sift flours a third time over egg mixture; fold ingredients together. Spread mixture into pan.
4 Bake sponge for 25 minutes. Turn sponge immediately onto a baking-paper-covered wire rack; turn top-side up to cool.
5 Meanwhile, dissolve coffee in the water in a small heatproof jug. Stir in marsala and coffee-flavoured liqueur; cool.
6 Beat mascarpone and icing sugar in a small bowl with electric mixer until smooth. Beat in cream and ⅓ cup of the coffee mixture.
7 Cut the sponge in half down the centre, then split each sponge half into two layers. Place one of the cake rectangles on a serving plate, cut-side up; brush with a quarter of the remaining coffee mixture then spread with ⅔ cup of mascarpone mixture. Repeat layering with cake (see notes), coffee mixture and mascarpone, finishing with the cake, cut-side down, and remaining mascarpone mixture spread on top and sides of cake. Refrigerate cake for 2 hours.
8 Just before serving, decorate cake with vienna almonds.

Raspberry and Nougat Ice-Cream Pudding

½ cup (110g) caster (superfine) sugar

1 cup (250ml) water

300g (9½ ounces) frozen raspberries

1 litre (4 cups) good-quality
vanilla ice-cream

100g (3 ounces) white chocolate,
chopped finely

150g (4½ ounces) firm almond nougat,
chopped finely

100g (3 ounces) frozen raspberries, extra

¼ teaspoon copha, melted

100g (3 ounces) white chocolate,
extra, melted

125g (4 ounces) fresh raspberries

1 Lightly oil a 2-litre (8-cup) pudding basin; line with two layers of plastic wrap.

2 Place sugar and the water in a small saucepan; stir over medium heat until sugar dissolves. Bring to the boil. Boil, uncovered, for 3 minutes. Remove pan from heat. Cool.

3 Process frozen raspberries with the cooled syrup until mixture forms a smooth sorbet. Spoon sorbet into pudding basin; smooth surface with the back of a spoon to level. Freeze for at least 2 hours or until sorbet is firm.

4 Spoon ice-cream into a large bowl and allow to soften slightly. Add chocolate and nougat, then crumble extra frozen raspberries over the top; stir until just combined. Spoon ice-cream mixture over firm sorbet layer in pudding basin, pressing down to ensure the ice-cream fills all the spaces. Cover with plastic wrap; freeze for 6 hours or overnight.

5 To serve, turn ice-cream out onto a chilled serving plate (wipe base and side of the basin with a warm cloth before removing, if needed); remove plastic wrap.

6 Combine copha and extra melted chocolate in a small jug; pour over the pudding. Serve pudding topped with fresh raspberries.

Tropical Fruit Salad with Lemon Grass and Ginger Granita

12 fresh lychees (300g)

½ small pineapple (350g)

½ small papaya (325g)

1 medium mango (430g)

2 gold kiwifruit (170g)

¼ honeydew melon (375g)

1 tablespoon lime juice

LEMON GRASS & GINGER GRANITA

1¼ cups (275g) caster (superfine) sugar

3 x 10cm (4-inch) sticks fresh lemon grass (20g), chopped coarsely

10cm (4-inch) piece fresh ginger (50g), peeled, sliced thinly

3 cups (750ml) water

2 tablespoons lime juice

1 Make lemon grass and ginger granita.

2 Peel lychees. Peel remaining fruit; cut into wedges. Place fruit and juice in a large bowl; toss gently to combine.

3 Divide fruit salad between serving bowls; top with granita.

LEMON GRASS & GINGER GRANITA Place sugar, lemon grass, ginger and the water in a medium saucepan over medium heat; stir until sugar is dissolved. Bring to the boil. Reduce heat; simmer, uncovered, for 1 minute. Stand for 30 minutes. Strain syrup into a large heatproof jug; stir in juice. Pour syrup mixture into a shallow 1-litre (4-cup) dish. Freeze for 1 hour. Use a fork to break up any ice crystals. Freeze for a further 4 hours, scraping with a fork every hour, or until frozen.

TIP You will need about 2 limes for this recipe.

DO-AHEAD The granita can be made a day ahead; cover and keep frozen.

Raspberry Trifle Torte

3 eggs

½ cup (110g) caster (superfine) sugar

½ cup (75g) cornflour (cornstarch)

2 tablespoons custard powder

1 teaspoon cream of tartar

½ teaspoon bicarbonate of (baking) soda

85g (3 ounces) raspberry jelly crystals

1 cup (250ml) boiling water

1 cup (250ml) cold water

⅓ cup (80ml) sweet sherry

600ml thickened (heavy) cream

250g (8 ounces) fresh raspberries

CUSTARD FILLING

¼ cup (35g) cornflour (cornstarch)

¼ cup (30g) custard powder

¼ cup (55g) caster (superfine) sugar

300ml pouring cream

¾ cup (180ml) milk

2 tablespoons sweet sherry

15g (½ ounce) butter

1 egg yolk

1 Preheat oven to 180°C/350°F. Grease a deep 22cm (9-inch) round cake pan; sprinkle with flour, shake out excess.

2 Beat eggs and sugar in a small bowl with an electric mixer for 5 minutes or until sugar dissolves. Transfer mixture to a large bowl. Fold triple-sifted cornflour, custard powder, cream of tartar and soda into egg mixture. Pour mixture into pan; bake for 25 minutes. Turn sponge immediately onto a baking-paper-covered wire rack to cool.

3 Meanwhile, stir jelly and the boiling water in a heatproof jug until dissolved. Stir in the cold water.

Rinse two deep 20cm (8-inch) round cake pans with cold water (do not wipe dry); divide jelly evenly between pans. Refrigerate until jelly is almost set.

4 Split cold sponge into three layers; sprinkle each cut side with sherry. Place bottom and middle sponge layer, cut-side down, on top of jelly in pans, pressing down firmly. Refrigerate 1 hour or until set. Cover remaining sponge layer with plastic wrap.

5 Make custard filling.

6 Beat cream in a small bowl with electric mixer until soft peaks form; fold ½ cup cream through custard filling. Refrigerate the remaining cream.

7 Line a dinner plate with a 45cm (18-inch) piece of plastic wrap; top with a second piece of plastic wrap in the other direction (you will have a cross). Working quickly, dip the cake pan with the bottom sponge layer in sink of hot water for 1 second or until jelly loosens from side of pan. Place plate on top of pan, quickly invert sponge and jelly onto plate. Clean and dry cake pan; carefully lift the plastic and cake back into pan. Top with half the custard filling.

8 Dip remaining cake pan in hot water for 1 second; holding plastic wrap out of the way, invert cake and jelly on top of the custard in other cake pan. Spread jelly with remaining custard filling. Place remaining sponge, cut-side down, on top of custard layer. Cover with plastic wrap; refrigerate for 3 hours or overnight.

9 Remove plastic wrap; place cake stand or serving plate on top of cake pan. Carefully invert torte onto a plate; remove plastic wrap. Spread remaining cream over top and side; serve topped with berries.

CUSTARD FILLING Combine cornflour, custard powder and sugar in a medium saucepan. Gradually stir in cream and milk; stir over medium heat until mixture boils and thickens. Remove from heat; stir in sherry, butter and egg yolk. Place custard in a medium bowl; cover surface with plastic wrap, cool.

Frozen White Chocolate Mousse with Espresso Jelly

250g (8 ounces) white chocolate, chopped

1 cup (250ml) thickened (heavy) cream

2 eggs, separated

2 teaspoons vanilla extract

2 tablespoons caster (superfine) sugar

ESPRESSO JELLY

2 tablespoons caster (superfine) sugar

2 tablespoons coffee-flavoured liqueur

1 cup (250ml) water

3 teaspoons instant espresso coffee

⅓ cup (80ml) boiling water

2½ teaspoons powdered gelatine

ALMOND PRALINE

½ cup (80g) blanched almonds

1 cup (220g) caster (superfine) sugar

½ cup (125ml) water

1 Cut eight 30cm (12-inch) squares of baking paper; fold in half diagonally to form triangles. Hold the apex of the triangle towards you, then roll the paper into a cone shape, bringing the three points of the triangle together. Staple the three points together. Place cones in tall glasses or jugs.

2 Stir chocolate and ¼ cup of the cream in a small saucepan over low heat until smooth. Transfer to a large bowl; cool for 5 minutes. Stir in egg yolks.

3 Beat remaining cream and extract in a small bowl with an electric mixer until soft peaks form. Fold cream into chocolate mixture.

4 Beat egg whites and sugar in a clean small bowl with electric mixer for 1 minute or until sugar is dissolved and soft peaks form. Fold egg whites into chocolate mixture, in two batches. Spoon mixture into paper cones. Freeze for 6 hours or overnight until firm.

5 Meanwhile, make espresso jelly and almond praline.

6 Turn jelly onto board; cut into 1cm (½-inch) cubes. Turn mousse cones onto serving plates, trimming bases to sit flat; discard paper cones. Spoon reserved coffee syrup onto plates, sprinkle with jelly and praline.

ESPRESSO JELLY Stir sugar, liqueur and the water in a small saucepan over high heat, without boiling, until sugar is dissolved. Stir in combined coffee and boiling water (or make ⅓ cup espresso coffee). Reserve ½ cup of the coffee syrup. Sprinkle gelatine over remaining coffee syrup in pan; stir over low heat until gelatine is dissolved. Cool for 15 minutes. Rinse a 15cm (6-inch) square cake pan with cold water; do not dry pan. Pour jelly into pan. Cover; refrigerate for 2 hours or until jelly is set.

ALMOND PRALINE Preheat oven to 180°C/350°F. Place nuts, in a single layer, on oven tray; roast for 5 minutes or until browned lightly. Chop nuts coarsely; return to tray lined with baking paper. Place sugar and the water in a small saucepan; stir over high heat, without boiling, until sugar dissolves. Bring to the boil; boil, uncovered, without stirring, for 10 minutes or until caramel in colour. Allow bubbles to subside; pour over nuts on tray. Cool. Break praline into pieces.

Christmas Eton Mess Wreath

250g (8 ounces) raspberries

1 tablespoon icing (confectioners') sugar, plus extra to dust

300g (9½ ounces) white chocolate Melts

200g (6½ ounces) coconut macaroons, quartered

6 raspberry french macaroons

6 strawberry french macaroons

250g (8 ounces) small strawberries

200g (6½ ounces) cherries

1 pomegranate (450g), halved, broken into small pieces

25g (¾ ounce) mini plain meringues

edible flowers, to decorate (optional)

¾ cup (180ml) thickened (heavy) cream, whipped, to serve

1 Place 75g (2½ ounces) of the raspberries in an airtight container; freeze for 2 hours.

2 Process frozen raspberries until finely chopped; return to the container, freeze until required. In the same food processor bowl, process 125g (4 ounces) of the remaining raspberries with icing sugar until pureed. Push puree through a fine sieve over a small bowl. Cover; refrigerate until required.

3 Place two sheets of baking paper, slightly overlapping on a work surface to create a wider sheet. Using a 40cm (16-inch) bowl, trace a circle; place a 30cm (12-inch) bowl in the centre, trace a second circle inside the first circle. You will now have a template for the chocolate ring.

4 Place chocolate in a medium heatproof bowl over a medium saucepan of gently simmering water (don't allow the bowl to touch water); stir until melted. Drop spoonfuls of chocolate inside the marked ring, then using the back of a spoon, spread chocolate thickly and evenly to fill ring. Stand until set.

5 Carefully transfer chocolate ring to a large serving board. Place coconut macaroons and french macaroons equally around the ring, layering with strawberries, cherries, pomegranate and remaining fresh raspberries. Crush mini meringues over the wreath, sprinkle with crumbled frozen raspberries and fresh flowers. Dust with icing sugar and drizzle with a little raspberry sauce.

6 Serve wreath with remaining raspberry sauce and whipped cream in separate small bowls, for guests to help themselves.

Peach and Nectarine Tart

60g (2 ounces) butter, softened

⅓ cup (75g) caster (superfine) sugar

1 egg

½ teaspoon orange blossom water

¾ cup (75g) almond meal

2 tablespoons plain (all-purpose) flour

2 x 375g (12-ounce) packets puff pastry

4 large peaches (880g)

1 nectarine (170g)

150g (4½ ounces) raspberries

¼ cup (35g) coarsely chopped roasted unsalted shelled pistachios

¼ cup (90g) honey

1 Beat butter and sugar in a small bowl with an electric mixer until creamy. Beat in egg and orange blossom water until combined. Stir in almond meal and flour.

2 Preheat oven to 220°C/425°F.

3 Roll out each packet of pastry on a floured sheet of baking paper into a 16cm x 34cm (6½-inch x 13½-inch) rectangle. Lift each pastry rectangle with paper onto an oven tray. Spread almond mixture thinly over pastry, leaving a 1cm (½-inch) border.

4 Cut peaches and nectarine in half; remove stones. Cut halves into thin wedges. Arrange fruit wedges, overlapping slightly, on almond mixture.

5 Bake for 30 minutes or until browned and pastry is cooked underneath. Serve tarts topped with raspberries and pistachios; drizzle with honey.

SERVING SUGGESTION Serve warm or cool with thick (double) cream or ice-cream.

Middle Eastern-style Fruit Salad

4 medium navel oranges (960g)

10 cardamom pods

1 cup (220g) caster (superfine) sugar

2 cups (500ml) water

1 vanilla bean, split lengthways,
   seeds scraped

2 medium carrots (240g),
   cut into matchsticks

1 pomegranate (450g)

4 medium blood oranges (960g)

6 medium peaches (900g), halved,
   stones removed, cut into wedges

⅔ cup (160ml) orange juice

½ cup (125ml) lemon juice

1 Using a vegetable peeler, peel rind from one navel orange. Place rind in a small saucepan with cardamom, sugar, the water and vanilla seeds and pod; stir over low heat until sugar dissolves. Add carrot and increase heat to medium; cook for 20 minutes or until syrup is thick and carrot is translucent. Using a fork, transfer candied carrot to a small bowl. Transfer unstrained syrup to a large bowl.

2 Remove seeds from pomegranate; reserve seeds. Using a small sharp knife, remove rind and pith from remaining navels and the blood oranges, following the curve of the fruit. Cut oranges into 5mm (¼-inch) thick rounds; add to the syrup with pomegranate seeds and peaches. Add juices to bowl; stir to combine.

3 Stir half the candied carrot into the fruit salad. Divide fruit salad among serving bowls, topped with remaining candied carrot.

Cakes
and
Puddings

Iced Christmas Cupcakes

You need alphabet and snowflake cutters, edible gold paint, available from cake decorator supply shops, and a new small artist's paintbrush. Use silver or gold paper cases for the cakes.

500g (1 pound) dried mixed fruit

125g (4 ounces) butter, chopped coarsely

½ cup (125ml) water

1 cup (200g) firmly packed dark
  brown sugar

¼ teaspoon bicarbonate of (baking) soda

2 tablespoons brandy

2 eggs, beaten lightly

½ cup (75g) plain (all-purpose) flour

½ cup (75g) self-raising flour

½ cup (75g) cornflour (cornstarch)

750g (1½ pounds) ready-rolled
  white icing

1 egg white, beaten lightly

1 Combine fruit, butter, the water, sugar and soda in a large saucepan; stir over medium heat until butter melts and sugar dissolves. Bring to the boil; remove from heat, stir in brandy. Transfer to a large heatproof bowl; cool to room temperature.

2 Preheat oven to 150°C/300°F. Line a 12-hole ¾-cup (180ml) texas muffin pan with paper cases.

3 Stir eggs into fruit mixture, then the sifted flours; divide mixture evenly among pan holes. Bake for 40 minutes or until a skewer inserted into the centre of the cake comes out clean. Cover hot cakes with a clean tea towel while still in the pan; cool cakes in pan.

4 To decorate: On a surface dusted with a little cornflour, knead icing until smooth. Roll out into a 5mm (¼-inch) thickness. Using a 5.5cm (2¼-inch) fluted cutter, cut out 12 rounds. Lightly brush tops of cakes with egg white; cover with icing rounds.

5 Using alphabet and snowflake cutters, cut out the letters to spell 'noel'. Use snowflake cutters to cut out snowflake shapes. Brush snowflakes with egg white, then secure on top of icing on some of the cakes.

6 Paint letters with edible gold paint. When completely dry, brush the bases with egg white; secure to cakes.

DO-AHEAD Cakes can be made up to 5 days ahead. Store in an airtight container at room temperature. If the weather is humid, decorate them the day before serving.

Notes

It is easier to chop the dried fruit by snipping with kitchen scissors. If the fruit sticks to the scissors, spray scissors lightly with cooking oil. Use a gluten-free ginger beer when using this mixture for the gluten-free Christmas cakes, checking that all ingredients are gluten free.

Two-in-One Basic Ginger Beer Fruit Mix

This basic fruit mix is enough to make a regular-sized fruit cake (see page 404) and a pudding (boiled or steamed) large enough to serve 12 (see page 403).

6 cups (1kg) sultanas

2 cups (300g) dried currants

2½ cups (375g) raisins, chopped coarsely

4⅓ cups (600g) pitted dried dates, chopped coarsely

½ cup (100g) red glacé cherries, quartered

1 cup (250g) glacé fruit (such as orange, pineapple, apricot, peach), chopped coarsely

¾ cup (250g) fig jam

1 tablespoon finely grated lemon rind

1 tablespoon finely grated orange rind

1½ tablespoons ground cinnamon

1½ tablespoons ground ginger

2 cups (500ml) ginger beer (see notes)

1 cup (250ml) dark rum

1 Combine dried fruit, jam, rinds and spices in a large bowl. Add ginger beer and rum; stir to combine.

2 Cover; stand at room temperature for 3 to 7 days, or longer if you like, stirring occasionally.

Gluten-free Christmas Cakes

Make sure you use a gluten-free ginger beer in the two-in-one basic ginger beer fruit mix, checking all the ingredients are gluten free.

250g (8 ounces) butter, softened

1 cup (220g) firmly packed dark
    brown sugar

4 eggs, at room temperature

1 cup (110g) almond meal

¾ cup (110g) gluten-free plain
    (all-purpose) flour

½ cup (75g) gluten-free self-raising flour

½ quantity of two-in-one basic ginger
    beer fruit mix (recipe page 399)

macadamias, pecans, walnuts, blanched
    almonds, to decorate

¼ cup (60ml) dark rum

ribbon or hessian strips, to decorate
    (optional)

1 Preheat oven to 160°C/325°F. Line base and sides of six deep 10cm (4-inch) round cake pans with three layers of baking paper, extending the paper 5cm (2 inches) over edge of pans.
2 Beat butter and sugar in a medium bowl with an electric mixer until smooth. Beat in eggs, one at a time. Transfer mixture to a large bowl; stir in almond meal and combined sifted flours, then fruit mix. Spoon cake mix into pans; smooth surface. Arrange nuts on the tops.
3 Bake cakes for 1½ hours or until cooked when tested. Brush tops of hot cakes with rum. Cover hot cakes tightly with foil; wrap in clean tea towels. Cool in pans overnight.
4 When cakes are cooled, turn out of pans. Decorate cakes with ribbon.

STORAGE These cakes will keep in an airtight container in the fridge for up to 3 months. Cakes are suitable to freeze.

Notes

You could also bake this cake mixture in a deep 22cm (9-inch) round or 20cm (8-inch) square cake pan at 150°C/300°F for 2½ to 3 hours.

Notes

If storing the pudding, cool completely. Wrap in plastic wrap and seal tightly in a freezer bag or airtight container. Pudding can be stored in the fridge for up to 2 months or frozen for up to 12 months.

Ginger Beer Steamed Christmas Pudding

See page 199 for helpful step-by-step images and information on how to prepare and cook a steamed pudding.

200g (6½ ounces) butter, softened

1 cup (220g) firmly packed dark
   brown sugar

3 eggs, at room temperature

½ quantity of two-in-one basic ginger
   beer fruit mix (recipe page 399)

1¼ cups (185g) plain (all-purpose) flour

3 cups (200g) soft breadcrumbs,
   made from 2-day-old bread

fresh figs and cherries, to decorate

1 Grease a 3-litre (12-cup) pudding steamer. Line the base with a round of baking paper. Place a large sheet of foil on the bench; top with a sheet of baking paper the same size. Fold a 5cm (2-inch) pleat lengthways through the centre of both sheets.

2 Beat butter and sugar in a small bowl with an electric mixer until combined. Beat in eggs, one at a time. Transfer mixture to a large bowl; stir in fruit mix, then stir in the flour and breadcrumbs, mix well.

3 Spoon mixture into steamer, level surface. Place pleated foil and paper, paper-side down, on top of pudding, with pleat running through the centre. Secure with kitchen string or lid. If using string, make a handle with string to make it easier to lift the steamer from the water.

4 Place steamer in a large saucepan with enough boiling water to come halfway up the side of the steamer; cover pan with a tight-fitting lid. Boil for 4 hours, replenishing with boiling water as necessary to maintain the water level.

5 Carefully remove pudding basin from the boiling water. If serving pudding hot, stand for 10 minutes before turning out. Before serving, top with figs and cherries.

SERVING SUGGESTION Serve with brandy custard, hard sauce or ice-cream.

Ginger Beer Fruit Cake

See pages 170 & 171 for helpful step-by-step images and information on how to prepare and cook a fruit cake.

250g (8 ounces) butter, softened

1 cup (220g) firmly packed dark brown sugar

4 eggs, at room temperature

1¼ cups (185g) plain (all-purpose) flour

1 cup (120g) almond meal

½ quantity of two-in-one basic ginger beer
  fruit mix (recipe page 399)

¼ cup (60ml) dark rum

¼ cup (80g) apricot jam

1kg (2 pounds) ready-made white icing

pure icing (confectioners') sugar, for dusting

silver cachous, to decorate

1 Preheat oven to 150°C/300°F. Line base and sides of a deep 25cm (10-inch) square cake pan with two layers of brown paper and two layers of baking paper, extending the papers 5cm (2 inches) over edges of the pan.

2 Beat butter and sugar in a medium bowl with an electric mixer until smooth. Beat in eggs, one at a time. Transfer mixture to a large bowl; stir in sifted flour, almond meal and fruit mix. Spoon the mixture into pan; smooth surface.

3 Bake cake for 2 hours or until cooked when tested with a skewer. If cake begins to overbrown, cover loosely with baking paper or foil.

4 Brush top of hot cake with rum. Cover hot cake tightly with foil; wrap in a clean tea towel. Cool in pan overnight.

5 When cooled, turn cake out; leave lining paper intact. Store in an airtight container in a cool, dry place.

6 To decorate, remove lining paper. Place cake, upside-down on a board or serving plate. Warm the jam in microwave oven for 30 seconds on HIGH (100%). Push jam through a small sieve into a bowl. Lightly brush top of cake with jam. Reserve 250g (8 ounces) of ready-made icing. Knead remaining icing together until smooth. Roll icing out on a smooth surface dusted well with sifted icing sugar into a 24cm (9½-inch) square, or large enough to fit the top of the cake. Lift icing; place on cake. Smooth icing by rubbing gently with a square of baking paper; trim edges. Knead remaining icing until smooth. Roll out until 3mm (⅛ inch) thick. Using a 3.5cm (1½-inch) star cutter, cut out about 36 stars. Place on a tray lined with baking paper. Allow to dry for several hours in a cool, dry place. If the weather is humid, keep in an air-conditioned room, if possible. Attach stars to the top of cake with a little of the remaining jam. Scatter with cachous.

STORAGE The cake will keep in an airtight container in a cool, dry place for up to 6 months. In humid weather, store in the fridge.

White Christmas Ice-Cream

1 vanilla bean

1¾ cups (430ml) milk

600ml thickened (heavy) cream

180g (5½ ounces) white chocolate, chopped coarsely

8 egg yolks

¾ cup (165g) caster (superfine) sugar

1 cup (130g) dried cranberries

2 tablespoons brandy

1 cup (140g) roasted unsalted shelled pistachios

2 teaspoons vegetable oil

1 Split vanilla bean lengthways; scrape seeds into a medium saucepan. Add pod, milk, cream and 50g (1½ ounces) of the chocolate; bring to the boil.

2 Meanwhile, whisk egg yolks and sugar in a medium bowl until thick and creamy; gradually whisk into hot milk mixture. Stir custard over low heat, without boiling, until thickened slightly. Cover surface of custard with plastic wrap; cool for 20 minutes.

3 Strain custard into a shallow container, such as an aluminium slab cake pan, cover with foil; freeze until almost firm.

4 Place custard in a large bowl, chop coarsely; beat with an electric mixer until smooth. Pour into a deep container, cover; freeze until ice-cream is firm. Repeat process two more times.

5 Meanwhile, place cranberries and brandy in a small bowl; stand for 15 minutes.

6 Stir cranberry mixture and nuts into ice-cream. Spoon ice-cream into eight ¾-cup (180ml) moulds. Cover; freeze 3 hours or until firm.

7 Stir remaining chocolate and oil in a small saucepan over low heat until mixture is smooth.

8 Dip each mould, one at a time, into a bowl of hot water for 1 second. Turn ice-creams onto serving plates; top with warm chocolate mixture.

Panettone Puds

Panettone is a sweet yeasted bread originally from Italy. Puds are best made just before serving; any fruit mince can be used.

340g (11 ounces) bought panettone, sliced thickly

1 cup (270g) cranberry and apple fruit mince (see page 445)

1 tablespoon icing (confectioners') sugar

CUSTARD

1 cup (250ml) pouring cream

¾ cup (180ml) milk

2 tablespoons caster (superfine) sugar

½ teaspoon vanilla extract

2 eggs

1 Preheat oven to 170°C/340°F. Grease six 1¼-cup (310ml) ovenproof teacups.

2 Make custard.

3 Layer panettone and half the fruit mince, overlapping panettone slightly, in cups. Dollop spoonfuls of remaining fruit mince over panettone. Pour custard over panettone.

4 Place cups in a large baking dish; add enough boiling water to come halfway up sides of cups. Bake puddings for 35 minutes or until set. Remove puddings from baking dish; stand for 10 minutes before serving, dusted with sifted icing sugar.

CUSTARD Bring cream, milk, sugar and extract to the boil in a small saucepan. Whisk eggs in a medium bowl; gradually whisk hot milk mixture into egg mixture.

Notes

If you can't decide whether to make a Christmas cake or a pudding, this recipe is the best of both worlds because it's just as delicious served hot as a pudding or cold as a cake. And it's not necessary to make it ages in advance: starting to prepare it a day or so ahead is just fine. Although the inclusion of irish whiskey makes it authentic, scotch, dark rum or brandy can be used instead.

Irish Pudding Cake

You will need to start this recipe at least a day ahead.

1½ cups (250g) pitted dried dates, chopped coarsely

1½ cups (250g) raisins, chopped coarsely

1¼ cups (200g) pitted prunes, chopped coarsely

1 cup (150g) dried currants

¾ cup (125g) sultanas

1 large apple (200g), grated coarsely

1½ cups (375ml) irish whiskey

1¼ cups (275g) firmly packed light brown sugar

185g (6 ounces) butter, softened

3 eggs, beaten lightly

½ cup (50g) ground hazelnuts

1½ cups (225g) plain (all-purpose) flour

1 teaspoon ground nutmeg

½ teaspoon bicarbonate of (baking) soda

½ teaspoon ground ginger

½ teaspoon ground cloves

1 Combine dried fruit, apple and 1 cup of the whiskey in a large bowl, cover tightly with plastic wrap; stand at room temperature overnight.

2 Preheat oven to 120°C/250°F. Grease a deep 20cm (8-inch) round cake pan; line with two thicknesses of baking paper, extending the paper 5cm (2 inches) above side.

3 Stir remaining whiskey and ½ cup of the sugar in a small saucepan over heat until sugar dissolves; bring sugar syrup to the boil. Remove pan from heat; cool syrup for 20 minutes.

4 Meanwhile, beat butter and remaining sugar in a small bowl with an electric mixer until just combined (do not overbeat). Beat in eggs, one at a time. Add egg mixture to fruit mixture; stir in ground hazelnuts, sifted dry ingredients and ½ cup of the cooled syrup. Spread cake mixture into pan.

5 Bake cake for 3½ hours. Brush cake with reheated remaining syrup, cover cake with foil; cool in pan.

STORAGE The cake will keep in an airtight container in a cool, dry place for up to 6 months. In humid weather, store in the fridge.

White Chocolate and Coconut Cake

180g (5½ ounces) white chocolate, chopped coarsely

125g (4 ounces) unsalted butter, chopped coarsely

1 cup (250ml) coconut cream

1¼ cups (275g) caster (superfine) sugar

2 eggs

2 teaspoons coconut extract

1¼ cups (185g) plain (all-purpose) flour

½ cup (75g) self-raising flour

⅓ cup (15g) flaked coconut

WHITE CHOCOLATE GLAZE

100g (3 ounces) white chocolate, chopped coarsely

¼ cup (60ml) pouring cream

1 Preheat oven to 140°C/280°F. Grease a deep 25cm (10-inch) fluted ring pan well; sprinkle with flour, shake out excess.

2 Place chocolate, butter, coconut cream and sugar in a medium saucepan; stir over low heat until smooth. Transfer mixture to a large bowl; cool for 15 minutes.

3 Whisk in eggs, extract and sifted flours until smooth. Pour mixture into pan.

4 Bake cake for 1 hour 20 minutes. Stand cake in pan for 5 minutes, before turning onto a wire rack to cool.

5 Meanwhile, make white chocolate glaze.

6 Drizzle cold cake with glaze; sprinkle with flaked coconut.

WHITE CHOCOLATE GLAZE Stir chocolate and cream in a small saucepan over low heat until smooth. Cool for 10 minutes.

STORAGE Cake will keep in an airtight container, in the fridge, for up to 1 week. Freeze uniced cake for up to 3 months.

Mojito Syrup Cake

500g (1 pound) butter

2 tablespoons finely grated lime rind

2 cups (440g) caster (superfine) sugar

6 eggs, separated

3½ cups (525g) self-raising flour

2 cups (500ml) buttermilk

1 small fresh coconut (700g)

3½ cups (875ml) thickened (heavy) cream

2 tablespoons finely chopped fresh mint

MOJITO SYRUP

2 cups (440g) caster (superfine) sugar

1 cup (250ml) white rum

1 cup (250ml) lime juice

⅓ cup finely chopped fresh mint

1 Preheat oven to 180°C/350°F. Grease two deep 20cm (8-inch) round cake pans; line bases with baking paper.

2 Beat butter, rind and sugar in a large bowl with an electric mixer until light and fluffy; beat in egg yolks. Stir in sifted flour and the buttermilk, in two batches.

3 Beat egg whites in a medium bowl with electric mixer until soft peaks form; fold into cake mixture, in two batches. Spread mixture evenly into pans.

4 Bake cakes for 50 minutes.

5 Make mojito syrup. Refrigerate half the syrup until cold; reserve remaining hot syrup.

6 Turn cakes, top-side up, onto wire racks over trays. Pour hot syrup over hot cakes. Cool.

7 Pierce the coconut 'eyes' with a strong metal skewer. Drain liquid from coconut. Tap coconut with hammer or meat tenderiser until husk cracks. Quarter coconut; peel away outer skin. Using a vegetable peeler, peel flakes from coconut flesh. You will need about 3 cups.

8 Beat cream and ½ cup of the cold syrup in a medium bowl with electric mixer until soft peaks form. Divide cream evenly into two bowls; stir chopped mint into one bowl of cream.

9 Split cakes in half. Place one cake layer on cake plate, cut-side up; brush with ¼ cup of the remaining cold syrup. Spread with one-third of the minted cream mixture. Repeat layers, finishing with cake. Spread plain cream mixture all over cake, then press coconut over cake.

MOJITO SYRUP Stir ingredients in a medium saucepan over high heat, without boiling, until sugar dissolves. Bring to the boil. Strain syrup into a medium heatproof jug; discard solids.

STORAGE Cake will keep in an airtight container, in the fridge, for up to 3 days.

Peach and Pistachio Cake Pots

4 small peaches (460g), halved

1 cup (280g) Greek-style yoghurt

2 medium apples (300g), grated coarsely

2 eggs, beaten lightly

¼ cup (60ml) milk

2 tablespoons honey

2 cups (240g) almond meal

2 teaspoons baking powder

⅓ cup (45g) roasted unsalted shelled pistachios, chopped coarsely

1½ tablespoons honey, extra

1 Preheat oven to 180°C/350°F. Cut 12 x 12cm (4-inch) squares from baking paper; line 12 x ⅓ cup (80ml) ovenproof pots with paper squares (see notes).

2 Thinly slice 3 of the peaches. Coarsely chop remaining peach; blend or process to a coarse puree. Fold peach puree through yoghurt in a small bowl. Cover; refrigerate until required.

3 Place apple, egg, milk, honey, almond meal and baking powder in a large bowl; mix until just combined. Spoon mixture into pots; push peach slices 2cm (¾ inch) into the top of the batter.

4 Bake cakes for 30 minutes or until a skewer inserted in the centre comes out clean.

5 Before serving, top cakes with pistachios; drizzle with extra honey. Serve warm or at room temperature with peach yoghurt.

DO-AHEAD This recipe is best made on the day of serving.

Notes

We used peat seedling pots available from hardware stores and garden nurseries. You can also cook the cakes in a 12-hole (⅓ cup/80ml) muffin pan, lined with baking paper squares.

Notes

Puddings can be cooked in two boilers at the same time or in batches; mixture will keep at room temperature for several hours. If you are giving puddings as gifts, hang the puddings in their cloths until cold; they can be stored, in the fridge, for up to 2 months, or frozen for up to 12 months.

Gluten-free Individual Boiled Puddings with Orange Custard

You will need to start this recipe at least a day ahead. You also need six 35cm (14-inch) squares pudding cloth (unbleached calico) and kitchen string. See page 199 for helpful step-by-step images and information on how to prepare and cook a steamed pudding.

1kg (2 pounds) mixed fruit

1 large green apple (200g), grated coarsely

½ cup (125ml) orange-flavoured liqueur

1 tablespoon finely grated orange rind

2 teaspoons mixed spice

2 teaspoons ground cinnamon

125g (4 ounces) butter, softened

½ cup (110g) firmly packed dark brown sugar

2 eggs

2 cups (140g) stale gluten-free white
   breadcrumbs

½ cup (60g) tapioca flour

1 cup (135g) gluten-free plain (all-purpose)
   flour, plus extra to spread on cloth

ORANGE CUSTARD

1½ cups (375ml) gluten-free vanilla custard

2 tablespoons orange-flavoured liqueur

1 Combine mixed fruit, apple, liqueur, rind, mixed spice and cinnamon in a large bowl. Cover with plastic wrap; stand at room temperature overnight.

2 Beat butter and sugar in a small bowl with an electric mixer until pale. Beat in eggs, one at a time. Stir egg mixture into fruit mixture. Stir in breadcrumbs and combined sifted flours.

3 Fill a boiler three quarters full of hot water, cover with a tight fitting lid; bring to the boil. Wearing thick rubber gloves and using tongs, dip pudding cloths, one at a time, into boiling water; boil for 1 minute, then remove. Squeeze excess water from cloth. Spread cloths on bench; rub 2 tablespoons of extra flour into centre of each cloth to cover an area about 20cm (8 inches) in diameter, leaving the flour a little thicker in centre. Divide pudding mixture equally among cloths; placing in centre of each cloth. Gather cloth around mixture, avoiding any deep pleats; pat into round shapes. Tie cloth tightly with string, as close to the mixture as possible Tie loops in string. Lower three puddings into boiling water. Cover; boil for 2 hours, replenishing with boiling water as necessary to maintain water level.

4 Lift puddings from water, one at a time, using a wooden spoon through string loops. Do not put pudding on bench; suspend from a spoon by placing over rungs of an upturned stool or wedging the spoon in a drawer. Twist ends of cloth around string to avoid them touching pudding; hang for 10 minutes. Repeat with remaining puddings.

5 Place puddings on a board; cut string, carefully peel back cloth. Turn puddings onto plate, then carefully peel cloth away completely. Stand for 20 minutes or until skin darkens and puddings become firm.

6 Make orange custard.

7 Serve puddings with custard.

ORANGE CUSTARD Combine ingredients in a small bowl.

Rich Chocolate Fruit Cake

See pages 170 & 171 for helpful step-by-step images and information on how to prepare and cook a fruit cake.

850g (1¾ pounds) canned pitted black cherries in syrup

1 cup (150g) raisins, chopped coarsely

¾ cup (120g) finely chopped pitted dried dates

½ cup (80g) sultanas

½ cup (95g) finely chopped pitted prunes

1 cup (200g) dried figs, chopped finely

1 cup (250ml) marsala

1 cup (120g) pecans

185g (6 ounces) butter, softened

2 teaspoons finely grated orange rind

1¼ cups (275g) firmly packed dark brown sugar

3 eggs

1¼ cups (185g) plain (all-purpose) flour

½ cup (75g) self-raising flour

2 tablespoons cocoa powder

2 teaspoons mixed spice

100g (3 ounces) dark (semi-sweet) chocolate, chopped finely

chocolate decoration (see tip) and icing (confectioners') sugar, to decorate (optional)

GANACHE

200g (6½ ounces) dark (semi-sweet) chocolate, chopped coarsely

½ cup (125ml) pouring cream

1 Drain cherries; reserve ⅓ cup syrup. Quarter cherries. Combine cherries with remaining fruit, ¾ cup of the marsala and reserved cherry syrup in a large bowl. Cover; stand overnight.

2 Preheat oven to 150°C/300°F. Grease a deep 22cm (9-inch) round cake pan; line with two layers of baking paper, extending the papers 5cm (2 inches) over edge of pan.

3 Process half the nuts until ground finely; chop the remaining nuts coarsely.

4 Beat butter, rind and sugar in a small bowl with an electric mixer until combined; beat in eggs, one at a time. Mix egg mixture into fruit mixture; stir in sifted dry ingredients, chocolate and ground and chopped nuts. Spread mixture into pan.

5 Bake cake for 3 hours. Brush hot cake with remaining marsala, cover with foil; cool in pan.

6 Make ganache.

7 Spread cake with ganache. Just before serving, top cake with chocolate decoration and dust with sifted icing sugar.

GANACHE Stir ingredients in a small saucepan over low heat until smooth. Refrigerate, stirring occasionally, for 20 minutes or until spreadable.

TIP We painted a branch of real holly roughly with melted dark chocolate to make the inedible decoration on the cake. Remove cake from fridge, then top with the chocolate decoration.

STORAGE Store un-iced cake in the fridge for up to 3 months. Once iced, the cake can be stored in the fridge for 2 weeks. Cut and bring to room temperature before serving.

Gluten-free Fruit and Almond Loaves

You will need to start this recipe at least 1 week ahead.

1kg (2 pounds) mixed dried fruit

1 tablespoon finely grated orange rind

⅔ cup (160ml) sweet sherry

150g (4½ ounces) butter, softened

⅔ cup (150g) firmly packed dark
  brown sugar

4 eggs

100g (3 ounces) marzipan, chopped

1 small apple (130g), grated coarsely

¾ cup (100g) almond meal

1¼ cups (185g) gluten-free plain
  (all-purpose) flour

1 cup (160g) blanched almonds

¼ cup (60ml) sweet sherry, extra

1 Combine fruit, rind and sherry in a large bowl; mix well. Cover with plastic wrap; stand in a cool, dark place for 1 week, stirring every day.

2 Preheat oven to 150°C/300°F. Line bases and sides of two 9cm x 21cm (3¼-inch x 8½-inch) loaf pans with two layers of baking paper, extending the papers 5cm (2 inches) above sides.

3 Beat butter and sugar in a small bowl with an electric mixer until just combined. Beat in eggs, one at a time. Mix egg mixture into fruit mixture. Stir in marzipan, apple, almond meal and sifted flour. Spread mixture into pans; decorate with nuts.

4 Bake loaves for 2 hours. Brush hot loaves with extra sherry, cover with foil; cool in pans.

The Night Before Frozen Christmas Ice-cream Cake

800g (1½-pound) square dark fruit cake

550g (1 pound) frozen mixed berries

1 litre (4 cups) good-quality vanilla bean
 ice-cream

2 tablespoons brandy or rum

½ teaspoon ground nutmeg

1½ teaspoons finely grated mandarin or
 orange rind

¼ cup (40g) dry-roasted almonds,
 chopped coarsely

10 vanilla flavour mini meringue drops

1 Grease a 20cm (8-inch) springform pan; line base and side with baking paper, extending the paper 3cm (1¼ inches) over edge of the pan.

2 Cut fruit cake into three slices horizontally. Place a square slice in the centre of the base of the pan. Using remaining slices, trim them to fit the gaps; reserve trimmings. Using your hands, flatten fruit cake to form a level base without gaps. Cut trimmings into small pieces.

3 Remove ½ cup frozen red berries, cut any strawberries in half. Press cut stawberries and red berries to the side of the pan using some ice-cream as 'glue'. Place the pan in the freezer for 10 minutes.

4 Spoon remaining ice-cream into a large bowl; stir in brandy, nutmeg, rind and nuts until combined. Spoon one-third of the ice-cream mixture into the pan; scatter with one-third reserved fruit cake, smooth surface with a spoon. Repeat with remaining ice-cream mixture and fruit cake. Freeze for 4 hours or overnight until firm.

5 Before serving, transfer to a serving plate; top with remaining berries and the meringues.

DO-AHEAD Ice-cream cake can be made up to 3 days ahead.

Chocolate Fig Panforte

You will need to start this recipe at least a day ahead.

¾ cup (110g) plain (all-purpose) flour

2 tablespoons cocoa powder

2 teaspoons ground cinnamon

1¾ cups (150g) coarsely chopped
   semi-dried figs

¼ cup (40g) finely chopped glacé orange

1 cup (160g) blanched almonds, roasted

1 cup (140g) hazelnuts, roasted

1 cup (120g) pecans, roasted

⅓ cup (115g) honey

⅓ cup (75g) caster (superfine) sugar

⅓ cup (75g) firmly packed light
   brown sugar

2 tablespoons water

100g (3 ounces) dark (semi-sweet)
   chocolate, melted

1 Preheat oven to 150°C/300°F. Grease a deep 20cm (8-inch) round cake pan; line base with baking paper.

2 Sift flour, cocoa and cinnamon into a large bowl; stir in fruit and nuts. Place honey, sugars and the water in a small saucepan; stir over low heat until sugar dissolves. Simmer, uncovered, without stirring, for 5 minutes. Pour hot syrup, then melted chocolate into fruit and nut mixture; mix well. Press mixture firmly into pan; press a 20cm (8-inch) round of baking paper on top.

3 Bake panforte for 40 minutes; cool in pan. Remove panforte from pan, discard baking paper; wrap in foil. Stand overnight before cutting into thin wedges to serve.

Kouglof

200g (6½ ounces) unsalted butter

½ cup (75g) raisins

¼ cup (60ml) kirsch

2 teaspoons finely grated orange rind

16 almond kernels

3⅓ cups (500g) plain (all-purpose) flour

1 teaspoon coarse cooking (kosher) salt

½ cup (110g) caster (superfine) sugar

5 teaspoons (14g) dried yeast

¾ cup (180ml) warm milk

4 eggs

½ cup (70g) slivered almonds

2 teaspoons icing (confectioners') sugar

1 Chop butter; stand at room temperature. Combine raisins, kirsch and rind in a small bowl.

2 Grease a 24cm (9½-inch) (top measurement) kouglof pan well. Place almond kernels in grooves of mould; refrigerate pan.

3 Sift flour and salt into a large bowl of an electric mixer with dough hook attached; add caster sugar, yeast, milk and eggs. Knead on low speed for 1 minute or until mixture forms a soft dough. Add butter. Increase speed to medium; knead for 10 minutes or until dough is smooth and elastic. Add raisin mixture and slivered almonds; knead until combined. Cover bowl; stand in a warm place for 1 hour or until dough has doubled in size.

4 Punch down dough; knead with electric mixer for 1 minute. Gently push dough into pan, to avoid disturbing the nuts. Cover; stand in a warm place for 1 hour or until dough has doubled in size.

5 Meanwhile, preheat oven to 180°C/350°F.

6 Bake kouglof for 40 minutes. Stand kouglof in pan for 5 minutes, before turning onto a wire rack to cool. Serve dusted with sifted icing sugar.

SERVING SUGGESTION Serve warm with whipped cream.

STORAGE Cake will keep in an airtight container at room temperature for about 1 week.

Orange, Date and Treacle Pudding

See page 199 for helpful step-by-step images and information on how to prepare and cook a steamed pudding.

1 cup (150g) finely chopped dried dates

⅓ cup (80ml) orange juice, warmed

60g (2 ounces) butter

¼ cup (90g) treacle

½ teaspoon bicarbonate of (baking) soda

1 cup (150g) self-raising flour

1 teaspoon mixed spice

⅓ cup (80ml) milk

1 egg

ORANGE SYRUP

¼ cup (55g) caster (superfine) sugar

2 tablespoons treacle

1 teaspoon finely grated orange rind

¼ cup (60ml) orange juice

25g (¾-ounce) butter

1 Grease a 2-litre (8-cup) pudding steamer. Place a large sheet of foil on the bench; top with a sheet of baking paper the same size. Fold a 5cm (2-inch) pleat lengthways through the centre of both sheets.

2 Combine dates and juice in a small bowl. Cover; stand for 20 minutes.

3 Melt butter with treacle in a small saucepan. Remove pan from heat, stir in soda; transfer mixture to a medium bowl. Stir in sifted flour and mixed spice, then combined milk and egg, in two batches. Stir in date mixture.

4 Spoon mixture into steamer, level surface. Place pleated foil and paper, paper-side down, on top of pudding, with pleat running through the centre. Secure with kitchen string or lid. If using string, make a handle with string to make it easier to lift the steamer from the water.

5 Place pudding steamer in a large saucepan with enough boiling water to come halfway up side of steamer; cover pan with tight-fitting lid. Boil for 1 hour, replenishing with boiling water as necessary to maintain water level. Remove steamer; stand pudding in steamer for 5 minutes before turning out.

6 Make orange syrup. Serve pudding with orange syrup.

ORANGE SYRUP Stir ingredients in a small saucepan over medium heat until smooth; bring to the boil. Reduce heat; simmer, uncovered, for 2 minutes.

DO-AHEAD This pudding is best made on the day and served hot.

Tropical Fruit Cakes

8 slices glacé pineapple (345g)

1 cup (180g) dried papaya

½ cup (90g) dried mango

½ cup (115g) glacé ginger

1 cup (140g) macadamia nuts

1 cup (170g) brazil nuts

2 eggs

½ cup (110g) firmly packed light
  brown sugar

1 tablespoon coconut-flavoured liqueur

100g (3 ounces) butter, melted

⅓ cup (50g) plain (all-purpose) flour

¼ cup (35g) self-raising flour

¼ cup (80g) apricot jam, warmed,
  strained

FRUIT & NUT TOPPING

3 slices glacé pineapple (170g)

¾ cup (135g) dried papaya

¼ cup (55g) glacé ginger

⅓ cup (45g) macadamia nuts

⅓ cup (55g) brazil nuts

½ cup (25g) coarsely grated fresh coconut
  (see notes)

1 Preheat oven to 150°C/300°F. Grease six deep 8cm (3¼-inch) round cake pans;
line with baking paper.

2 Coarsely chop fruit. Combine fruit and nuts in a large bowl.

3 Beat eggs and sugar in a small bowl with an electric mixer until thick and creamy.
Add liqueur, butter and sifted flours; beat until combined. Stir egg mixture into fruit
mixture. Press mixture firmly into pans.

4 Make fruit and nut topping; gently press topping evenly over cake mixture.

5 Bake cakes for 1¾ hours. Turn cakes, top-side up, onto a wire rack; brush tops with jam.
Leave to cool.

FRUIT & NUT TOPPING Coarsely chop fruit; combine with nuts and coconut in a bowl.

DO-AHEAD Cakes can be made a month ahead; store in an airtight container..

Notes

We used Malibu for the coconut-flavoured liqueur in this recipe. You can buy flaked coconut instead of the fresh coconut, if you prefer. Cover cakes with foil halfway through baking time if fruit on top starts to brown.

Notes

Muslin is a loosely-woven cotton fabric that can be used to separate liquid from solids. Use Grand Marnier, Curaçao or Cointreau for an orange-flavoured liqueur.

Orange Marmalade and Cranberry Cake

You will need to start this recipe at least a day ahead.

1 cup (130g) dried cranberries

1 cup (250ml) orange-flavoured liqueur

ORANGE MARMALADE

1 large orange (300g), unpeeled

1 cup (250ml) water

1½ cups (330g) caster (superfine) sugar

185g (6 ounces) butter, softened

3 eggs

1 cup (120g) almond meal

1 cup (150g) plain (all-purpose) flour

½ cup (75g) self-raising flour

CRANBERRY GLACÉ ICING

3 cups (480g) pure icing (confectioners') sugar

¼ cup (60ml) cranberry juice

1 Combine cranberries and liqueur in a small bowl. Cover; stand overnight.

2 Meanwhile, for the orange marmalade, cut unpeeled orange into eight wedges; slice wedges thinly crossways. Tie seeds in a small muslin bag; place orange pieces and seeds into small bowl with the water. Cover, stand overnight.

3 Transfer the orange mixture, including muslin bag, into a medium saucepan; bring to the boil.

Reduce heat; simmer, covered, stirring occasionally, for 40 minutes or until rind is tender. Add sugar to pan; stir over high heat, without boiling, until sugar dissolves. Bring to the boil; boil, uncovered, stirring occasionally, for 20 minutes or until marmalade jells when tested. Strain marmalade through sieve into a small heatproof bowl. Reserve marmalade and rind mixtures separately, cool. Discard seeds.

4 Preheat oven to 150°C/300°F. Grease a 20cm (8-inch) baba or fluted ring pan well; sprinkle with flour, shake out excess.

5 Beat butter and marmalade in a small bowl with electric mixer until combined. Beat in eggs, one at a time (mixture will curdle at this stage but will come together later). Transfer mixture to a large bowl; stir in almond meal, sifted flours, cranberry mixture and rind mixture. Spread mixture into pan.

6 Bake cake for 1¼ hours. Stand cake in pan for 5 minutes, before turning onto a wire rack to cool.

7 Meanwhile, make cranberry glacé icing.

8 Drizzle cold cake with icing.

CRANBERRY GLACÉ ICING Sift icing sugar into a medium heatproof bowl; stir in enough juice to make a stiff paste. Stir mixture over a medium pan of simmering water until icing is spreadable.

STORAGE Iced cake will keep in an airtight container at room temperature for up to 1 week. Freeze uniced cake for up to 3 months.

Edible Gifts

Triple-Choc Brownie

125g (8 ounces) butter, chopped coarsely

200g (6½ ounces) dark (semi-sweet) chocolate, chopped coarsely

½ cup (110g) caster (superfine) sugar

2 eggs, beaten lightly

1¼ cups (185g) plain (all-purpose) flour

150g (4½ ounces) white chocolate, chopped coarsely

100g (3 ounces) milk chocolate, chopped coarsely

1 teaspoon icing (confectioners') sugar

1 Preheat oven to 170°C/340°F. Grease a 20cm (8-inch) round springform pan; line base and side with baking paper.

2 Stir butter and dark chocolate in a medium saucepan over low heat until almost smooth. Remove from heat; cool for 10 minutes.

3 Stir caster sugar and eggs into chocolate mixture, then stir in sifted flour and white and milk chocolates. Spread mixture into pan.

4 Bake brownie for 30 minutes or until a skewer inserted in the centre comes out with moist crumbs. Cool in pan. Just before serving, dust with sifted icing sugar.

Mini Fruit Mince Tarts

2 cups (300g) plain (all-purpose) flour

2 tablespoons custard powder

⅓ cup (55g) icing (confectioners') sugar

200g (6½ ounces) butter, chopped

1 egg

1 tablespoon iced water, approximately

1¼ cups (320g) bottled fruit mince

2 teaspoons finely grated orange rind

½ cup (40g) natural flaked almonds

FRANGIPANE

125g (4 ounces) unsalted butter, softened

⅓ cup (75g) caster (superfine) sugar

2 teaspoons finely grated lemon rind

2 eggs

2 egg yolks

1 cup (120g) almond meal

1 Process flour, custard powder and icing sugar until combined. Add butter; process until combined. Add egg and enough of the water to process to a soft dough. Wrap dough with plastic wrap; refrigerate for 30 minutes.

2 Lightly grease three 12-hole (1½ tablespoon/30ml) mini muffin pans. Roll 3 level teaspoons of pastry into a ball; gently press over base and side of a pan hole. Repeat with remaining pastry – you may have a little pastry left over. Refrigerate pastry cases for 30 minutes.

3 Make frangipane.

4 Preheat oven to 180°C/350°F. Combine fruit mince and rind in a small bowl. Fill each pastry case with 1½ teaspoons of the fruit mince. Top with 2 level teaspoons of frangipane; spread to the edge. Sprinkle with flaked almonds.

5 Bake tarts for 25 minutes or until pastry is browned. Twist tarts in pan to loosen before removing. Cool tarts on a wire rack.

FRANGIPANE Beat butter, sugar and rind in a small bowl with an electric mixer until combined. Add eggs and egg yolks; beat until just combined. Stir in almond meal.

TIP Natural flaked almonds are flaked almonds with the skin on.

DO-AHEAD Tarts can be made a week ahead or frozen for up to 3 months. Refresh tarts by heating in a 160°C/325°F oven for 5 minutes or until warm, then allow to cool before serving.

Apple Cherry Pies

You will need a 6.5cm (2¾-inch) round cutter for this recipe.

3 medium apples (450g), peeled, chopped finely

¼ cup (55g) caster (superfine) sugar

1 star anise

2 tablespoons water

300g (9½ ounces) frozen pitted cherries, quartered

1 tablespoon cornflour (cornstarch)

1 egg white, beaten lightly

2 teaspoons caster (superfine) sugar, extra

PASTRY

1⅔ cups (250g) plain (all-purpose) flour

⅓ cup (75g) caster (superfine) sugar

150g (4½ ounces) cold butter, chopped

1 egg yolk

1 Make pastry.

2 Combine apple, sugar, star anise and half the water in a medium saucepan; bring to the boil. Reduce heat; simmer, covered, for 5 minutes or until apple is tender. Add cherries; simmer for 2 minutes. Stir in blended cornflour and the remaining water; stir over heat until mixture boils and thickens. Remove from heat; cool for 10 minutes. Discard star anise.

3 Preheat oven to 200°C/400°F. Grease 18 holes of two 12-hole (2-tablespoon/40ml) deep flat-based patty pans.

4 Roll two-thirds of the pastry between sheets of baking paper until 3mm (⅛-inch) thick; cut out 18 x 6.5cm (2¾-inch) rounds from pastry. Press rounds into pan holes. Refrigerate for 20 minutes.

5 Roll remaining pastry between sheets of baking paper to make a 20cm (8-inch) square; cut into 5mm (¼-inch) wide strips. Spoon fruit mixture into cases, brush edges of pastry with egg white. Lattice pastry strips over fruit filling; trim any excess pastry. Brush lattice with egg white; sprinkle with extra sugar.

6 Bake pies for 20 minutes. Stand pies in pan for 10 minutes; transfer to a wire rack to cool.

PASTRY Process flour, sugar and butter until crumbly. Add egg yolk; process until combined. Knead dough on a floured surface until smooth. Wrap dough in plastic wrap; refrigerate for 30 minutes.

Cranberry and Apple Fruit Mince

2⅔ cups (325g) dried cranberries

2½ cups (200g) finely chopped dried apples

2 cups (320g) finely chopped raisins

1 cup (250g) finely chopped dried cherries

¾ cup (150g) finely chopped dried figs

½ cup (85g) mixed peel

½ cup (115g) glacé ginger, chopped finely

3 medium apples (450g), peeled, grated

1½ cups (330g) firmly packed light brown sugar

½ cup (160g) raspberry jam

1 tablespoon finely grated orange rind

¼ cup (60ml) orange juice

2 teaspoons mixed spice

½ teaspoon ground clove

1 cinnamon stick, halved

1⅔ cups (330ml) orange-flavoured liqueur

1 Mix ingredients in a large bowl until combined. Cover bowl with plastic wrap.

2 Store mixture in a cool dry place for 1 month before using; stir mixture every 2 or 3 days.

Lemon, Honey and Pistachio Biscotti

½ cup (110g) caster (superfine) sugar

1 egg

¾ cup (110g) plain (all-purpose) flour

⅓ cup (50g) self-raising flour

2 teaspoons finely grated lemon rind

½ cup (70g) unsalted pistachios, roasted

¼ cup (50g) pepitas (pumpkin seed kernels)

¼ cup (35g) sunflower seed kernels

1 tablespoon honey

2 teaspoons caster (superfine) sugar, extra

1 Preheat oven to 180°C/350°F. Grease an oven tray.

2 Whisk sugar and egg in a medium bowl until combined; stir in sifted flours and rind, then nuts, seeds and honey. Turn dough onto a lightly floured work surface; shape into a 20cm (8-inch) log. Place log on tray; sprinkle with extra sugar.

3 Bake for 30 minutes or until golden. Cool on tray.

4 Reduce oven to 150°C/300°F.

5 Using a serrated knife, cut the log diagonally into 5mm (¼-inch) slices. Place slices, in a single layer, on ungreased oven trays. Return biscotti to oven for 20 minutes or until dry and crisp, turning halfway through baking time. Cool on wire racks.

STORAGE Biscotti will keep in an airtight container for at least a month.

Fruit and Nut Logs

Candied clementines are available from specialty food stores and delicatessens. Edible rice paper is a product used in making confectionery and is available from specialist food shops and online.

150g (4½ ounces) dark (semi-sweet) chocolate

1 cup (170g) coarsely chopped dried figs

¾ cup (100g) dried cherries

1 teaspoon finely grated orange rind

¼ cup (60ml) brandy

⅔ cup (90g) roasted unsalted pistachios

⅔ cup (70g) coarsely chopped roasted walnuts

⅓ cup (60g) finely chopped candied clementines

¼ cup (55g) finely chopped glacé ginger

½ teaspoon ground cinnamon

¼ teaspoon mixed spice

2 sheets edible rice paper, measuring 15cm x 23cm (6 inches x 9¼ inches)

1 Chop half of the chocolate finely. Chop remaining chocolate coarsely. Place coarsely chopped chocolate in a small heatproof bowl over a small saucepan of simmering water (don't let water touch base of bowl); stir until melted.

2 Process figs, cherries, rind and half the brandy until fruit is chopped finely. Transfer mixture to a large bowl; stir in nuts, clementines, ginger, spices, finely chopped and melted chocolate.

3 Spoon half the mixture down a long side of each rice paper sheet. Roll each sheet to enclose filling and make a log shape. Pinch along top of each log to make a triangle shape; brush rice paper with remaining brandy.

4 Wrap fruit and nut logs in baking paper; stand overnight at room temperature. Serve logs sliced thickly.

White Choc-mint Candy Cane Bark

375g (12 ounces) white chocolate Melts

1¼ cups (45g) rice bubbles

⅓ cup (25g) shredded coconut

75g (2½ ounces) candy canes, chopped

1 tablespoon silver cachous

1 tablespoon tiny silver cachous

1 Grease a 23cm x 32cm (9-inch x 13-inch) swiss roll pan; line base and opposite sides with baking paper.

2 Place chocolate in a medium heatproof bowl over a medium saucepan of simmering water (don't let water touch base of bowl); stir until smooth. Remove bowl from heat; stir in rice bubbles and coconut.

3 Working quickly, spread chocolate mixture onto lined tray as thinly as possible; sprinkle with candy canes and cachous. Refrigerate until set. Break into pieces to serve.

TIP While we used two different sizes of silver cachous, you could use just any size, colour or combination you prefer.

When it comes to take-home treats, it's all about packaging. Add a personal touch for each guest with festive tags and ribbon.

JEWELLED ROCKY ROAD

PREP TIME 25 MINUTES
(+ REFRIGERATION) **MAKES** 35

300g (9½ ounces) toasted marshmallows
  with coconut, chopped coarsely
½ cup (40g) flaked almonds, roasted
4 slices glacé pineapple (125g), chopped
½ cup (125g) chopped glacé peaches
½ cup (100g) chopped glacé citron
450g (14½ ounces) white chocolate,
  melted

1 Grease a 20cm x 30cm (8-inch x 12-inch)
rectangular pan; line base and two long sides
with baking paper, extending the paper
5cm (2 inches) over long sides.
2 Combine marshmallow, nuts and fruit in a
large bowl. Working quickly, stir in chocolate;
spread mixture into pan, pushing mixture
down firmly to flatten.
3 Refrigerate rocky road until set before
cutting into squares.

STORAGE Rocky road will keep in an
airtight container for about 4 weeks.

FRUIT & NUT SNACK MIX

PREP + COOK TIME 25 MINUTES
(+ COOLING) **MAKES** 2¼ CUPS

½ cup (75g) unsalted raw cashews
½ cup (80g) almond kernels
⅓ cup (65g) coarsely chopped dried figs
⅓ cup (30g) dried apple
⅓ cup (65g) pepitas (pumpkin seed kernals)
¼ cup dried cranberries

1 Preheat oven to 180°C/350°F. Line an oven tray with baking paper.
2 Combine nuts, figs, dried apple and pepitas in a medium bowl; spread evenly on tray.
3 Bake mixture for 15 minutes or until golden. Cool; stir through cranberries.

Fruit Mince Swirls

You will need a fluted 7cm (2¾-inch) round cutter for this recipe.

475g (15 ounces) bottled fruit mince

½ cup (125g) finely chopped glacé peaches

⅓ cup (45g) finely chopped toasted slivered almonds

¼ cup (30g) almond meal

2 teaspoons brandy or orange juice

4 sheets ready-rolled puff pastry

2 tablespoons icing (confectioners') sugar, plus extra for dusting

1 egg, beaten lightly

1 tablespoon milk

vanilla sugar, for dusting (optional)

1 Preheat oven to 220°C/425°F. Grease two oven trays; line with baking paper.

2 Combine fruit mince, peaches, slivered almonds, almond meal and brandy in a medium bowl.

3 Place a sheet of pastry on work surface; sift 1 tablespoon of the icing sugar over pastry. Place another sheet of pastry on top, pressing down firmly. Roll pastry up tightly, then mark log into 24 pieces, about 1cm (½ inch) apart. Repeat with remaining pastry and icing sugar.

4 Cut six pieces from the log at a time. Dust board with extra sifted icing sugar; place pieces, cut-side up, on board. Roll out each piece into an 8cm (3¼-inch) round.

5 Spoon 1 tablespoon of the fruit mince mixture onto the centre of three rounds. Brush edges with combined egg and milk. Top with other three rounds, press edges to seal. Trim each pie with a fluted 7cm (2¾-inch) round cutter to neaten the edges. Place on trays. Repeat to make a total of 24 pies. Brush pie tops lightly with remaining egg and milk mixture.

6 Bake pies for 12 minutes or until well browned. Transfer pies to wire racks to cool. Just before serving, dust pies with vanilla sugar.

DO-AHEAD These pies can be made several days ahead; keep in an airtight container. Refresh pies in a 180°C/350°C oven for 10 minutes or until warm.

Notes

These fudgy cakes are delicious
served warm or cold. For a
delicious dessert, remove paper
case from cold cake and place on
a microwave-safe serving plate;
reheat cake in microwave oven
and serve with thick (double)
cream or vanilla ice-cream.

Rum, Raisin and Cranberry Chocolate Cakes

300g (9½ ounces) dark (semi-sweet)
  chocolate, chopped

185g (6 ounces) unsalted butter, chopped

¼ cup (25g) cocoa powder

1 cup (220g) firmly packed light
  brown sugar

¾ cup (165g) caster (superfine) sugar

2 teaspoons vanilla extract

4 eggs, beaten lightly

1½ cups (225g) plain (all-purpose) flour

¼ cup (60ml) dark rum

½ cup (75g) raisins, chopped coarsely

½ cup (65g) dried cranberries,
  chopped coarsely

½ cup (70g) roasted unsalted pistachios,
  chopped coarsely

1 Preheat oven to 170°C/340°F. Line 18 holes of two 12-hole (⅓-cup/80ml) muffin pans
with paper cases.

2 Place chocolate and butter in a large saucepan; stir over low heat until smooth.
Whisk in sifted cocoa and sugars; cool for 15 minutes.

3 Stir in extract and egg, then sifted flour and rum. Stir raisins, half the cranberries and
half the nuts into chocolate mixture. Spoon mixture evenly into paper cases; sprinkle
with remaining cranberries and nuts.

4 Bake cakes for 30 minutes. Cool cakes in pan.

STORAGE These cakes will keep in an airtight container, in the fridge, for up to 1 week.
Bring to room temperature before serving. Freeze cakes for up to 3 months.

Macadamia and Maple Tarts

½ cup (110g) firmly packed brown sugar

1 tablespoon cornflour (cornstarch)

2 tablespoons maple syrup

25g (¾ ounce) unsalted butter, melted

2 eggs

2 tablespoons pouring cream

1 teaspoon finely grated orange rind

1 cup (140g) unsalted macadamias

2 teaspoons icing (confectioners') sugar

PASTRY

1¼ cups (185g) plain (all-purpose) flour

¼ cup (55g) caster (superfine) sugar

125g (4 ounces) cold unsalted butter, chopped coarsely

1 egg

1 Make pastry.

2 Grease six deep 10cm (4-inch) round loose-based flan tins. Divide pastry into six portions. Roll portions, one at a time, between sheets of baking paper into rounds large enough to line flan tins. Lift rounds into tins; press into sides, trim edges. Prick bases all over with a fork. Refrigerate for 30 minutes.

3 Preheat oven to 200°C/400°F. Place tins on an oven tray; line pastry in each with baking paper then fill with dried beans or uncooked rice. Bake for 10 minutes. Carefully remove paper and beans; bake a further 5 minutes. Stand pastry cases in tins to cool.

4 Reduce oven to 160°C/325°F. Combine brown sugar and flour in a medium bowl; whisk in syrup, melted butter, eggs, cream and rind. Divide nuts among cases; pour over maple mixture.

5 Bake tarts for about 25 minutes; cool. Refrigerate tarts for 30 minutes. Just before serving, dust tarts with sifted icing sugar.

PASTRY Process flour, sugar and butter until crumbly. Add egg; process until combined. Knead on a floured surface until smooth. Wrap pastry in plastic wrap; refrigerate 30 minutes.

Chocolate Orange Truffles with Boozy Prunes and Ginger

You will need to start this recipe at least a day ahead.

½ cup (125ml) thickened (heavy) cream

450g (14½ ounces) dark (semi-sweet) chocolate, chopped coarsely

½ cup (50g) cocoa powder, plus extra

BOOZY PRUNES & GINGER

⅓ cup (60g) finely chopped pitted prunes

2 tablespoons finely chopped glacé ginger

2 teaspoons finely grated orange rind

1 tablespoon orange-flavoured liqueur

1 Make boozy prunes and ginger.

2 Place cream and chocolate in a medium heatproof bowl over a medium saucepan of simmering water (don't let water touch base of bowl); stir until smooth. Stand at room temperature until mixture starts to thicken. Stir in prune mixture. Refrigerate mixture for 2 hours or until firm.

3 Sift cocoa into a medium bowl. Roll level tablespoons of chocolate mixture into balls; roll in cocoa. Place on a tray; refrigerate until firm.

4 Remove truffles from the fridge 30 minutes before serving. Dust with extra sifted cocoa.

BOOZY PRUNES & GINGER Combine ingredients in a small bowl. Cover; stand overnight.

STORAGE Store truffles in an airtight container in the refrigerator for up to 3 weeks. Truffles, without cocoa coating, can be frozen for up to 3 months. Remove from freezer 1 hour before serving, then dust with cocoa.

Cheese and Seed Biscuits

150g (5 ounces) cold butter

1¼ cups (185g) plain (all-purpose) flour

pinch cayenne pepper

1 cup (120g) coarsely grated mature
cheddar

½ cup (40g) coarsely grated parmesan

2 tablespoons sesame seeds

2 tablespoons poppy seeds

1 Coarsely grate butter into processor bowl, add flour and cayenne pepper; process until crumbly. Add cheeses; process until dough comes together. Turn dough onto floured surface; knead until smooth.

2 Roll dough into two 15cm (6-inch) logs. Sprinkle sesame seeds in a shallow tray; sprinkle poppy seeds in another shallow tray. Roll each log in one type of seed. Wrap logs in plastic wrap; refrigerate for 1 hour or until firm.

3 Meanwhile, preheat oven to 180°C/350°F. Line oven trays with baking paper.

4 Cut logs into 5mm (¼-inch) slices. Place slices, about 2.5cm (1 inch) apart, on trays.

5 Bake biscuits for 15 minutes. Cool on trays.

STORAGE Biscuits will keep for up to 1 week in an airtight container, or freeze for up to 3 months. To refresh biscuits, place them in a single layer on oven trays, and bake at 180°C/350°F for 5 minutes; cool on trays.

Notes

These savoury biscuits are perfect for entertaining. Give them as a gift to the hostess so she can offer them with cheese, fruit or on their own accompanied with a glass of sparkling wine or festive punch.

Notes

If you don't have a silicone
muffin pan, turn this recipe
into rocky road. Melt the
chocolate and mix with
the remaining ingredients;
spread into a shallow
baking-paper-lined tray
and, when it's almost set,
cut into squares.

Chocolate Bonbons

You will need two 12-hole (1-tablespoon/20ml) silicone mini muffin pans for this recipe.

125g (4 ounces) turkish delight

⅓ cup (45g) roasted unsalted shelled pistachios, chopped coarsely

40g (1½ ounces) mini white marshmallows

⅓ cup (45g) dried cranberries

370g (12 ounces) dark (semi-sweet) chocolate, chopped coarsely

1 Using lightly oiled scissors, chop turkish delight into small squares.

2 Sprinkle half the turkish delight, half the nuts, half the marshmallows and half the cranberries into holes of two 12-hole (1-tablespoon/20ml) silicone mini muffin pans.

3 Place chocolate in a medium saucepan; stir over low heat until smooth. Pour chocolate into pan holes, making sure chocolate runs to the base. Sprinkle tops with remaining turkish delight, nuts, marshmallows and cranberries; press gently into chocolate. Refrigerate for 2 hours or until set.

4 Turn bonbons out of pans; wrap individually in cellophane.

STORAGE Store bonbons in an airtight container in the fridge.

Rudolf the Reindeer Cookies

You will need a 9cm (3¼-inch) round cutter and 10 ice-block sticks for this recipe.

90g (3 ounces) butter, softened

1 egg, at room temperature

½ cup (110g) firmly packed light
   brown sugar

⅓ cup (25g) desiccated coconut

⅓ cup (35g) wheat germ

⅔ cup (100g) wholemeal plain
   (all-purpose) flour

⅓ cup (50g) white self-raising flour

½ teaspoon mixed spice

20 pretzels (40g)

¼ cup (45g) dark (semi-sweet) choc Bits

10 giant choc orange balls (70g)

1 Beat butter, egg and sugar in a small bowl with an electric mixer until combined.
Stir in coconut, wheat germ and sifted flours and mixed spice. Wrap dough in plastic wrap;
refrigerate for 30 minutes.

2 Roll dough between sheets of baking paper until 5mm (¼-inch) thick. Place on tray;
refrigerate for 30 minutes.

3 Preheat oven to 180°C/350°F. Grease oven trays; line with baking paper.

4 Using a 9cm (3¼-inch) round cutter, cut 10 rounds from dough, re-rolling scraps as
necessary. Place rounds about 7.5cm (3 inches) apart on trays. Slide an ice-block stick under
each cookie; press down firmly. Position two pretzels on each cookie (as pictured) for antlers;
press down firmly. Decorate cookies with choc Bits for eyes and mouths.

5 Bake cookies for 12 minutes. Immediately press choc orange balls onto hot cookies
for noses. Cool on trays.

TIP If the choc orange balls don't stick to the cookies, secure them with a little dab of
melted chocolate.

STORAGE Decorated cookies can be stored in an airtight container for up to 1 week.

Chocolate Pistachio Shortbread

½ cup (70g) roasted unsalted shelled
  pistachios

250g (8 ounces) unsalted butter, softened

1 cup (160g) icing (confectioners') sugar

1¼ cups (185g) plain (all-purpose) flour

½ cup (100g) rice flour

⅓ cup (35g) dutch-processed cocoa

1 Preheat oven to 160°C/325°F. Line two large oven trays with baking paper.

2 Process half the nuts until finely ground; finely chop remaining nuts.

3 Beat butter and sifted icing sugar in a small bowl with an electric mixer until light and fluffy. Transfer mixture to a large bowl; stir in sifted flours, cocoa and ground nuts, in two batches. Turn dough onto a floured surface; knead until smooth.

4 Divide dough into six portions; place three portions on each tray. Using your hands, press each portion into a 12cm (4¾-inch) round, so the rounds are about 2.5cm (1 inch) apart. Using fingertips, pinch edges of rounds to make frills. Mark each round into 6 wedges; prick wedges with a fork. Sprinkle rounds with chopped nuts.

5 Bake shortbread for 45 minutes. Cool on trays before cutting into wedges.

STORAGE Shortbread will keep in an airtight container at room temperature for up to 2 weeks.

Cinnamon Eggnog French Macaroons

You will need a piping bag fitted with a 1cm (½-inch) plain tube for this recipe.

1¼ cups (200g) icing (confectioners') sugar

¾ cup (90g) almond meal

¼ cup (20g) desiccated coconut

1 teaspoon ground cinnamon

3 egg whites

¼ cup (55g) caster (superfine) sugar

2 teaspoons icing (confectioners') sugar, extra

EGGNOG CUSTARD

1 tablespoon cornflour (cornstarch)

1 tablespoon custard powder

1 tablespoon caster (superfine) sugar

½ cup (125ml) milk

15g (½ ounce) butter

1 egg yolk

2 tablespoons brandy

1 Grease oven trays; line with baking paper.

2 Process icing sugar, almond meal, coconut and cinnamon until fine; sift through a fine sieve into a medium bowl, discard any large pieces.

3 Beat egg whites and caster sugar in a small bowl with an electric mixer until firm peaks form and sugar is dissolved. Fold in almond mixture, in two batches.

4 Spoon mixture into a piping bag fitted with a 1cm (½-inch) plain tube. Pipe 4cm (1½-inch) rounds, about 2.5cm (1 inch) apart, on trays. Tap trays on bench so macaroons spread slightly. Dust with sifted extra icing sugar. Stand for 30 minutes or until macaroons are dry to touch.

5 Make eggnog custard.

6 Preheat oven to 150°C/300°F.

7 Bake macaroons for 20 minutes. Cool on trays. Sandwich macaroons with about 1 teaspoon of custard. Dust with a little more sifted icing sugar before serving.

EGGNOG CUSTARD Combine cornflour, custard powder and sugar in a small saucepan; gradually stir in milk. Stir over heat until mixture boils and thickens. Remove from heat; stir in butter, egg yolk and brandy. Cover surface directly with plastic wrap; cool.

STORAGE Filled macaroons are best eaten the day they are made. Unfilled macaroons will keep in an airtight container, at room temperature, for up to 3 days or will freeze for 3 months.

Notes

The custard can be made
several days ahead;
store in the fridge.
Return custard to room
temperature before using.

Gingerbread People

You will need a 13cm (5¼-inch) gingerbread man cutter and a small piping bag with a small plain tube for this recipe.

125g (4 ounces) butter, softened

½ cup (110g) firmly packed light
   brown sugar

½ cup (180g) treacle

1 egg yolk

2½ cups (375g) plain (all-purpose) flour

1 tablespoon ground ginger

1 teaspoon mixed spice

1 teaspoon bicarbonate of (baking) soda

ROYAL ICING

1 egg white

1½ cups (240g) pure icing
   (confectioners') sugar

1 teaspoon lemon juice

1 Beat butter and sugar in a small bowl with an electric mixer until combined. Beat in treacle and egg yolk. Transfer mixture to a large bowl; stir in sifted dry ingredients. Turn dough onto a floured surface; knead until smooth. Divide dough in half. Wrap each half in plastic wrap; refrigerate for 30 minutes.

2 Preheat oven to 160°C/325°F. Grease and line oven trays with baking paper.

3 Roll each dough half between sheets of baking paper until 5mm (¼-inch) thick. Using a 13cm (5¼-inch) gingerbread man cutter, cut out 12 gingerbread people, re-rolling scraps as necessary. Place shapes, about 2.5cm (1 inch) apart, on trays.

4 Bake gingerbread for 10 minutes. Stand on trays for 10 minutes, before transferring to wire racks to cool.

5 Make royal icing. Spoon icing into a small piping bag fitted with a small plain tube. Using picture as a guide, decorate gingerbread people with royal icing.

ROYAL ICING Beat egg white in a small bowl with an electric mixer until just broken up. Gradually beat in sifted icing sugar until firm peaks form; stir in juice. Cover surface directly with plastic wrap.

STORAGE Gingerbread peopl will keep in an airtight container for up to 1 week.

Fruit Butters

*You will need sterilised jars for this recipe.
See page 482 for information on sterilising
jars. Make sure you grate the rind from the
citrus fruit before juicing. Store the butters
in sterilised jars in the fridge.*

PASSIONFRUIT BUTTER

4 eggs, beaten lightly, strained

185g (6 ounces) unsalted butter, chopped

¾ cup (165g) caster (superfine) sugar

⅓ cup (80ml) lemon juice

1 cup (250ml) passionfruit pulp

LIME BUTTER

4 eggs, beaten lightly, strained

185g (6 ounces) unsalted butter, chopped

1½ cups (225g) caster (superfine) sugar

½ cup (125ml) lime juice

¼ cup (60ml) lemon juice

1 tablespoon finely grated lime rind

green food colouring

BLOOD ORANGE BUTTER

4 eggs, beaten lightly, strained

185g (6 ounces) unsalted butter, chopped

¾ cup (165g) caster (superfine) sugar

1 cup (250ml) blood orange juice

1 tablespoon finely grated blood orange rind

1 For the passionfruit butter, place ingredients in medium heatproof bowl over a medium
saucepan of simmering water. Stir until mixture thickly coats the back of a wooden spoon.
Remove from heat immediately. Stand bowl in sink of cold water, stirring occasionally,
for 10 minutes to stop cooking process. Pour into hot sterilised jars; seal.
2 For lime butter, combine ingredients except rind and colouring in a medium heatproof bowl;
cook as per passionfruit butter. Stir in rind and colouring before pouring into hot sterilised jars.
3 For blood orange butter, combine ingredients except rind in a medium heatproof bowl;
cook as per passionfruit butter. Stir in rind before pouring into hot sterilised jars.

Notes

If you don't have a piping bag and small plain tube, you can use a small strong plastic bag instead. Spoon the icing into a corner of the bag, twist the bag to close it. Snip the corner from the bag, then use it to pipe the icing.

Giant Father Christmas Cookies

You will need to start this recipe at least a day ahead. You will need a piping bag fitted with a small plain tube (see notes).

125g (4 ounces) unsalted butter, softened

1 egg, at room temperature

½ cup (110g) caster (superfine) sugar

1⅔ cups (250g) plain (all-purpose) flour

12 dried currants (2g)

12 tic tacs (5g)

½ cup (40g) shredded coconut

red food colouring

black writing gel

ROYAL ICING

1 egg white

1½ cups (240g) pure icing (confectioners')
  sugar

2 tablespoons lemon juice, approximately

1 Preheat oven to 180°C/350°F. Line two oven trays with baking paper.

2 Beat butter, egg and sugar in a small bowl with an electric mixer until combined; stir in sifted flour, in two batches. Wrap dough in plastic wrap; refrigerate for 30 minutes.

3 Roll dough between sheets of baking paper until 5mm (¼-inch) thick; refrigerate for 15 minutes.

4 Using the template (on page 482), cut out six Father Christmas shapes from dough, re-rolling scraps as necessary. Place shapes about 2.5cm (1 inch) apart on trays. Press currants onto cookies for eyes. Bake for 15 minutes. Cool on trays.

5 Make royal icing.

6 Half-fill a piping bag fitted with a small plain tube with royal icing. Using picture as a guide, pipe icing in an unbroken line to outline the white parts of the hat and pompom; stand until icing has dried. Secure tic tacs to faces with a little royal icing to make eyebrows.

7 Spread a thin layer of the icing over one cookie for the beard, press some of the coconut onto icing before it dries. Repeat with remaining cookies.

8 Stir enough of the remaining lemon juice into icing to make it the consistency of pouring cream. Carefully spoon or pipe icing inside the outlines of the hat for white fur and pompom; stand several hours or until icing is dry.

9 Colour remaining icing red, pipe or spoon onto hats; stand until dry. Use writing gel to make noses on the cookies.

ROYAL ICING Beat egg white in a small bowl with electric mixer until just broken up. Gradually beat in sifted sugar, 1 tablespoon at a time. Beat in 1 teaspoon of the lemon juice. Cover surface directly with plastic wrap.

STORAGE Cookies will keep in an airtight container for 2 weeks.

Gluten-free Mini Gingerbread Houses

You need a piping bag fitted with a fine piping tube.

125g (4 ounces) butter, softened

½ cup (175g) golden syrup or treacle

½ cup (110g) firmly packed dark brown sugar

2½ cups (335g) gluten-free plain (all-purpose) flour

1 tablespoon ground ginger

1 teaspoon ground cinnamon

¼ teaspoon ground cloves

1 tablespoon xanthan gum

pure icing (confectioners') sugar, for dusting

ROYAL ICING

1½ cups (240g) pure icing (confectioners') sugar

1 egg white

1 teaspoon lemon juice

1 Using the templates from page 482, trace and cut out the shapes using firm card board.

2 Beat butter, syrup and brown sugar in a medium bowl with an electric mixer until creamy and paler in colour. Add combined sifted flour, spices and gum; stir until mixture just comes together. Knead dough gently on a surface dusted with gluten-free plain flour until smooth. Wrap dough in plastic wrap; refrigerate for 30 minutes or until firm.

3 Preheat oven to 180°C/350°F. Grease two oven trays; line with baking paper.

4 To make side walls: roll one-third of the dough on a surface dusted with gluten-free flour until 3mm (⅛-inch) thick. Using wall template, cut out 16 squares; place 3cm (1¼ inches) apart on trays.

5 Bake for 10 minutes or until lightly golden. Slide paper and walls from trays onto a wire rack to cool. Cool and reline trays (see notes).

6 To make front and back walls: repeat with rolling half the remaining dough. Using end wall template, cut out 16 walls; place on trays. Bake as directed in step 5.

7 To make roof: repeat rolling remaining dough. Using roof template, cut out 16 rectangles; place on trays. Bake as directed in step 5.

8 Make royal icing. Fill piping bag fitted with a fine piping tube (no. 2). Pipe icing onto shapes, attaching side walls with front and back walls to make a house (hold in place for a few minutes to stabilise, if necessary). Pipe along the top edge with a little icing; position roof (hold in position, if necessary). Repeat with remaining pieces to make a total of 8 houses. Stand for 30 minutes or until icing is set.

9 Using picture as a guide decorate houses with royal icing. Stand for 30 minutes or until set. Just before serving, dust with sifted icing sugar.

ROYAL ICING Sift icing sugar through a fine sieve into a bowl. Lightly beat egg white in a small bowl with electric mixer until mixture is just broken up – do not whip into peaks. Beat in the icing sugar, a tablespoon at a time, to reach the required consistency. When icing reaches the right consistency, stir in juice. Cover surface directly with plastic wrap until ready to use.

Notes

Cool oven trays between baking gingerbread shapes; reline with baking paper before the next batch. Don't overcook the shapes; they will feel soft when cooked, but will crisp on standing. Gingerbread houses will keep in an airtight container for up to 1 week.

STERILISING JARS

It's important the jars be as clean as possible; make sure your hands, the preparation area, tea towels and cloths etc, are clean, too. The aim is to finish sterilising the jars and lids at the same time the preserve is ready to be bottled; the hot preserve should be bottled into hot, dry clean jars. Jars that aren't sterilised properly can cause deterioration of the preserves during storage. Always start with cleaned washed jars and lids, then following one of these methods:

(1) Put jars and lids through the hottest cycle of a dishwasher without using any detergent.

(2) Lie jars down in a boiler with the lids, add enough cold water to cover, then place the lid on. Bring to the boil over a high heat and boil for 20 minutes.

(3) Stand jars upright, without touching, on a wooden board on the lowest shelf in the oven. Turn the oven to the lowest possible temperature and leave jars to heat for 30 minutes.

Remove jars from the oven or dishwasher with a towel, or from the boiling water with tongs and rubber-gloved hands; the water will evaporate from hot wet jars quite quickly. Stand jars upright and not touching each other on a wooden board, or a bench covered with a towel. Fill jars as directed in the recipe; secure the lids tightly, holding jars firmly with a towel or an oven mitt. Leave at room temperature to cool before storing.

Giant Father Christmas Cookies Template
(recipe page 479)

Gluten-free Mini Gingerbread House Templates
(recipe page 480)

ROOF
3.5cm x 6cm
(1½ inches x 2½ inches)

SIDE WALLS
5cm x 5cm
(2 inches x 2 inches)

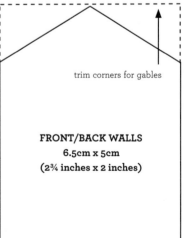

trim corners for gables

FRONT/BACK WALLS
6.5cm x 5cm
(2¾ inches x 2 inches)

Glossary

ALLSPICE also called pimento or jamaican pepper; tastes of nutmeg, cumin, clove and cinnamon. Available whole or ground.

ALMONDS

blanched brown skins removed.

flaked paper-thin slices.

meal also called ground almonds.

slivered small pieces cut lengthways.

vienna toffee-coated almonds.

BAKING POWDER a raising agent consisting mainly of two parts cream of tartar to one part bicarbonate of soda.

BAY LEAVES aromatic leaves from the bay tree available fresh or dried; adds a peppery flavour.

BEANS

borlotti also called roman beans or pink beans, can be eaten fresh or dried. Interchangeable with pinto beans due to their similarity in appearance – pale pink or beige with dark-red streaks.

broad (fava) available dried, fresh, canned and frozen. Fresh should be peeled twice (discarding the outer long green pod and the beige-green inner shell); frozen beans have had their pods removed but the beige shell still needs to be removed.

butter cans labelled butter beans are, in fact, cannellini beans. Also another name for lima beans, sold both dried and canned; a large beige bean having a mealy texture and mild taste.

green also known as french or string beans (although the tough string they once had has generally been bred out of them), this long thin fresh bean is consumed in its entirety once cooked.

BEETROOT (BEETS) a firm, round root vegetable.

BICARBONATE OF SODA also known as baking soda.

BLOOD ORANGE a virtually seedless citrus fruit with blood-red-streaked rind and flesh; sweet, non-acidic, salmon-coloured pulp and juice having slight strawberry or raspberry overtones. The juice can be drunk straight or used in cocktails, sauces, sorbets and jellies; can be frozen for use in cooking when the growing season finishes. The rind is not as bitter as an ordinary orange.

BURGHUL also called bulghur wheat; hulled steamed wheat kernels that, once dried, are crushed into various-sized grains. Is not the same as cracked wheat.

BUTTER we use salted butter unless stated otherwise; 125g is equal to 1 stick (4 ounces).

BUTTERMILK originally the term given to the slightly sour liquid left after butter was churned from cream, today it is made from no-fat or low-fat milk to which specific bacterial cultures have been added.

CACHOUS also called dragées; minuscule metallic-looking-but-edible confectionery balls used in cake decorating; available in silver, gold or various colours.

CAPERS the grey-green buds of a warm climate shrub, sold either dried and salted or pickled in a vinegar brine; tiny young ones, called baby capers, are available in brine or dried in salt.

CAPSICUM (BELL PEPPER) also called pepper; discard seeds and membranes before use.

CARAWAY SEEDS the small, half-moon-shaped dried seed from a member of the parsley family; adds a sharp anise flavour when used in both sweet and savoury dishes.

CARDAMOM a spice native to India and used extensively in its cuisine; can be purchased in pod, seed or ground form.

CELERIAC (CELERY ROOT) tuberous root with knobbly brown skin, white flesh and a celery-like flavour. Keep peeled celeriac in acidulated water to stop discolouring. It can be eaten raw in salads; used in soups and stews; boiled and mashed; or sliced thinly and deep-fried as chips.

CHEESE

blue mould-treated cheeses mottled with blue veining.

bocconcini from the diminutive of "boccone", meaning mouthful in Italian; walnut-sized, baby mozzarella. A delicate, semi-soft, white cheese traditionally made from buffalo milk.

fetta Greek in origin; a crumbly textured goat's- or sheep-milk cheese with a sharp, salty taste. Ripened and stored in salted whey.

goat's made from goat's milk, has an earthy, strong taste. Available in soft, crumbly and firm textures, in various shapes and sizes, and sometimes rolled in ash or herbs.

haloumi a Greek Cypriot cheese with a semi-firm, spongy texture and very salty sweet flavour. Ripened and stored in salted whey; best grilled or fried, and holds its shape well on being heated. Eat while still warm as it becomes tough and rubbery on cooling.

mascarpone an Italian fresh cultured cream product made in much the same way as yoghurt. Whiteish to creamy yellow in colour, with a soft, creamy buttery-rich, luscious texture.

mozzarella soft, spun-curd cheese; from southern Italy. Traditionally made from water-buffalo milk, now generally made from cow milk. The most popular pizza cheese because of its low melting point and elasticity when heated.

parmesan also called parmigiano; is a hard, grainy cow's-milk cheese originating in Italy. Reggiano is the best variety.

pecorino the generic Italian name for cheeses made from sheep milk. A hard, white to pale-yellow cheese, matured for 8 to 12 months. If you can't find it, use parmesan cheese.

ricotta a soft, sweet, moist, white cow's-milk cheese with a low fat content (8.5%) and a slightly grainy texture. The name roughly translates as "cooked again" and refers to ricotta's manufacture from a whey that is itself a by-product of other cheese making.

CHERVIL a mildly fennel-flavoured member of the parsley family with curly dark-green leaves. Available both fresh and dried but is best used fresh; its delicate flavour diminishes the longer it's cooked.

CHICKPEAS (GARBANZO BEANS) also called channa; an irregularly round, sandy-coloured legume. Has a firm texture, even after cooking, a floury mouth-feel and a robust nutty flavour; available canned or dried (reconstitute for several hours in cold water before use).

CHILLI use rubber gloves when handling fresh chillies as they can burn your skin. We use unseeded chillies because the seeds contain the heat; use fewer chillies rather than seed the lot.

flakes also sold as crushed chilli; dehydrated deep-red extremely fine slices and whole seeds.

long red available both fresh and dried; a generic term used for any moderately hot, long, thin chilli (about 6cm to 8cm long).

red thai (serrano) also called scuds or bird's eye chillies; tiny, very hot and bright red.

CHINESE COOKING WINE also called shao hsing or chinese rice wine; made from fermented rice, wheat and sugar. Substitute mirin or sherry.

CHOCOLATE

dark (semi-sweet) also known as luxury chocolate; made of a high percentage of cocoa liquor and cocoa butter, and little added sugar.

Melts small discs of compounded milk, white or dark chocolate ideal for melting and moulding.

white contains no cocoa solids but derives its sweet flavour from cocoa butter. It is very sensitive to heat.

CHOCOLATE HAZELNUT SPREAD also called Nutella; made of cocoa powder, hazelnuts, sugar and milk.

CHORIZO sausage of Spanish origin, made of coarsely ground pork and highly seasoned with garlic and chilli. They are deeply smoked, very spicy and dry-cured so that they do not need cooking.

CINNAMON available both in the piece (called sticks or quills) and ground into powder; one of the world's most common spices.

CLOVES dried flower buds of a tropical tree; can be used whole or ground; has a strong scent and taste so use sparingly.

COCOA POWDER also known as unsweetened cocoa; cocoa beans (cacao seeds) that have been fermented, roasted, shelled and ground into powder then cleared of most of the fat content.

dutch-processed is treated with an alkali to neutralise its acids. It has a reddish-brown colour, a mild flavour and easily dissolves in liquids.

COCONUT

cream obtained commercially from the first pressing of the coconut flesh alone, without the addition of water; the second pressing (less rich) is sold as coconut milk. Available in cans and cartons at most supermarkets.

desiccated concentrated, dried, unsweetened and finely shredded coconut flesh.

extract synthetically produced from flavouring, oil and alcohol.

flaked dried flaked coconut flesh.

milk not the liquid found inside the fruit (coconut water), but the diluted liquid from the second pressing of the white flesh of a mature coconut (the first pressing produces cream). Available in cans and cartons at most supermarkets.

shredded unsweetened thin strips of dried coconut flesh.

CORIANDER (CILANTRO) bright-green-leafed herb with both pungent aroma and taste. Used as an ingredient in a wide variety of cuisines. Both the stems and roots of coriander are used in cooking: wash well before chopping. Coriander seeds are dried and sold either whole or ground, and neither form tastes remotely like the fresh leaf.

CORNFLOUR (CORNSTARCH) available made from corn or wheat; used as a thickening agent.

CORNICHON French for gherkin, a very small variety of cucumber. Pickled, they are a traditional accompaniment to pâté; the Swiss always serve them with fondue.

COUSCOUS a fine, dehydrated, grain-like cereal product made from semolina; it swells to three or four times its original size when liquid is added. It is eaten like rice with a tagine, as a side dish or salad ingredient.

CRANBERRIES available dried and frozen; they have a rich, astringent flavour and can be used in cooking sweet and savoury dishes. The dried version can usually be substituted for or with other dried fruit.

CREAM

pouring also called pure or fresh cream. It has no additives. Minimum fat content 35%.

thick (double) dolloping cream with a minimum fat content of 45%.

thickened (heavy) a whipping cream containing a thickener. Minimum fat content 35%.

CREAM OF TARTAR the acid ingredient in baking powder; added to confectionery mixtures to help prevent sugar from crystallising. Keeps frostings creamy and improves volume when beating egg whites.

CRÈME FRAÎCHE a mature, naturally fermented cream with a velvety texture and slightly tangy, nutty flavour. Minimum fat content 35%. A French variation of sour cream, it boils without curdling and is used in sweet and savoury dishes.

CUMIN also called zeera or comino; resembling caraway in size, cumin is the dried seed of a plant related to the parsley family. Available dried as seeds or ground, it has a spicy, almost curry-like flavour.

CUSTARD POWDER instant mixture used to make pouring custard; it is similar to North American instant pudding mixes.

DUKKAH an Egyptian specialty spice mixture made up of roasted nuts, seeds and an array of aromatic spices.

EDAMAME (shelled soy beans) available frozen from Asian food stores and some supermarkets.

EGGPLANT also called aubergine. Ranging in size from tiny to very large and in colour from pale green to deep purple.

EGGS we use large chicken eggs weighing an average of 60g unless stated otherwise. If a recipe calls for raw or barely cooked eggs, exercise caution if there is a salmonella problem in your area, particularly in food eaten by children and pregnant women.

FENNEL also called finocchio or anise; a crunchy green vegetable slightly resembling celery that's eaten raw in salads; fried as an accompaniment; or used as an ingredient in soups and sauces. Also the name given to the dried seeds of the plant, which have a stronger licorice flavour.

FISH SAUCE called naam pla (Thai) or nuoc naam (Vietnamese); the two are almost identical. Made from pulverised salted fermented fish (most often anchovies); has a pungent smell and strong taste. Available in varying degrees of intensity, use according to taste.

FLOUR
gluten-free plain (all-purpose) a blend of gluten-free flours and starches (may include corn, potato, tapioca, chickpea and rice flours).
plain (all-purpose) unbleached wheat flour; is the best for baking as the gluten content ensures a strong dough for a light result.
rice very fine, almost powdery, gluten-free flour made from ground white rice.

self-raising plain flour sifted with baking powder; make at home in the proportion of 1 cup flour to 2 teaspoons baking powder.
wholemeal also called wholewheat; milled with the wheat germ so is higher in fibre and more nutritional than plain flour.

GELATINE we use dried (powdered) gelatine; it's also available in sheets called leaf gelatine. Three teaspoons of dried gelatine (8g sachet) is about the same as four gelatine leaves. The two types are interchangeable but leaf gelatine gives a much clearer mixture than dried gelatine.

GINGER
fresh also called green or root ginger; the thick gnarled root of a tropical plant.
glacé fresh ginger root preserved in sugar syrup; crystallised ginger can be used if rinsed with warm water and dried before using.
ground also called powdered ginger; used as a flavouring in baking but cannot be substituted for fresh ginger.

GLACÉ CHERRIES also called candied cherries; boiled in a heavy sugar syrup and then dried.

GLACÉ FRUIT fruit such as peaches, pineapple and orange cooked in a heavy sugar syrup then dried.

GLUCOSE SYRUP also called liquid glucose, made from wheat starch. Available at most supermarkets.

GOLDEN SYRUP a by-product of refined sugarcane; pure maple syrup or honey can be substituted. Treacle is a similar product, however, it is more viscous and has a stronger flavour and aroma than golden syrup (which has been refined further and contains fewer impurities).

HORSERADISH purchased in bottles at the supermarket in two forms: horseradish cream and prepared horseradish. These cannot be substituted one for the other in cooking but both can be used as table condiments.

KAFFIR LIME LEAVES also known as bai magrood and looks like two glossy dark-green leaves joined end to end, forming a rounded hourglass shape. Dried leaves are less potent so double the number if using them as a substitute for fresh; a strip of fresh lime peel may be substituted for each kaffir lime leaf.

KITCHEN STRING made of a natural product, so it neither affects the flavour of the food it's tied around nor melts when heated.

KUMARA the Polynesian name of an orange-fleshed sweet potato often confused with yam; good baked, boiled, mashed or fried similarly to other potatoes.

LEMON GRASS also called takrai, serai or serah. A tall, clumping, lemon-smelling and tasting, aromatic tropical grass; the white lower part of the stem is used, finely chopped, in much of the cooking of South-East Asia.

LYCHEES a small fruit from China with a hard shell and sweet, juicy flesh. The white flesh has a gelatinous texture and musky, perfumed taste. Discard the rough skin and seed before using in salads or as a dessert fruit. Also available canned in a sugar syrup.

MAPLE SYRUP (PURE) distilled from the sap of sugar maple trees. Maple-flavoured syrup or pancake syrup is not an adequate substitute for the real thing.

MARZIPAN made from ground almonds, sugar and glucose. Similar to almond paste, however, is not as strong in flavour, has a finer consistency and is more pliable. Cheaper brands often use ground apricot kernels and sugar.

MIRIN a Japanese champagne-coloured cooking wine, made of glutinous rice and alcohol. It is used expressly for cooking and should not be confused with sake.

MIXED DRIED FRUIT a combination of sultanas, raisins, currants, mixed peel and cherries

MIXED PEEL candied citrus peel.

MIXED SPICE a classic spice mix generally containing caraway, allspice, coriander, cumin, nutmeg and ginger, although cinnamon and other spices can be added.

MUSHROOMS, BUTTON small, cultivated white mushrooms with a mild flavour. When a recipe in this book calls for an unspecified mushroom, use button.

MUSTARD

dijon pale brown, creamy, distinctively flavoured, fairly mild french mustard.

wholegrain also known as seeded. A French-style coarse-grain mustard made from crushed mustard seeds and dijon-style french mustard.

NIGELLA SEEDS also called kalonji or black onion seeds. Tiny, angular seeds, black on the outside and creamy within, with a sharp nutty flavour that is enhanced by frying briefly in a dry hot pan before use. Available from most Middle-Eastern and Asian food shops.

NORI a type of dried seaweed used in Japanese cooking as a garnish, flavouring or for sushi. Sold in thin sheets, plain or toasted (yaki-nori).

NUTMEG a strong and pungent spice ground from the dried nut of an evergreen tree native to Indonesia. Usually found ground but the flavour is more intense from a whole nut, available from spice shops, so it's best to grate your own.

OIL

cooking spray we use a cholesterol-free spray made from canola oil.

olive made from ripened olives. Extra virgin and virgin are the first and second press, respectively, and are considered the best; the "extra light" or "light" name on other types refers to taste not fat levels.

peanut pressed from ground peanuts; the most commonly used oil in Asian cooking because of its high smoke point (capacity to handle high heat without burning).

sesame made from roasted, crushed, white sesame seeds; a flavouring rather than a cooking medium.

vegetable sourced from plants.

ONION

green (scallions) also called (incorrectly) shallot; an immature onion picked before the bulb has formed, having a long, bright-green edible stalk.

red also known as spanish, red spanish or bermuda onion; a large, sweet tasting, purple-red onion.

shallots also called french shallots, golden shallots or eschalots. Small and elongated, with a brown-skin, they grow in tight clusters similar to garlic.

spring crisp, narrow green-leafed tops and a round sweet white bulb larger than green onions.

PANCETTA an Italian unsmoked bacon; pork belly is cured in salt and spices then rolled into a sausage shape and dried for several weeks.

PAPRIKA ground dried sweet red capsicum (bell pepper); there are many types available, including hot, sweet, mild and smoked.

PINE NUTS also called pignoli; not a nut but a small, cream-coloured kernel from pine cones. They are best roasted before use to bring out the flavour.

POLENTA also called cornmeal; a flour-like cereal of dried corn (maize). Also the name of the dish made from it.

POMEGRANATE a fruit about the size of an orange, with a yellowish shell that turns a rich red colour as it matures. Inside the inedible husk are hundreds of seeds, each wrapped in an edible lucent-crimson pulp having a tangy sweet-sour flavour.

molasses not to be confused with pomegranate syrup or grenadine (used in cocktails); pomegranate molasses is thicker, browner, and more concentrated in flavour – tart and sharp, slightly sweet and fruity. Brush over grilling or roasting meat, seafood or poultry, add to salad dressings or sauces. Buy from Middle Eastern food stores or specialty food shops.

PRESERVED LEMON whole or quartered salted lemons preserved in a mixture of water, lemon juice or olive oil, and occasionally with spices such as cinnamon, coriander and clove. Use the rind only and rinse well under cold water before using.

PROSCIUTTO a kind of unsmoked Italian ham; salted, air-cured and aged. There are many styles of prosciutto, one of the best being Parma ham, from Italy's Emilia Romagna region, traditionally lightly salted, dried then eaten raw.

RICE, WILD not a true member of the rice family but a very dark brown seed of a North American aquatic grass; has a distinctively nutty flavour and crunchy, resilient texture. Sold on its own or in a blend with basmati or long-grained white rice.

ROCKET (ARUGULA) also rugula and rucola; peppery green leaf eaten raw in salads or used in cooking. Baby rocket leaves are smaller and less peppery.

SAFFRON stigma of a member of the crocus family, available ground or in strands; imparts a yellow-orange colour to food once infused. The quality can vary greatly; the best is the most expensive spice in the world.

SAGE pungent herb with narrow, grey-green leaves; slightly bitter with a slightly musty mint aroma. Refrigerate fresh sage wrapped in a paper towel and sealed in a plastic bag for up to 4 days. Dried sage comes whole, crumbled or ground.

SASHIMI fish sold as sashimi has to meet stringent guidelines regarding its handling. Seek local advice from authorities before eating any raw seafood.

SESAME SEEDS black and white are the most common of this small oval seed, however there are also red and brown varieties. The seeds are used as an ingredient and as a condiment. Roast the seeds in a frying pan over low heat.

SILVER BEET (SWISS CHARD)
also called, incorrectly, spinach; has fleshy stalks and large leaves. Prepare as you would spinach
SNOW PEAS also known as mangetout; a variety of garden pea, eaten pod and all (although you may need to string them). Used in stir-fries or eaten raw in salads.
SOY SAUCE
dark deep brown, almost black in colour; rich, with a thicker consistency than other types. Pungent but not particularly salty; good for marinating.
japanese an all-purpose low-sodium soy sauce with more wheat content than its Chinese counterparts; fermented in barrels and aged. The sauce to choose if you only want one variety.
light thin in consistency and, while paler than the others, the saltiest tasting; used in dishes in which the natural colour of the ingredients is to be maintained. Not to be confused with salt-reduced or low-sodium soy sauces.
SPINACH also called english spinach and incorrectly, silver beet. Baby spinach leaves are best eaten raw in salads; the larger leaves should be added last to soups, stews and stir-fries, and should be cooked until barely wilted.
STAR ANISE a dried star-shaped pod whose seeds have an astringent aniseed flavour; commonly used to flavour stocks and marinades.
SUGAR
brown a soft, finely granulated sugar retaining molasses for its characteristic colour and flavour.
caster (superfine) finely granulated table sugar.
demerara small-grained golden-coloured crystal sugar.
icing (confectioners') also known as powdered sugar; pulverised granulated sugar crushed together with a small amount of cornflour.
palm also called nam tan pip, jaggery, jawa or gula melaka; made from the sap of the sugar palm tree.

Light brown to black in colour and usually sold in rock-hard cakes; substitute with brown sugar.
pure icing (confectioners') also known as powdered sugar.
SUMAC a purple-red, astringent spice ground from berries growing on shrubs that flourish wild around the Mediterranean; adds a tart, lemony flavour to dips and dressings and goes well with barbecued meat. Can be found in Middle-Eastern food stores.
THYME a member of the mint family, it has tiny grey-green leaves that give off a pungent minty, light-lemon aroma. Dried thyme comes in both leaf and powder form. Dried thyme should be stored in a cool, dark place for no more than 3 months. Fresh thyme should be stored in the refrigerator, wrapped in a damp paper towel and placed in a sealed bag for no more than a few days.
TOMATOES
canned whole peeled tomatoes in natural juices; available crushed, diced or chopped, sometimes unsalted or reduced salt.
mixed medley contains a mix of grape, baby roma, Zebrino and cherry tomatoes. Each has a distinct shape, size and flavour with colours ranging from yellow, to red and brown with stripes.
paste triple-concentrated tomato puree.
roma (egg) also called plum; smallish, oval-shaped tomatoes are much used in Italian cooking.
truss small vine-ripened tomatoes with the vine still attached.
TREACLE thick, dark syrup not unlike molasses; a by-product of sugar refining.
VANILLA
bean dried, long, thin pod from a tropical golden orchid; the minuscule black seeds inside the bean are used to impart a luscious vanilla flavour in baking and desserts. A bean can be used three or four times.

extract made by extracting the flavour from the vanilla bean pod; pods are soaked, usually in alcohol, to capture the authentic flavour.
paste made from vanilla pods and contains real seeds. Is highly concentrated – 1 teaspoon replaces a whole vanilla pod. Found in most supermarkets in the baking section.
VIETNAMESE MINT not a mint at all, but a pungent and peppery narrow-leafed member of the buckwheat family. Not confined to Vietnam, it is also called cambodian mint, pak pai (Thailand), laksa leaf (Indonesia), daun kesom (Singapore) and rau ram in Vietnam.
VINEGAR
balsamic originally from Modena, Italy, there are now many balsamic vinegars on the market. Quality can be determined up to a point by price; use the most expensive sparingly.
cider made from fermented apples.
rice wine is a vinegar used in Asian cooking. Made from rice wine lees (sediment left after fermentation), salt and alcohol.
WATERCRESS a slightly peppery, dark-green leafy vegetable commercially cultivated but also found growing in the wild.
WITLOF (BELGIAN ENDIVE) related to and confused with chicory. A versatile vegetable, it tastes as good cooked as it does raw.
WOMBOK (NAPA CABBAGE) also called chinese or peking cabbage; elongated in shape with pale green, crinkly leaves, this is the most common cabbage in South-East Asia.
YEAST (dried and fresh), a raising agent used in dough making. Granular (7g sachets) and fresh compressed (20g blocks) yeast can almost always be substituted one for the other when yeast is called for.
YOGHURT we use plain full-cream yoghurt in our recipes unless specifically noted otherwise.
Greek-style plain yoghurt that has been strained in a cloth (muslin) to remove the whey and to give it a creamy consistency.

Conversion Chart

MEASURES

One Australian metric measuring cup holds approximately 250ml; one Australian metric tablespoon holds 20ml; one Australian metric teaspoon holds 5ml.

The difference between one country's measuring cups and another's is within a two- or three-teaspoon variance, and will not affect your cooking results. North America, New Zealand and the United Kingdom use a 15ml tablespoon. All cup and spoon measurements are level. The most accurate way of measuring dry ingredients is to weigh them. When measuring liquids, use a clear glass or plastic jug with the metric markings.

We use large eggs with an average weight of 60g.

DRY MEASURES

metric	imperial
15g	½oz
30g	1oz
60g	2oz
90g	3oz
125g	4oz (¼lb)
155g	5oz
185g	6oz
220g	7oz
250g	8oz (½lb)
280g	9oz
315g	10oz
345g	11oz
375g	12oz (¾lb)
410g	13oz
440g	14oz
470g	15oz
500g	16oz (1lb)
750g	24oz (1½lb)
1kg	32oz (2lb)

LIQUID MEASURES

metric	imperial
30ml	1 fluid oz
60ml	2 fluid oz
100ml	3 fluid oz
125ml	4 fluid oz
150ml	5 fluid oz
190ml	6 fluid oz
250ml	8 fluid oz
300ml	10 fluid oz
500ml	16 fluid oz
600ml	20 fluid oz
1000ml (1 litre)	1¾ pints

LENGTH MEASURES

metric	imperial
3mm	⅛in
6mm	¼in
1cm	½in
2cm	¾in
2.5cm	1in
5cm	2in
6cm	2½in
8cm	3in
10cm	4in
13cm	5in
15cm	6in
18cm	7in
20cm	8in
22cm	9in
25cm	10in
28cm	11in
30cm	12in (1ft)

OVEN TEMPERATURES

The oven temperatures in this book are for conventional ovens; if you have a fan-forced oven, decrease the temperature by 10-20 degrees.

	°C (Celsius)	°F (Fahrenheit)
Very slow	120	250
Slow	150	300
Moderately slow	160	325
Moderate	180	350
Moderately hot	200	400
Hot	220	425
Very hot	240	475

The imperial measurements used in these recipes are approximate only.
Measurements for cake pans are approximate only. Using same-shaped cake pans of a similar size should not affect the outcome of your baking. We measure the inside top of the cake pan to determine sizes.

Index

Published in 2017 by Bauer Media Books, Australia.
Bauer Media Books is a division of Bauer Media Pty Ltd.

Bauer Media Books

Publisher Jo Runciman

Editorial & food director Sophia Young

Director of sales, marketing & rights Brian Cearnes

Editorial director-at-large Pamela Clark

Creative director Hannah Blackmore

Managing editor Stephanie Kistner

Senior designer Gayna Murphy

Food editor Elizabeth Macri

Operations manager David Scotto

Cover & additional photography

Photographer James Moffatt

Stylist Vivien Walsh

Photochef Angela Devlin

Photochef assistant Sharon Kennedy

Cover recipes
Three-in-one mix fruit mince pies, page 174;
Iced Christmas cupcakes, page 396.

The publisher would also like to thank
Wild Lotus Florist, for the fresh pine floral wreath
and pine tree trimmings (cover, pages 1, 2, 3, 4, 5)
wildlotusflorist.com.au
Yael Grinham, for the blue and white paper flowers
and paper flower wreath (pages 234, 235)
yaelgrinham.com

Printed in China
by Leo Paper Products Ltd

National Library of Australia
Cataloguing-in-Publication entry
Title Christmas : the complete collection /
Pamela Clark
ISBN 9781742458717 (hardback)
Notes Includes index.
Subjects Christmas cooking. Cooking. Cookbooks.
Other Creators/Contributors
Clark, Pamela (Food director), editor.
Also Titled Australian women's weekly

© Bauer Media Pty Limited 2017
ABN 18 053 273 546

Published by Bauer Media Books,
a division of Bauer Media Pty Ltd,
54 Park St, Sydney; GPO Box 4088,
Sydney, NSW 2001, Australia
Ph +61 2 9282 8618; Fax +61 2 9126 3702
www.awwcookbooks.com.au

Order books
phone 136 116 (within Australia)
or order online at
www.awwcookbooks.com.au

Send recipe enquiries to
recipeenquiries@bauer-media.com.au